FAMILIA

ULSTER GENEALOGICAL REVIEW

Ulster
Genealogical
& Historical
Guild

NUMBER 36

2020

COVER IMAGE

Sake Deen Mahomed
Coloured lithograph by T. M. Baynes after himself
images@wellcome.ac.uk http://wellcomeimages.org
© Wellcome Library, London, Wellcome Images

BACK COVER IMAGE

*State Line – For Glasgow, Belfast, Dublin, Londonderry & Liverpool
– Austin Baldwin & Co., genl. agents*, New York: J. Ottmann Lith.
© COURTESY OF LIBRARY OF CONGRESS PRINTS AND PHOTOGRAPHS DIVISION

Published 2020
by Ulster Historical Foundation
www.booksireland.org.uk
www.ancestryireland.com

ISBN 978-1-913993-04-7

Printed by Gutenberg Press Limited
Design and production by Dunbar Design

CONTENTS

EDITORIAL

There is a wide-ranging chronological and subject spread in the articles in this edition of *Familia*, from the Ulster Plantation in the early seventeenth century to the recent Troubles period. Andrew Kane's forensic examination of the available evidence associated with the 1718 migration from English-planted County Londonderry adds interesting detail to its near-legendary and pioneering reputation. The account by Bill McGee and William Roulston of the Makgee family's migration from Dumfries outlines an intriguing angle on a Catholic Scottish family settling in plantation County Tyrone.

That critical period in Irish history, the late eighteenth century, is well served from differing perspectives. Brett Hannam narrates, with appropriate illustrations, the several influences of Robert Jephson in a fast-changing political landscape. Brian White recounts the role his Bryson forebears played in the 1798 rebellion and their subsequent adventures as exiles. Tom Bartlett's review article reflects on significant Ulster participants in and observers of the 1798 Rebellion, two of them influential female voices. Jonathan Chambers' nicely illustrated account of his forebear, George Washington Chambers, is a model family search and a rattling good account. Ian Montgomery's :eighteenth century draws attention to a new and important nominal source, the Belfast Poor's Money List 1753.

Sean Worgan's consideration of John Bulmer Hobson, an Ulster Quaker Nationalist, and Patrick Maume's study of the Donegal Unionist, James Alexander Rentoul, cast informative perspectives on political developments in the quarter century leading to the outbreak of World War One that prepared the way for the political landscape on this island that continues in one form or another today. Richard

McMinn's review article is a thoroughgoing consideration of four recent titles that continue the assessment he has been making in recent editions of a range of issues arising from, as the title indicates, the decade of centenaries 1912–22. Studies of Arthur Griffith and Richard Mulcahy are accompanied by considerations of Protestant Nationalism pre- and post-Partition and the only-now-being-addressed question of the treatment of returning GAA members who fought for the allied cause in WWI. Amanda Croft examines the part played by the iconography of artist Harry Clarke's work in developing an identity for the newly-formed Free State.

The aftermath of this decade of upheaval, specifically the cruelty of the post-partition civil war as it unfolds in Seán Enright's book on executions, is judiciously, in every sense, appraised by Patrick Butler. Paddy Fitzgerald assesses the thesis at the heart of David Fitzpatrick's posthumously published book on the Americanisation of Irish society. He also considers a range of individual experiences of mostly Ulster immigrants to Colonial America described in *Transatlantic Lives* edited by Linde Lunney, James Quinn and William Roulston (Research Director, UHF, whose continuing editorial support I take this opportunity to acknowledge gratefully). Anthony Malcomson casts an approving eye over Richard Butler's book on the construction of courthouses and prisons in Ireland in the latter half of the eighteenth century. Tom Bartlett reviews the extent to which piracy stalked the coasts of southern Ireland early in the seventeenth century as described in Connie Kelleher's *The Alliance of Pirates*. Brenda Collins considers Alice Johnson's analysis of the role the middle classes in industrialising Belfast's accelerating nineteenth-century growth.

Titles relating to the modern era include *Reporting the Troubles*, assessed by Dennis Kennedy, himself a vastly experienced journalist. David Steers, a Non-Subscribing Presbyterian cleric, assesses the responses of a range of Presbyterian voices during and after the post-1968 civil unrest. Gerry Cleary recommends Professor Brian Walker's published thoughts on identity issues arising from the pre- and post-1998 peace process and its sometimes sticky aftermath. Trevor Parkhill reports on books by two local sporting heroes, footballer and fund-raiser Liam Beckett and Lady Mary Peters, Ulster's 1972 Munich Olympics gold medallist who has called on her many female friends in

EDITORIAL

the athletics world to serve as an example to aspiring young athletes. Daragh Smyth's *Earthing the Myths*, a comprehensive account of the myths and legends of early Ireland, completes the reviews section.

James Bartlett's account of the stranger-than-fiction life of Dean Mahomed, 'Irish-Indian travel writer, curry entrepreneur and shampooer to Kings', not only provides a most appropriate image for the front cover but draws attention to an issue of much current concern.

VALETE

There can be no more sobering reminder of time marching on than the realisation that three of last year's contributors, two of them *Familia* regulars, have sadly passed away in recent months and whose wisdom will be much missed – Jonathan Bardon and D. George Boyce, both first-division Irish historians, and David S. Cook, first non-Unionist Lord Mayor of Belfast (1978–9) and enthusiastic local historian. *Requiescant in pace*.

TREVOR PARKHILL

NOTES ON CONTRIBUTORS

JAMES BARTLETT is a freelance journalist, broadcaster and author in Los Angeles who has published, in *Familia* and elsewhere, on topics of Irish historical and genealogical interest.

THOMAS BARTLETT is Emeritus Professor of Irish History, University of Aberdeen. His most recent monograph is *Ireland: a History* (Cambridge, 2010) and he is general editor of a four-volume *History of Ireland* (Cambridge, 2018).

PATRICK BUTLER is a Belfast-based barrister, presently specialising in public inquiry work. He was president of the Belfast Literary Society 2017–18.

JONATHAN CHAMBERS from Lecale, County Down, is a barrister and graduate of Oxford University. He was a winner of the RHS Prize for History and remains a keen amateur historian.

LESLIE CLARKSON is Emeritus Professor of Social History, Queen's University Belfast.

GERRY CLEARY is a former Assistant Professor in the International College, I Shou University, Kaohsiung, Taiwan, Republic of China. He is currently an Open Learning Tutor, Queen's University Belfast.

BRENDA COLLINS is a Visiting Research Fellow in the School of History, Anthropology, Philosophy and Politics, Queen's University Belfast, and retired curator, Lisburn Museum.

AMANDA CROFT has lectured in art history in further and higher education for over 30 years. Specialising in twentieth-century and contemporary Irish art, she also runs *Arttalks: Artwalks.*

ROBSON DAVISON, a retired civil servant, taught history in Ballyclare High School and Belfast Royal Academy before becoming a member of the Department of Education Inspectorate.

PATRICK FITZGERALD is Lecturer and Development Officer, Mellon Centre for Migration Studies, Ulster American Folk Park, Omagh, and an Honorary Research Fellow in History at Queen's University Belfast.

BRETT HANNAM is Chief Executive of the Strategic Investment Board. He has published two books on the history of County Armagh and is writing a biography of Robert Jephson.

ANDREW KANE is Research Consultant with Ulster Historical Foundation and Trustee of the North of Ireland Family History Society. He published *The Town Book of Coleraine* (2016) where his family have lived for some 12 generations.

NOTES ON CONTRIBUTORS

DENNIS KENNEDY is a historian who has worked in journalism in Ireland north and south, USA and Ethiopia, and as a lecturer in European Studies at Queen's University Belfast (1993–2001).

BILL McGEE, a retired Wisconsin civil servant, has published on his Scots-Irish family in the *Directory of Irish Family History Research* and the *Dumfries & Galloway Family History Society Newsletter*.

RICHARD McMINN is a former Principal of Stranmillis University College, Belfast, where he also taught Irish history, and is a former Trustee of the National Museums Northern Ireland.

ANTHONY MALCOMSON, archivist and historian, was Director of PRONI 1988–1998. He has published extensively on Irish politics and aristocratic society *c.* 1725–1832.

PATRICK MAUME is a researcher with the Royal Irish Academy's *Dictionary of Irish Biography* who has published widely on nineteenth- and twentieth-century Irish history and literature.

IAN MONTGOMERY is an archivist retired from the Public Record Office of Northern Ireland. He also worked on the Belfast City Archive Project cataloguing records of the former Belfast Corporation.

TREVOR PARKHILL is editor of *Familia* and former Keeper of History, Ulster Museum.

WILLIAM ROULSTON is Research Director, Ulster Historical Foundation.

DAVID STEERS is a Non-Subscribing Presbyterian minister based in County Down and edits the theological journal *Faith and Freedom*.

BRIAN WHITE was born in Canada, educated at Cambridge and is now retired from the Northern Ireland Civil Service. His research interests include the Bryson and Robb families.

SEAN WORGAN, born and raised in Dagenham, England, is third generation Irish on his mother's side, English on his father's. His 2011 Keele University Ph.D. was on Bulmer Hobson.

'98

3d.

WHO FEARS TO SPEAK?

Who was Andrew Bryson?
The Bryson family of County Down
and the rebellion of 1798

B. R. D. WHITE

The story of the Bryson family of north County Down has
been described as one of the 'most remarkable' case histories
arising from the United Irish rebellion of 1798.[1] Interest,
understandably, has focussed on the extraordinary letter written
during the early 1800s in New York by Andrew Bryson
(1779–?1813) in which he gave a vivid account of his
experiences as a convicted rebel whose punishment was
compulsory enlistment into the British army and service on the
fever-ridden island of Martinique.[2]

There is, of course, a wider family story, parts of which have appeared
in print.[3] However, the narrative has significant gaps and, worse,
there is confusion arising from the fact that there were *three* (not just
two) members of the Bryson family called Andrew who, during the late
1790s, were active rebels in the same small part of County Down.[4]

The purpose of this article is to fill out the story of the Bryson family,
to describe its role at a critical juncture in Irish history and, where
possible, to clarify matters where uncertainty about identification has
arisen. In doing so, the author draws not only on public documents but
also on family records held by descendants of the Brysons.[5] These papers
– genealogies, wills, leases and memoirs – provide a framework of
people, places and relationships which help to make sense of the public
record. Sadly, however, the Bryson family archive is incomplete as much
of it, including letters written from America, was deliberately destroyed
in 1874.[6]

THE ANDREW BRYSONS: DISAMBIGUATION

Before discussing the role of the Brysons in the United Irish movement and in the rebellion of 1798, it is worth identifying the three rebels called Andrew Bryson and indicating how they will be distinguished. They were:

- Andrew (1749–1834), hereafter 'Andrew Sr';
- His second son, Andrew (1779–?1813), hereafter 'Andrew Jr'; and
- Andrew Sr's nephew, Andrew (1767–1842), hereafter 'Andrew of Ballysallagh'.

THE BRYSON FAMILY

Family tradition is that the Bryson family came originally to north Down in the company of the Blackwood family of Ballyleidy in the parish of Bangor. The first firmly attested member of the family is Andrew Sr's father, also called Andrew (1704–64), who farmed at Ballysallagh, a townland immediately to the west of Ballyleidy, on land leased from the Blackwoods.[7] He had four sons: in order, William (who was the father of Andrew of Ballysallagh), Samuel, James and Andrew Sr.

It seems possible that Andrew Sr was the product of a second marriage. Under the terms of his father's will, he and his mother, Jean Findly, were left an inheritance that was distinct from that of his older brothers and this settlement may reflect land that she brought to the marriage.[8] In 1770 Andrew Sr married Isabella Barr, known as Sibella, the daughter of David Barr, a farmer of the Cottown (or Cotton), a townland in the parish of Bangor.[9] At some point Andrew Sr established himself on a farm there. At the same time, it would seem, he had business interests in Newtownards or at least a close association with that town: the freehold record of 1785 documenting his holding at the Cottown describes him as 'Bryson Andrew N. T. Ards'.[10] It is likely that his business interests included tanning, probably in connection with Kennedy family of Flush Hall, Newtownards, known to have owned a tannery.[11]

Andrew Sr had six daughters and two sons. Both sons, David (1776–1845) and Andrew Jr, were active in the United Irish revolt, as was at

THE BRYSON FAMILY OF COUNTY DOWN

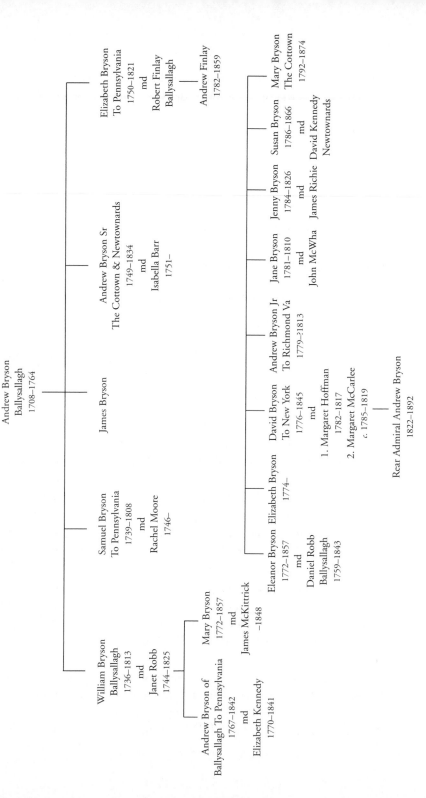

least one of the daughters, Elizabeth (Eliza) (b. 1774).[12] Andrew of Ballysallagh was the only son of Andrew Sr's eldest brother, William (c.1736–1813). William farmed at Ballysallagh but like other members of the Bryson family had business interests ('concerns' as he called them) in Newtownards.[13]

ANDREW BRYSON SR (1749–1834)

It is not clear when Andrew Sr first became involved in the United Irish movement. He may have been the Bryson who met Wolfe Tone in Belfast in 1792 [14] but this seems unlikely. The surname 'Bryson' is cited four times by Tone in his diary without any accompanying forename and, in the main, scholars who have edited Tone's papers have concluded that the references were to Rev. James Bryson (d. 1796),[15] a Presbyterian minister and a founder member of the Belfast Reading Society, later the Linen Hall Library.[16]

Rev. James Bryson is known to have been kinsman of the Ballysallagh and Cottown Brysons. This fact is confirmed in Andrew Jr's letter to his sister in which he recounts an offer to meet the widow of his relative, the Rev. Andrew Bryson, late of Dundalk, who was the Rev. James Bryson's son.[17] What degree of kinship existed between the two Andrews is not specified. However, during the late 1800s it was believed by descendants of the Bryson family of Ballysallagh that Rev. James Bryson was the James, brother of Andrew Sr, referred to in his father's will.[18] This information was in genealogical notes, probably written in the 1890s, contained in a Bryson family Bible.[19] In contrast, the *Dictionary of National Biography* says that Rev. James was the son of a John Bryson who died aged 102 (sic) in Holywood, County Down, and was probably of Donegal extraction.[20] Another Bryson active in Belfast liberal politics at that time who may have met Tone was the merchant, William Bryson, who in 1792 was among the proposers of 'a petition to Parliament in favour of our Roman Catholic brethren' and who was the father-in-law of Samuel Neilson, editor of the *Northern Star*, the liberal Belfast newspaper.[21]

Whether or not Andrew Sr met Tone, it would seem that by the late 1790s he had achieved senior rank in the military organisation of the United movement. In one government document he is referred to as 'Andw Bryson, N. Ards, Lt Col'.[22] In another, dated 31 March 1798, he is described as 'Col. Com. Co. Down" ('Com' stands for 'Committee').[23] Andrew Sr is also, quite obviously, the Colonel Bryson referred to in *Betsy Gray, or Hearts of Down,* the factually-based, if somewhat embellished, story of events in north Down during the 1798 rebellion told by local man, W. G. Lyttle.[24] In the lead-up to the 1798 rebellion the name 'Andrew Bryson' appears in a number of contemporary sources and there is nothing to suggest otherwise than that person being referred to was Andrew Sr. These instances are as follows.

In October 1796 an attempt was made on the life of Rev. John Cleland, the Church of Ireland rector of Newtownards. He was the agent of the Londonderrys of Mount Stewart and, as a magistrate, a zealous persecutor of the United Irish movement. Cleland survived when the assailant's pistol misfired. A spy reported that 'Andw Bryson 'had been among the five men who cast lots to choose the assassin'.[25] Subsequently (and presumably to deflect attention away from themselves), Andrew Bryson along with James Jackson, the Newtownards apothecary who had also been among those drawing lots, contributed to the reward fund set up to find the perpetrator, subscribing two guineas and three guineas respectively.[26]

In June 1797 the Belfast press reported that 'Andrew Bryson was brought in prisoner from Newtownards – charged with seditious practices'.[27] Swept up in Lieutenant-General Lake's campaign to disarm the United Irish movement, Andrew Sr was one of a number of suspects who found themselves being held in the Artillery Barracks in Belfast.[28] (In later life Andrew Sr's youngest daughter, Mary, remembered when as a four-year-old she saw 'the soldiers putting her mother on a white horse and taking her away to compel her to tell where her husband was hiding, while she poor child was screaming to them not to take away her ma'.[29] If the remembered age was correct, this incident would have come from that time.)

In addition to the information surrounding the Cleland assassination attempt, there was a report from 1797 that an 'Andrew Bryson' had been involved in an attempt to procure the manufacture of pikes and had purchased iron in Newtownards for the purpose. Unfortunately, the Millisle blacksmith who had been engaged to make the weapons, one Miskelly, was an informer. As the Andrew Bryson implicated in this scheme was later described as having been 'committed a close prisoner without fire or candle etc'[30] there can be little doubt that it was Andrew Sr, then languishing in Belfast, who Miskelly had betrayed. By the summer of 1797 the United Irish movement had been compromised by government agents. Meetings of the County Down colonels, including one in Saintfield a few days before Andrew Sr's arrest took place, had been penetrated by a spy, Nicholas Maginn (various spellings) of Saintfield, who held high rank as 'a member of the Provincial and County Committees and also a Colonel in the Military System of the United Irishmen'.[31]

Andrew Sr was again in the press in November 1797 when he and 11 or 12 other prisoners (the newspaper reports are not consistent) appeared in the court of King's Bench in Dublin as the result of an action of *habeas corpus* brought by Robert Emmett and William Sampson. The action challenged the prisoners' continued incarceration without trial in the Artillery Barracks in Belfast. The court duly found that it was unlawful for the prisoners to be confined for more than a few days in a place that was not 'a legal prison' by a person who was not 'a known officer of the law'. Moreover, as the only charge against the prisoners, that of treasonable practices, was bailable under the common law, the court 'was bound to release them on bail'. In consequence, 'each of the prisoners was […] bailed to appear at the next assizes for the county of Antrim, and discharged.'[32] In the event, Andrew Bryson and others actually appeared at the Down assizes on 9 April 1798 only to be discharged 'there being no prosecution'.[33]

On 31 March 1798, shortly before he was due to appear in court in Downpatrick, Andrew Sr attended a meeting of colonels in Newtownards. On this occasion, the meeting decided not to transact any business but to adjourn instead to Greyabbey. To quote the spy, Maginn, who duly reported the meeting to the Revd John Cleland, 'Andrew Brison' was among those who believed that it was too dangerous to hold a meeting in Newtownards 'whear such a man as Mr Cleland resided as Magistrate and no dute might have spies under him'.[34]

At some point prior to the outbreak of the rebellion, Andrew Sr may have been arrested again. According to Lyttle, Andrew Sr was being held prisoner in the Newtownards market-house when it was attacked by insurgents in June 1798 and he was released by them.[35] Whatever the truth of this, Andrew Sr did become involved directly in the rebellion, specifically as a member of the committee that took over the administration of rebel-held Newtownards.

There is no evidence that Andrew Sr took part in any of the fighting. As if to confirm this, among the depositions taken by the authorities with a view to the prosecution of offenders is one from Archibald Davidson of Drumhirk which gives detail about the doings of named individuals but merely states that the 'deponent saw Andw Bryson apparently active amongst the Rebels'.[36] As will be shown below, the depositions and reports subsequent to the rebellion which name 'Andrew Bryson' as being on active service refer explicitly either to his nephew (Andrew of Ballysallagh) or to Andrew Jr. In a petition drafted at some point between 1807 and 1813, Andrew Sr's wife was to claim that her husband had 'taken the benefit of his Majesty's Gracious Proclamation in the year 1797 by swearing allegiance to his Majesty and entering into securities' and furthermore that he 'had never borne arms against the legitimate government of the country'.[37] The latter statement may have been literally true, if somewhat disingenuous.

Whether or not Andrew Sr played a significant part in the military aspects of the rebellion, he was obviously of continuing concern to the authorities:

- In the notice published on 18 July 1798, by Major-General Nugent, commander of the northern district, 'Andrew Bryson, of Newtownards' was listed among 'those who have secreted themselves in the County of Down' and for the 'apprehension' of whom a reward of fifty guineas was offered: those who harboured him would 'suffer as capital offenders, and their property be destroyed'.[38]
- In the General Pardon Act 1798, 'Andrew Bryson, of Newtownards, in the county of Down, tanner' is listed among those specifically excepted from its provisions.[39] (Although this Act only received Royal Assent on 6 October 1798, its complexities meant that it had been in gestation since at least the beginning of July.)[40]
- In the so-called Surrender Act of 1798, 'Andrew Bryson, of Newtownards, county Down' is listed among persons who 'have been engaged in the rebellion' who were required before 1 December 1798 'to surrender themselves, and abide by their trials respectively, … on pain of being attainted of High Treason'.[41]

Durey believes that these references relate to Andrew Jr who, he suggests, had been fast-tracked to the rank of colonel to fill the gaps in the hierarchy created by arrests.[42] This surmise appears to have resulted from a misreading of the evidence, including a lack of awareness of the existence of Andrew of Ballysallagh. It might be noted that Andrew Jr was a few months over the age of 19 at the time of the rebellion and it is unlikely that he would have been promoted over the head of his very capable older brother, David, or indeed his cousin Andrew of Ballysallagh, both identified as a captains during the rebellion itself.[43] It seems equally improbable that a youngster's capture would be worth fifty guineas.

Following the rebellion, it is told, Andrew Sr attempted to evade capture. According to a family story, on one occasion he avoided arrest by hiding in the bed of a servant girl in the house of his widowed sister, Mrs Elizabeth Finlay (1750–1821) of Ballysallagh, while she distracted the soldiers with a supper of bread and cream. In this account, Andrew Sr then 'made his escape to Scotland and from that to America.[44]' Whether or not the story of hiding in a servant's bed is true, his journey into exile in the United States was in reality more complicated.

In mid-August 1798 following the spate of bloodletting, the overarching aim of the authorities was to 'disorganize the North',[45] that is to neutralise the leadership of the United Irish movement. The authorities in County Down, however, faced a dilemma. As a result of changes made by the new lord lieutenant, Lord Cornwallis, who had arrived in office in June and who had been unimpressed by the standards of justice that he found,[46] the death penalty had become harder to obtain.[47] In consequence, given Cornwallis' 'reluctance to countenance the death sentence except for clearly proven crimes', General Nugent concluded that the best option would be to remove captured rebel leaders from the country and send them abroad 'either at their own expense or to serve [in the army]'.[48] However, even convicting the leaders of offences that would merit transportation was not guaranteed.

The government hoped to use the informer, Nicholas Maginn: General Nugent was convinced that, if he could be induced to appear in court 'many of the Principals to save their lives & Properties would have been forward to prosecute even their best friends'.[49] However, Maginn refused to turn King's evidence, and the authorities were forced to take a different tack. On 23 August 1798 Nugent issued a proclamation which, in effect, offered prisoners exile abroad and freedom from prosecution in return for certain securities.[50] For men fearful that, even in the absence of Maginn, other damning evidence might be found, this would have been a tempting proposition. In the case of Andrew Sr (and Dr James Jackson) there was indeed another potential Crown witness, Henry Gordon, a United Irish officer who following capture had been 'turned'.[51]

It is not clear when Andrew Sr came into custody. By late September, however, he seems to have been among a number of prisoners that Nugent was anxious to 'get rid of' who were negotiating to be allowed to take passage to America on the ship, *Pallas*.[52] Although such lenient treatment might seem directly at odds with the terms of the General Pardon Act, that legislation specifically allowed the people excepted from its provisions, such as Andrew Sr, to be pardoned 'upon condition of banishment, or such other condition or conditions as his Majesty, in his royal wisdom, think [sic] fit to impose'.[53] They were, however, compelled to apply individually for this conditional pardon, although it 'was seldom refused'.[54] It might be noted that the fact that Andrew Sr went voluntarily into exile does not necessarily mean that no court action had been taken against him. Dr James Jackson, for example, was convicted in Newtownards on 9 August 1798 and sentenced to stand in the pillory on three market days and to a period of six months in Downpatrick gaol, but he nevertheless left Ireland with Andrew Sr on board the *Pallas* less than two months later.[55]

On 8 October 1798 when the *Pallas* departed from Belfast, Andrew Sr was in the company of other United Irishmen who, in the words of the *Belfast News-Letter*, 'had accepted the terms of the Proclamation'[56] and were thereby banishing themselves to the United States. Andrew Sr's son, David, was with him.[57] It should be noted that the *Pallas* was also carrying a number of United Irishmen who had not come to terms with the government and who had been smuggled on board. Whether David had government permission to be on the *Pallas* is not known.

The voyage of the *Pallas* was ill-starred. Having left Belfast, she met severe headwinds off Lough Swilly and was forced back to Larne harbour, arriving on 11 October.[59] Setting off once more on 17 October, the *Pallas* encountered further bad weather, culminating on

31 October in a severe storm off Cape Clear which carried away her bowsprit, stanchions and railings and, worse, 'nearly the whole of the rudder'.[60] Fortunately, the storm had abated by 3 November and the captain was able to fashion a makeshift steering system. This involved organising the male passengers into watches which, for four hours at a time, pulled two steering ropes to port or starboard under the direction of the helmsman.[61]

There was a debate about where the *Pallas* should go. The illegal fugitives in particular did not want to land in Ireland and favoured the Western Isles. The captain and others sought a harbour where repairs might be effected. In reality, the impossibility of sailing against the wind was probably the determining factor. On 11 November, after over a week of gruelling work on the steering ropes, the *Pallas* reached the harbour of Cork, the safe arrival of the vessel being recorded in an address of thanks from the passengers to the ship's 'clever and energetic' captain for his 'unremitting and effectual exertions'.[62]

According to one source, David left again for the United States on 1 January 1799, presumably with his father.[63] How they achieved this and from where is not clear. Possibly it was on this occasion that Andrew Sr was in Scotland. It is known that a fellow passenger (and also former member of the Newtownards rebel committee), William Heron, took ship from Cork initially to Liverpool but then to Belfast where he was 'taken up' and brought into custody at Mount Stewart. This prompted the furious letter from Lord Londonderry to his son, Viscount Castlereagh, already quoted from, denouncing the 'traitorous' Newtownards committee. In it Londonderry also railed against Andrew Bryson and Doctor Jackson, suggesting that 'wilfully landing in Ireland after Transportation' be made 'Felony of Death'.[64] General Nugent, who was asked to look into Londonderry's concerns, confirmed that he had 'given Directions for the Apprehension of Andrew Bryson & Doctor Jackson, should they appear in the North' but he did 'not understand that they [had] returned to the County Down from Cork'. He concluded saying that Bryson, Jackson and Heron 'deserve no favour from Government'.[65]

It is not known whether, apart from David, other members of Andrew Sr's immediate family went to the United States at this time, although his daughter, Eliza, was there in 1805 [66] and other females in the family visited.[67] What is certain, however, is that his wife, Sibella, remained in Ireland and was one of four attorneys appointed by Andrew Sr in in 1801 or 1802 'authorized to settle his affairs'.[68]

The reference to 'settling ... affairs' might suggest that the whole family was considering emigration. However, by 1805 with more settled times returning, Andrew Sr's eldest daughter, Nelly Robb, was counselling him against selling up his Irish property and warning him of the 'inconveniences' of 'beginning a new business at your advanced stage in life'.[69] In the event, Andrew Sr did not remain in the United States. By early 1806 his wife was contemplating applying for 'protections' that would allow him to return. In a letter to David, her brother, Nelly explained that to this end their mother was seeking the assistance of 'Lady Hillsborough' (the widow of the second marquess of Downshire). In doing so, Nelly explained, Sibella Bryson was hoping to exploit 'the very great enmity between the houses of Hillsborough and Londonderry' and the latter's then current political weakness. (Following the death of William Pitt, the Londonderrys were, according to Nelly, 'nearly as much out of power as the Brysons were three weeks after the rebellion'.)[70]

It is known that Andrew Sr had come back by the beginning of 1810, his presence in Ireland being confirmed in a letter written by his brother, William.[71] The precise timing and circumstances of his return are not clear, although it would seem that the move had not been properly sanctioned by the authorities, leaving open the possibility of re-arrest and re-conviction with unpleasant consequences.[72] Fear of this fate stimulated his wife to petition the duke of Richmond, the lord lieutenant of Ireland, in office between April 1807 and June 1813, for permission for her husband to remain. The petition, must have been successful.[73] With a date of registry of 19 July 1814, Andrew Sr of Cottown put himself on the list of £50 freeholders entitled to vote in elections, not the action of a man trying to avoid detection.[74]

Andrew Sr died at his home in the Cottown on 23 May 1834. According to an obituary:

> He was ... until the last hour of his existence, a firm and consistent friend to civil and religious liberty; his undeviating adherence to those

principles subjected him, at a melancholy period in Irish history, to very serious sacrifices, both of a personal and pecuniary nature. His memory will always be held in respect, by every true friend to genuine liberty.[75]

ANDREW BRYSON OF BALLYSALLAGH (1767–1842)

Andrew Bryson of Ballysallagh was the only son of William Bryson (1736–1813), one of the brothers of Andrew Sr. He had two sisters. One of these was married to James McKittrick, another United Irishman who was 'out' in 1798[76] and who, after initially being sentenced to fourteen years transportation, went into exile in the United States for several years before coming back to Ulster. In time he had draper's shop in Newtownards where he continued to agitate for liberal causes[77] as later did his son, John.[78] In January 1791 Andrew married Elizabeth Kennedy of Ballymaglaff, parish of Comber. They had 12 children, of whom six sons and three daughters survived childhood.

Information about Andrew of Ballysallagh derives in large measure from a book published privately by one of his American descendants.[79] This includes not only family trees but also transcripts of letters that Andrew received from his Bryson relatives during the early 1800s and several second-hand accounts of his experiences during and after the rebellion provided by descendants. According to these accounts, which are inconsistent, Andrew of Ballysallagh was a 'captain in the Irish Rebellion of 1798', was captured at some point, possibly in the immediate aftermath of the battle of Ballynahinch but managed to escape on his way to the gallows by a ruse or bribery. There are other stories about evading capture and escape. One describes how he was taken on board ship in a barrel; another has him being hidden in a coal hold; others describe two attempts to get away from Ireland, the first one ending in shipwreck, the second one with his family being successful.[80] In a separate story, current in the family in Ireland in the late 1800s, it is told that at some point 'Andrew was hailed by [a] patrol and asked how he was out so late. He said that his wife was going to be confined & he was running for the doctor & begged not to be detained, so he got off.'[81]

His descendants' belief that Andrew of Ballysallagh was a United Irish officer is corroborated by contemporary records. In a deposition taken by James Cleland in early July 1798, the deponent, James Barr of

Ballysallagh, claimed to have gone 'with a party of arm'd Men to Scraba, and when there was commanded by Andw Bryson (son of Wm Bryson of Ballysallagh) who acted as his Captain'. Later, the deponent stated, Andrew was in action at Ballynahinch where 'he drew up the Men and commanded the party'.[82] (Another deponent, Robert Smith of Ballysallagh was less certain about rank. Smith deposed that Andrew, 'son of William Bryson of Ballysallagh', was 'at the camp on Tuesday evening [i.e. at Ballynahinch on 12 June]' and that he 'thought he was an officer but does not know whether he was or not'.)[83] That Andrew of Ballysallagh was captured at some point is confirmed by an eyewitness who was present when 'Capt. Andrew Bryson of the Newtownards Company [was] taken near Killyleagh last Tuesday' (i.e. 10 July).[84] Subsequently, on 18 July 1798, 'Andw Bryson', residence 'Ballysallagh', was referred to as 'Captain' in a list of rebel officers drawn up in connection with their prosecution.[85]

As for the stories surrounding Andrew of Ballysallagh's attempts to get away by sea, the accounts given by his descendants could be consistent with him being one of the fugitives who was smuggled aboard the ship *Pallas* and who had to be hidden from the authorities when the vessel was forced back to Larne. Being forced back to Cork by the Hallowe'en storm would have caused even greater anxiety. In January 1799, this time with his wife and their two surviving children, Andrew left Ireland, possibly from Londonderry. He was at sea on 2 February 1799 when his wife gave birth to his third surviving son (another Andrew (1799-1864)). The family arrived at Philadelphia about 1 March 1799 before travelling to Uniontown, Fayette County, Pennsylvania, where they settled. Andrew's uncle, Samuel Bryson (1739–1808), was already resident in the locality.[86]

In Pennsylvania the Bryson family multiplied. In 1834 one of David Bryson's sons spent twelve days in Uniontown visiting 'cousins "to the third or fourth generations"' concluding of his host, Andrew, 'Such a quantity of Brysons I never saw before – think of a man having nine children and twenty nine grandchildren – as Goldsmith says in his Vicar of Wakefield – what a great Benefactor to mankind is such a man'.[87] This branch of the Bryson family subsequently spread widely in the United States, among its members, six generations later, being the author Bill Bryson.

ANDREW BRYSON JR (1779–?1813)

Andrew Jr's story is known almost entirely from the letter he wrote to his sister in the early 1800s.[88] He was just 19 years old in June 1798, the time of the rebellion. Durey believes that, like his older brother David, Andrew Jr was a tanner,[89] but that is surely based on the erroneous belief that he is the 'Bryson' cited in the General Pardon Act.[90] In the rebellion itself, Andrew Jr seems to have played a relatively low-key role. He was possibly the 'Andrew Bryson' referred to in the account given by the Newtownards butcher, Jack Saunders, as forming part of the guard that he (Saunders) escaped past in order to get to Belfast.[91] He was also referred to in the deposition made by George Crawford of Whitespots who stated that 'young Andw Bryson was said to be an officer' although Crawford 'did not see him act'.[92] There is, however, no other record of Andrew Jr's involvement in the rebellion, of the charges brought against him, or of the trial where he was sentenced to serve for life overseas in the British army. What had he done to deserve this fate? Certainly Andrew Jr does not seem to have been engaged in actual fighting as he claims to have seen a man die for the first time when he was onboard ship to the West Indies in 1799.[93]

As it happens, the court martial records of two men who subsequently served alongside Andrew Jr in the West Indies have survived so it is possible to see the sorts of offence which they had committed. John Sibbet of Killinchy, who was sentenced 'in consideration of his youth' to serve abroad 'for his natural life', was convicted of 'breaking into the house of Mr Potter and carrying arms'.[94] John Purse was convicted of 'acting as a traitor and rebel' but more specifically of taking arms and furniture from James Rose Clealand's house in Newtownards and of 'being in arms as a rebel in Ballynahinch in the action which took place there'. Purse's ostensibly more lenient sentence of service abroad for 14 years took into account his guilty plea and, possibly as well, the fact that he had received a gunshot wound during the battle.[95]

Having been sentenced, it was the day after Christmas 1798 when Andrew Jr left the prison tender in Belfast harbour bound for New Geneva, County Waterford, where military barracks had been converted into an extensive prison Why Andrew Jr was not allowed to go into exile with his father must be a matter of conjecture. According to Durey, hopes of being treated leniently by Lord Cornwallis, the lord lieutenant, depended on 'the universal support of one's kin'. In Andrew Jr's case, according to the letter to his sister, his prospects of more lenient treatment were undermined by an uncle. Durey, curiously, suggests that this was a reference to his *cousin*, Rev. William Bryson of Antrim.[96] The family, however, has always considered the culprit to have been his actual uncle, his mother's brother, Henry Barr, a British army doctor.[97] Nevertheless, it is not clear why Andrew Jr alone and not his father (or brother) came to be Henry Barr's target if, indeed, Dr Barr was the offender.

Arriving in the West Indies in April 1799, Andrew Jr was assigned to the 43rd Regiment of Foot serving on Martinique, which was, for European soldiers, one of the most unhealthy islands in the West Indies.[98] Despite almost immediately falling very sick, Andrew Jr's overriding aim was to escape from the island by persuading some friendly ship's captain to smuggle him off. In the event, Andrew Jr was saved by his brother. According to the account given by a nephew, when David Bryson learned where Andrew Jr had been taken, he chartered a vessel in New York and went looking for him.

> He cruised about among the islands and called … at the place where he knew his brother was stationed … saw him among the convicts, and put his finger to his lips as a sign he did not wish to be recognised. In the evening he landed for water again, … made arrangements for a future landing, when he got him into his boat, rowed to the vessel, weighed anchor and off to New York.[99]

According to another source, the arrangement on the island was made with the help of a slave.[100]

After arriving in New York, Andrew Jr began the long letter to his sister, Nelly Robb, describing events after December 1798. The implication from the letter is that Andrew Jr on arrival in the United States entered into commerce. According to one source, he succeeded in making his fortune.[101] Nevertheless, unequivocal information about him after 1802 is limited. In New York naturalisation documents from the Court of Common Pleas dated 24 December 1802, there is a record of a 'Bryson, Andrew, late of parish of Bangor, Co. of Down, Ire.' who is described as being a 'grocer', that is to say what would now be called a wholesaler.[102] This is probably a reference to Andrew Jr as, in her petition seeking permission for Andrew Sr's return home to be regularised, Sibella Bryson said that her husband 'had never claimed the privileges of an American citizen'.[103] (By 1802, neither father nor son, however, would actually have completed the necessary time qualification for citizenship, although the court may merely have been recording the preliminary stages of naturalisation.)[104]

By early 1806, Andrew Jr was no longer resident in New York. It may be inferred that this was the point at which he moved to Richmond, Virginia.[105] It is probably not a coincidence, therefore, that a business called 'Andrew Bryson & Co.' is recorded as leasing land there on 4 November 1806[106] or that, by July 1807, an Andrew Bryson was partnership as a general merchant with John Parkhill (1786–1856), a native of Londonderry.[107] They advertised their core business as hardware and ironmongery but Bryson & Parkhill also sold tea, coffee, spirits and tobacco and acted as property agents.[108] The partnership was 'dissolved by mutual consent' in September 1811, with Bryson receiving payments from Parkhill.[109] The last direct record of Andrew Jr in the possession of the family is the letter written in September 1812 datelined 'Natches' (presumably Natchez, Mississippi,) which he sent to his cousin, Andrew of Ballysallagh, then living in Pennsylvania.

It now seems clear that Andrew Jr died on either 6 or 7 October 1813, and is the 'Andrew Bryson' whose death notice appeared in the Richmond *Virginia Argus* describing him as 'late merchant of this city'.[110] He is also presumably the person, despite the wrong age being recorded, who was memorialised in St John's church cemetery, Henrico County, Virginia, the stone reading 'in memory of Andrew BRYSON, who departed this life 7th Oct, 1813 aged 35 years'.[111] In his last known letter, written a year earlier while in New Orleans, he describes himself as having had 'quite a bilious attack'.[112] His health may, of course, have been compromised by his privations on Martinique.

Finally, in regard to Andrew Jr, there is also the intriguing possibility that, during the War of 1812, he had once again taken up arms against the British. It has been claimed that the Bryson memorialised in the St John's cemetery had served for 10 days in March 1813 as a private in the 19th regiment (Ambler's) Virginia militia.[113] Certainly, an Andrew Bryson did serve in that unit,[114] but the information given in the document about this individual is at variance with what is known about Andrew Jr.[115]

DAVID BRYSON (1776–1845)

David Bryson was born 29 October 1776. It is clear from his subsequent achievements in the leather trade that David must have served a successful apprenticeship as a tanner, probably in Newtownards. By the age of 19 he was acquiring land in north Down in his own name, a piece 'known as the sheep park' containing nearly eighteen acres and a meadow of over two acres.[116]

David was active during the 1798 rebellion. In a deposition following the rebellion he was identified as being captain of the 'Newton company' and described as exercising it at Scrabo.[117] Whatever his role, David was able to go to America with his father, although whether under the terms of the government's proclamation or illicitly is not clear. In New York, David began his work as a tanner and currier, soon moving to premises at 48 Frankfort Street, in an area known as the Swamp, where the Brooklyn bridge now stands and where the city's leather trade was then concentrated. He prospered as a leather merchant[118] and by 1817 had founded and was director of the Phoenix Bank.[119] In 1845, the year of his death, he was listed among the wealthy citizens of New York with an estate of $400,000 (the equivalent to about $4,430,000,000 today).[120]

From an early point David became involved in New York politics. He was a founder member and from 1802 onwards a frequent secretary of the Hibernian Provident Society. This had been set up to give relief to Irish immigrants, in particular members of the society and their families, but it also gave political support to New York Republicans.[121] David was also involved in the early days of the Tammany Society, the organisation that was, in the second half of the nineteenth century, to secure a power base among Irish emigrants and come to dominate Democratic politics in the city. He was a sachem (senior office bearer) in the society.[122] It is recorded that David owned a building called Harmony Hall where it said that the 'Swamp clique would sometimes mature their plans before giving them the broader endorsement of Tammany'.[123] David also took a more formal role in politics and from 1828 to 1831 represented Fourth Ward on the corporation of New York

City. In 1835 according to a commentator from County Down, 'Mr Bryson has immense influence in New York at Elections [...]. He is chairman of the nominating Committee. He has made his fortune, filled up his tanholes and has nothing to do but to appoint Representatives to Congress.'[125]

David was married twice: first, in 1809 to Margaret Hoffman (1789–1817) with whom he had a son and a daughter and then in 1819 to Margaret McCartee (*c.* 1785–1825) with whom he had two sons and two daughters. He also had an adopted daughter, born in 1803, who on his death received an equal share of that part of his estate which did not come from his marriages.[126] This suggests that she was his natural daughter.

POSTSCRIPT: REAR-ADMIRAL ANDREW BRYSON (1822–92)

As chance would have it, the Bryson family was to have one more brush with the cause of Irish independence: in 1866, when armed members of the Fenian Brotherhood invaded the Niagara peninsula of Canada West (modern-day Ontario), crossing the Niagara River from Buffalo, New York. The person involved was yet another Andrew Bryson, the third son of David Bryson (second by his second marriage). In June, with the substantive rank of commander in the United States Navy, he was the captain of the side-wheel steamer, U.S.S. *Michigan,* stationed on Lake Erie, guarding the United States border. Capt. Bryson (to use his courtesy title) was by then a battle-hardened veteran of the American Civil War, having commanded a Union monitor in the Carolinas and a gunboat on the Mississippi.

The Fenian attack on the Niagara peninsula was part of a wider plan by the Brotherhood to capture Canada, to exchange it for Irish independence. Although unrealistic, the raid on Canada West, involving about 850 men, many of them civil war veterans, had some initial success against the less-experienced British and Canadian troops.[127] Capt. Bryson had prior warning of the invasion attempt and had made preparations to prevent it but found his ship temporarily immobilised during the night of the main river crossing, his pilot having been suborned by the Fenians. Once daylight came and he could take *Michigan* into action, however, Capt. Bryson was able to interdict

Fenian supplies crossing the Niagara River and bring the invasion quickly to an end.[128] He secured in the process about 700 prisoners.[129]

It is hard to believe that Capt. Bryson was unaware of his family history, the circumstances which had forced his father to cross the Atlantic, and the irony of events which found him working, in effect, alongside British military authorities against Irish revolutionaries. His duty as an American officer, however, was clear. In the immediate aftermath of the incursion, a delegation of British officers went on board *Michigan.* There Capt. Bryson and other senior Americans were able to assure the British that they were under strict orders to prevent infractions of international law and, indeed, 'had prevented many reinforcements from getting across to the British territory on the two previous nights.'[130] Although there was little prospect that the Fenians' plans would have succeeded, it had been 'the small flotilla headed by the *Michigan*' which had 'stood between them and real carnage in Canada'.[131] Andrew Bryson ended his naval career as Rear Admiral in command of the United States' South Atlantic squadron. He died in Washington D.C. on 7 February 1892.

CONCLUSION

Although members of the Bryson family suffered physical hardship, destruction of property[132] and serious financial loss following the battle of Ballynahinch, they were more fortunate than the luckless men and women killed or who, after a brief appearance before a court martial, were flogged or (to use the newspaper cliché of the day) 'launched into eternity' from the gallows. They were also fortunate to have left material which enables their story to be told today. The writing of this article has shown how it is possible to combine family papers and family history with public papers and published history not only to give a fuller insight into the role played by the individual members of a family in shaping important events such the uprising in 1798 and in creating the society which emerged in its aftermath but also a better understanding of how the authorities at the time sought to re-impose control and order.

NOTES

1 Peter Gilmore, Trevor Parkhill and William Roulston, *Exiles of '98: Ulster Presbyterians and the United States* (Belfast, 2018), p. 153.

2 Andrew Bryson, New York, to his sister (Eleanor Jane (Nelly) Robb), 28 May 1801, transcript in possession of the author; also available as Public Record Office of Northern Ireland (PRONI), T1373/5; an edited version can be found in Michael Durey, *Andrew Bryson's Ordeal: An Epilogue to the 1798 Rebellion* (Cork, 1998). (Where copies of family papers are available in the Public Record Office of Northern Ireland, the author cites a PRONI reference.)

3 For example, Gilmore et al., *Exiles of '98*; Kerby A Miller, Arnold Schrier, Bruce D. Boling, and David N. Doyle, *Irish Immigrants in the Land of Canaan: Letters and Memoirs from Colonial and Revolutionary America, 1675–1815* (New York, 2003), p. 641 fn 58.

4 Sadly, this confusion is particularly obvious in Michael Durey's introduction to *Andrew Bryson's ordeal*. For an example of mix-up in a popular publication see Nick Barratt, 'At home with Bill Bryson', in *Your Family History*, July 2010, p. 20.

5 Family papers in the possession of Mrs S. N. White, Helen's Bay, Co. Down; Mrs Ellen Robb Iyengar, Palo Alto, California; and the author (see footnote 2).

6 Fulfilling a promise, on the day of the funeral of Mary Bryson (1792–1874), a great niece burned, unread, papers still in the family home: see transcript of a letter (undated but written in 1894) from Elizabeth Simpson née Crickard to Andrew Bryson (1851–1918), PRONI, T1373/5.

7 Actually, there are two townlands, Ballysallagh Major and Ballysallagh Minor, but contemporary, non-formal references typically referred to both together as 'Ballysallagh'.

8 Will of Andrew Bryson of Ballysalloch Minor, 7 May 1764, PRONI, T1454/4/1.

9 The Cottown had been acquired in 1672 by William Hamilton, a Belfast merchant. He was the great grandfather of William Drennan, the physician, founding member of the Society of United Irishmen and political reformer who eventually inherited the townland in two tranches in 1806 and 1807. For the complex trail of inheritance see *The Drennan-McTier Letters*, ed. Jean Agnew (3 vols, Dublin, 1998), i pp xxiii-xv.

10 PRONI, D654/A3/1B.

11 Andrew Sr is described as a tanner in the General Pardon Act of 1798 (38 Geo. III, c. 55 [Ire]); for the Kennedys of Flush Hall see, e.g. *Banner of Ulster*, 7 Jan. 1848.

12 Regarding Eliza, see W. G. Lyttle, *Betsy Gray or, hearts of Down; a tale of Ninety-eight* (reprint, Newcastle, Co. Down, 1988), pp 37, 105. She was probably the Bryson daughter involved in the theft of wheat and oats from James Rose Clealand: see Kenneth Robinson, North Down and Ards in 1798 (Bangor, 1998), p. 83.

13 William Bryson to Andrew, formerly of Ballysallagh, 26 Feb. 1801, transcribed in Homer C. Nycum, *Some Brysons and Swearingens* (Ann Arbor, Michigan, no date), p. 215.

14 Gilmore et al., Exiles of '98, p. 153. See also *Life of Theobald Wolfe Tone compiled and arranged by William Theobald Wolfe Tone*, ed. Thomas Bartlett, (Dublin, 1998), pp 132, 994. Bartlett through his indexing implies that the Bryson who Tone dined with in Belfast on 12 July 1792 was Andrew Bryson.

15 'Bryson' is named in Tone's diary on 17, 18 and 19 Oct. 1791 and 12 July 1792. That Tone was referring to the Rev. James Bryson, see *The Autobiography of Theobald Wolfe Tone (1763–98)*, ed. R. Barry O'Brien (2 vols, London, 1893), i, 96; *The Writings of Theobald Wolfe Tone*, eds T. W. Moody, R. B. McDowell and C. J. Woods (3 vols, Oxford, 1998), i, 138 fn 2; *Life of Theobald Wolfe Tone*, ed. Bartlett, pp 122-3, 994.

16 John Anderson, *History of the Belfast Library and Society for Promoting Knowledge, commonly known as the Linen Hall Library, chiefly taken for the Minutes of the Society and published in connection with the centenary celebration in 1888* (Belfast, 1888), p. 11.

17 Andrew Bryson, New York, to his sister, 28 May 1801, PRONI, T1373/5.

18 Will of Andrew Bryson of Ballysalloch Minor, 7 May 1764, PRONI, T1454/4/1.

19 Possibly written by Elizabeth Simpson, née Crickard, great granddaughter of Andrew Sr, in answer to a query from an American Bryson relative. There are no (other) obvious errors in these notes.

20 Leslie Stephen (ed.), *Dictionary of National Biography*, (63 vols, London, 1885–1900), vii, 169-70.

21 R. R. Madden (ed. V. F. O'Reilly), *The United Irishmen; Their Lives and Times* (8 vols, New York, 1910–11) i, 278-9, viii, 165.

22 List of Captains, Colonels and other United Irishmen, PRONI, D714/3/23, pp 198, 200.

23 Black Book of the Rebellion in the North, PRONI, D272/1.

24 Lyttle, *Betsy Gray*, p.37 and elsewhere.

25 Espionage report made by Nicholas Maginn, PRONI, D714/2/24.

26 *Belfast News-Letter*, 31 Oct. 1796.

27 Ibid., 26 June 1797.

28 *Dublin Evening Post*, 21 Nov. 1797.

29 Elizabeth Simpson to Andrew Bryson (1851–1918), PRONI, T1373/5.

30 Humphrey Galbraith, Donaghadee, to Lord Downshire, PRONI, D607/E/365.

31 *Report of the Secret Committee of the House of Commons with appendix* (Dublin 1798), pp 131 and 137.

32 *Saunders's News-Letter*, 22 Nov. 1797; Dublin Evening Post, 25 Nov. 1797.

33 Belfast News-Letter, 13 Apr. 1798.

34 *Report of the Secret Committee*, p. 156; 'At a Meeting of Com in Newton Ards for thee lower half for thee County…', PRONI, D714/2/19.

35 Lyttle, *Betsy Gray*, p. 105.

36 Deposition of Archibald Davidson of Drumhirk taken by James Clealand, 19 June 1798, PRONI, D714/3/7.

37 Petition of Isabella Bryson, parish of Bangor, to Charles, duke of Richmond (undated), PRONI, T1454/3/2. In fact, the 'Proclamation' taken advantage of was made in 1798, after the rebellion.

38 For example, *Belfast News-Letter*, 20 July 1798.

39 38 Geo. III, c. 55 [Ire].

40 Charles Ross (ed), *Correspondence of Charles, First Marquis Cornwallis* (3 vols, London, 1859), ii, 359.

41 38 Geo. III, c. 80 [Ire].

42 Durey, *Andrew Bryson's Ordeal*, pp 7 and 9. It is clear that Durey was not aware that Andrew Bryson of Ballysallagh was a third individual, see for example Durey, *Andrew Bryson's Ordeal*, pp 1–2.

43 Deposition of George Crawford of Whitespots taken by James Cleland, 29 July 1798, PRONI, D714/3/20; deposition of John Barr of Ballysallagh taken by James Cleland, 5 July 1798, PRONI, D714/3/11c.

44 Elizabeth Simpson to Andrew Bryson (1851–1918), PRONI, T1373/5.

45 General Nugent to Edward Cooke, 14 Aug. 1798, NAI, RP 620/39/172.

46 Cornwallis to Major-General Ross, 24 July 1798, in Ross, *Cornwallis Correspondence*, ii, 368-9.

47 Thomas Bartlett, 'Clemency and compensation: the treatment of defeated rebels and suffering loyalists after the 1798 rebellion' in Jim Smyth (ed), *Revolution, Counter-Revolution and Union: Ireland in the 1790s* (Cambridge, 2000), p. 107.

48 Bartlett, 'Clemency and compensation', p. 112 quoting General Nugent to Leslie, 9 Aug. 1798, Scottish Record Office [now the National Records of Scotland], GD 26/9/527/1/7; see also Alex. Marsden, Dublin Castle, to General Nugent, 29 Aug. 1798, PRONI, D272/39.

49 General Nugent, Belfast, to Lord Castlereagh, Dublin, 26 July 1798, N.A.I., R.P. 620/3/32/11.

50 A Proclamation, Belfast, 23 Aug. 1798, NAI, RP 620/39/197.

51 List appended to General Nugent's letter to Edward Cooke, 14 Aug. 1798, NAI, RP 620/39/172; see also Gilmore et al., *Exiles of '98*, p. 165.

52 General Nugent, Belfast to Lord Castlereagh, 25 Sept. 1798, NAI, RP 620/40/99. That he was allowed to go, see Lord Londonderry to Lord Castlereagh, NAI, RP 620/8/85/13.

53 38 Geo. III c. 55 [Ire] s. 8.

54 Ross, *Cornwallis Correspondence*, ii, 360.

55 Sentence of James Jackson, 3 August 1798, NAI, RP 620/2/15/53; Gilmore et al., *Exiles of '98*, p. 171.

56 *Belfast News-Letter,* 9 Oct. 1798

57 Inferred from Samuel Bryson, Glasgow, to Samuel Finlay, Ballysallagh, 10 Mar. 1799, PRONI, T1373/4.

58 John Caldwell, Jr, Particulars of history of a north county Irish family, p. 119, PRONI, T3541/5/3.

59 The same storm did considerable damage the French man-of-war, *Hoche*, before the Battle of Tory Island (12 October 1798), ultimately leading to its capture and to Wolfe Tone being taken prisoner (William James, *The Naval History of Great Britain from the Declaration of War by France in 1793 to the Accession of George IV* (6 vols, London, 1837), ii, PP 127–9.

60 By coincidence, damage caused to a British man-of-war by the same storm had enabled the French squadron under Commodore Savary to escape its pursuers. This had been the last French attempt to land troops in Ireland during 1798 (James, *Naval history of Great Britain*, ii, 147).

61 Caldwell, Particulars of history of a north county Irish family, pp 119–20, PRONI, T3541/5/3. The steering ropes would have been attached to either a long hawser or a spar trailed behind the ship. Jury systems of this kind are described in John Harland, *Seamanship in the Age of Sail* (London, 1984), pp 302–03.

62 Caldwell, Particulars of history of a north county Irish family, pp 119–20, PRONI, T3541/5/3; *Belfast News-Letter*, 20 Nov. 1798.

63 Samuel Bryson, Glasgow, to Samuel Finlay, Ballysallagh, 10 Mar. 1799, PRONI, T1373/4.

64 Lord Londonderry to Lord Castlereagh, NAI, RP 620/8/85/13.

65 General Nugent to Alexander Marsden, ?27 Mar. 1799, NAI, RP 620/8/85/13.

66 Inferred from Nelly Robb, Ballysallagh, to Andrew Bryson Sr, New York, 22 Mar. 1805, PRONI, T1454/3/1.

67 Mary Bryson may have lived in New York for a period (see Elizabeth Simpson to Andrew Bryson (1851–1918), PRONI, T1373/5). Eliza was living at the Cottown in 1831 when her father drafted his will (PRONI, T1373/17).

68 William Bryson, Ballysallagh, to Andrew Bryson, formerly of Ballysallagh, 1 Mar. 1802, in Nycum, *Some Brysons and Swearingens*, p. 216.

69 Nelly Robb, Ballysallagh, to Andrew Bryson Sr, New York, 22 Mar. 1805, PRONI, T1454/3/1.

70 Nelly Robb, Ballysallagh, to David Bryson, New York, 22 Mar. 1806, PRONI, T1454/3/3. According to the letter, protection was also being sought for David Bryson and 'discharge for Andw [Jr]'.

71 William Bryson, Newtownards, to Andrew Bryson, formerly of Ballysallagh, Uniontown, Pennsylvania, 27 Feb. 1810 transcribed in Nycum, *Some Brysons and Swearingens*, p. 221.

72 For example, James Finlay, court-martialled in Newtownards in 1798, indicted for 'returning and being at large' at Downpatrick assizes, April 1804 (*Saunders's News-Letter*, 16 Apr. 1804).

73 Petition of Isabella Bryson to Charles, duke of Richmond, undated, PRONI, T1454/3/1. The reference in it to 'intercourse with America' being closed would suggest a date either while the Embargo Act (10th Congress, sess. 1, Ch. 5) was in force or after news of the United States' declaration of war in 1812 had been received in Ireland.

74 PRONI, D654/A3/1E.

75 *Newry Examiner and Louth Advertiser*, 31 May 1834.

76 For example, PRONI, D714/3/9.

77 Gilmore et al., *Exiles of '98*, p. 182. He had returned by August 1802, see Nycum, *Some Brysons and Swearingens*, p. 213.

78 For example, *Northern Whig*, 24 May 1832.

79 Nycum, *Some Brysons and Swearingens*.

80 Ibid., pp 4, and 228–9.

81 Elizabeth Simpson to Andrew Bryson (1851–1918), PRONI, T1373/5.

82 Deposition of John Barr of Ballysallagh, 5 July 1798, PRONI, D714/3/11c. Also cited was Andrew of Ballysallagh's first cousin, Andrew Finlay of Ballysallagh, who was the son of Andrew Sr's widowed sister, Elizabeth.

83 Deposition of Robert Smith of Ballysallagh, 8 July 1798, PRONI, D714/3/12.

84   Dean William Annesley, Oakley, to Lord [Downshire], 14 July 1798, PRONI, D607/F/320.

85   List of officers in the rebel army, according to information, Lisburn, 18 July 1798, PRONI, D162/98. (In order to advance the claim that Andrew Jr had been promoted to a colonelcy, Durey suggests that this list was based on 'outdated information' (Durey, *Andrew Bryson's Ordeal*, p.108). However, the Andrew Bryson listed is clearly not Andrew Jr!)

86   Nycum, *Some Brysons and Swearingens*, pp 4, 5, and 228.

87   Cornelius Bryson, New York, to John Murdock, Pittsburgh, 7 Dec. 1834, PRONI, T1373/18.

88   Andrew Bryson, New York, to his sister, 28 May 1801, PRONI, T1373/5.

89   Durey, *Andrew Bryson's ordeal*, p. 2.

90   38 Geo. III, c. 55 [Ire].

91   H. Galbraith, Belfast, to Edward Hull, Stranraer, 13 June 1798, PRONI, D607/F/235.

92   Deposition of George Crawford of Whitespots, 29 July 1798, PRONI, D714/3/20.

93   Andrew Bryson Jr to his sister, 28 May 1801, PRONI, T1373.

94   Proceedings of court martial of John Sibbett of Killinchy, Downpatrick, 22 June 1798, NAI, RP 620/2/15/2.

95   Proceedings of court martial of John Purse, Newtownards, 31 July 1798, NAI, RP 620/2/15/61.

96   Durey, *Andrew Bryson's ordeal*, p. 10; Andrew Bryson Jr to his sister, 28 May 1801, PRONI, T1373.

97   Elizabeth Simpson to Andrew Bryson (1851–1918), PRONI, T1373/5.

98   Sir Richard George Augustus Levinge, Bt, *Historical Record of the Forty-Third Regiment, Monmouthshire Light Infantry, with a roll of the officers and their services from the period of embodiment to the close of 1867* (London, 1868), pp 93–4; British Library, West Indian Papers, Stowe MS 921.

99   According to Mrs Caroline Simpson (née Crickard), Andrew Jr's great niece, 'These particulars were obtained from Alexander Robb (1800–88 [sic]), who was the eldest son of Mrs Nelly Robb the sister to whom Andrew wrote these letters'. PRONI, T1373.

100 Frank W. Norcross, *A History of the New York Swamp* (New York, 1901), p.113.

101 Norcross, *The New York Swamp*, p.113.

102 Kenneth Scott (ed), *Early New York Naturalizations: Abstract of Naturalization Records from Federal, State and Local Courts, 1792–1840* (Baltimore, 1981), p. 206.

103 Petition of Isabella Bryson, PRONI, T1454/3/1.

104 7th Congress, sess. 1, Ch. 28.

105 Norcross, *The New York Swamp*, p.113.

106 Information contained in private communication from J. B. Martin, Killinchy.

107 *Virginia Argus*, 18 July 1807; Parkhill papers held in the Wilson Library at the University of North Carolina, see https://finding-aids.lib.unc.edu/01826/#folder_2#1 (28 Feb. 2020).

108 For example, *Virginia Argus*, 2 Sept. 1808; 13 Apr. 1810.

109 *The Enquirer* (Richmond), 24 Sept. 1811.

110 *Virginia Argus*, 11 Oct. 1813.

111 L. W. Burton (J. S. Moore (ed)), *Annals of Henrico Parish, Diocese of Virginia, and especially of St John's Church, the present mother church of the parish, from 1611 to 1844* (Richmond, Virginia, 1904), p. 417.

112 Nycum, *Some Brysons and Swearingens*, pp 214.

113 The Society of the War of 1812 in the Commonwealth of Virginia, Myron E. Lyman, Sr (compiler), 'Information on War of 1812 veterans buried in Virginia' (10 Nov. 2009), p. 7, (http://usgwarchives.net/va/statewide/warof1812/w1812vetinfo.pdf) (24 Feb. 2020).

114 National Archives and Records Administration, *Index to the Compiled Military Service Records for the Volunteer Soldiers who Served during the War of 1812*, Washington, D.C.

115 According to the Society of the War of 1812 in the Commonwealth of Virginia, the Andrew Bryson memorialised was born in Scotland and emigrated from 'Dundalk County, Louth, Scotland during period 1786 to 1796'.

116 Assignment, Joseph Walker, Bangor, to David Bryson, Newtownards, 31 Jan. 1795, PRONI, T1373/3.

117 Deposition of George Crawford of White Spots, PRONI, D714/3/20.

118 Norcross, *History of the New York Swamp*, p. 113.

119 Ibid., p. 114; *The History of Manufacturers Hanover Trust Company Courtesy of the JPMorgan Chase Archives* (https://www.chasealum.org/article.html?aid=198) (retrieved 24 June 2019); Walter Barratt, *The Old Merchants of New York City* (New York, 1864), p. 282.

120 *Wealth and Biography of the wealthy citizens of New York City, comprising and alphabetical arrangement of persons estimated to be work $100,000, and upwards, with the sums appended to each name; being useful to banks, merchants, and others* (6th ed., New York, 1845) in Henry Wysham Lanier, A Century of Banking in New York, 1822–1922 (New York, 1922), p. 5; for relative value see www.measuringworth.com (11 Feb. 2020).

121 John D Crimmins, *St Patrick's Day: Its Celebration in New York and other American Places, 1737–1845* (New York, 1902), pp 108–10; 145–6 and passim.

122 *Proceedings of the Tammany Society, or Columbian Order, on laying the cornerstone of their new hall in fourteenth street, and celebrating the ninety-first anniversary of the declaration of American independence, at Irving Hall, Thursday, July 4th, 1867, also, a brief history of the origin and earlier history of the society* (New York, 1867), p. 142.

123 Norcross, *History of the New York Swamp*, p. 9.

124 D. T Valentine, *Manual of the corporation of the city of New York for the years 1842 & 3* (New York, 1842), pp 224–5.

125 John S. Crawford, New York, to Mrs Wm Sharman Crawford, Crawfordsburn, Bangor, County Down, 9 Nov. 1835, PRONI, D856.

126 Andrew Robb, Hogtown, Florida, to Mrs John Murdock, Pittsburgh, Mar. 1846, PRONI, T1454/5/2. She was Mrs Eliza Purse, née Wright.

127 John R. Grodzinski, 'Fenian Raids' in *The Canadian Encyclopedia* (https://www.thecanadianencyclopedia.ca/en/article/fenian-raids) (14 Oct. 2019).

128 Bradley A. Rodgers, *Guardian of the Great Lakes: The U.S. Paddle Frigate Michigan* (Ann Arbor, Michigan, 1996), pp 110–7.

129 Report of Col R. W. Lowry, 4 June 1866 in Fred G. Ketcheson, *The Fenian Raid at Fort Erie, June the first and second, 1866 : With a map of the Niagara peninsula, shewing the route of the troops, and a plan of the Lime Ridge battle ground* (Toronto, 1866), p 83.

130 Ibid., p 82.

131 Rodgers, *Guardian of the Great Lakes*, p. 116.

132 Colonel Atherton to General Nugent, 20 June 1798, quoted in R. R. Madden, *the United Irishmen* (2nd series, 2 vols, London, 1843), ii, p. 429.

A daguerreotype of the George Washington Chambers family

The Lecale Diaspora on the American Frontier
General George Washington Chambers (1793–1875)
Fighter at the War of 1812, Hat Seller,
Judge, General and Confederate[1]

JONATHAN CHAMBERS

INTRODUCTION

In a previous article by the author, in the *Lecale Review*[2] the life of Dr James Chambers of Tullynaskeagh (*c.* 1765–1801) and his fatal duel on the Kentucky frontier was examined in some detail. His story was discovered as a consequence of the reading of calfskin and copper-plate family histories of the Chambers family of Tullynaskeagh written and completed by the author's ancestor (and amateur historian) Francis Chambers (22 June 1771–24 March 1862) of Ballywarren, Ballee, County Down.[3] According to Francis Chambers,

[James Chambers] was educated for a minister. He preached in the Ballee Meeting House in the year 1783; but owing to an unknown cause, he sailed for America, and the Rev. Mr Patterson, was partly charged as the cause of it, which caused the family to join the Down Congregation. James was of a hasty temper and when in America, a dispute arising, ended in a duel in which he fell; he left one son, named Washington with whom William Lewis was in America.

WHO WAS WASHINGTON CHAMBERS? A SUBSEQUENT HISTORIAN'S RESEARCHES

A subsequent history of the Chambers family of Tullynaskeagh was written in 1977 by John Arthur ('Jack') Chambers (1895–1984). Jack Chambers was a very gentle and interesting person whom the author had the pleasure to meet when in his early youth and when Jack was in his latter years. Although he spoke little of it, Jack had served with distinction with 'C' and 'D' Companies of the 13th Battalion Royal Irish Rifles in the First World War between 1915 and 1918. He served in both Flanders and in Italy. Interestingly he drove a Chambers Car, a converted ambulance, from the Belfast University Street Works to the Western Front in 1915. Jack subsequently worked for Chambers Cars Limited on his return from the war.[4]

May 1915, France. A Chambers ambulance of the type donated by the Ulster Liberal Association and other bodies to the Red Cross and the the type donated by the Ulster Liberal Volunteer Force. Jack Chambers, right, supervises two Red Cross drivers

His wartime experiences appear not to have dimmed his interest in history. Pre-war as a boy he both transcribed the history written by Francis Chambers[5] and made what further researches he could then do to try and determine whether Washington Chambers might be traced. The common and exasperating 'brick wall' experienced by most family and local historians is summed up by Jack Chambers in the following thoughtful passage in his history written in 1977.[6]

One hundred and seventeen years after Mr. James Chambers laid down his pen, I take up mine to carry on his history of the Chambers family. He tells his story so objectively that it is only with difficulty that one can deduce where he himself fits into the picture. The Story is of a family anciently established at the end of the sixteenth century in a farm in Lecale, which sent branches out over parts of Ulster and reaching to the United States of America. When the story stops it is sad to note that almost all the offshoots of the main stem have reached a dead end. It is highly probable however that if complete records were available it would be found that of the many of our name now scattered over Ulster, a few at least sprang originally from Tullynaskeagh. There is a tradition that the Chambers families in the Banbridge and Laurencetown district are descended from an early John Chambers of Tullynaskeagh. One Downpatrick family represented by R. I. Chambers lately deceased, who carried on a business of Painter and Decorator, and W. J. Chambers also deceased who had a farm at Chapletown, are definitely a collateral branch, though the relationship is so distant that it is scarcely recognised on either side.

It is fascinating but now useless to speculate whether the Washington Chambers born in U.S.A. had any descendants, but the story indicates a definite possibility of very distant Chambers cousins in America.

THE AUTHOR'S FURTHER SEARCHES FOR WASHINGTON CHAMBERS[7]

By 2016, when the present author's searches began, the sources available to the amateur historian were completely different from those which Jack Chambers had to call on. Public records depositories[8], online non-copyright works[9], newspaper archives[10], museums[11], historical societies[12], and other family historians' and genealogists' research were online, digitised and fully searchable. The author was able to determine and give some context to the lives of both the son of Dr James Chambers – George Washington Chambers (1793–1875) and his younger sister Margaret Chambers (1796–1848; d. Natchez, Mississippi). George Washington Chambers may also have had a number of other siblings including Stephen, Benjamin, Maria and another unnamed sister.[13]

GEORGE WASHINGTON CHAMBERS FIGHTER AGAINST THE BRITISH IN THE WAR OF 1812, HAT SELLER, JUDGE, GENERAL AND CONFEDERATE

The first lead in the search for George Washington Chambers came from an online source in the following historical transcript found online.[14]

CHAMBERS, GEN. GEORGE. Louisville, Ky. Born 1793; his death was announced at the annual reunion of June, 1875, as one of the 19 old soldiers who had died since the 1874 reunion. He was a son of Dr. James Chambers, who was killed in a duel with John Rowan, at Bardstown, 3 Feb. 1801. His mother was Jude, a daughter of Judge Benjamin Sebastian. His father, Dr. James, was a colonel in the American Revolution, the son a volunteer in 1812. "Judge for twenty years without intermission, of the thousands of cases litigated before him not one was ever reversed by the Court of Appeals. When only 15 years of age he could split rails at the rate of 100 per day. He first learned the hat business, then studied law. He was married three times. He had a beautiful female child born unto him in his 74th year, which was made occasion for an assembly of the Bar, and the presentation of a silver cup to his little daughter, Maggie White." He died near Louisville 8 Jan. 1875, aged 81. One of his daughters, Martha M., died 1 Aug. 1836, aged 19 years. One George and one George M. Chambers listed in AG: *Louisville Daily Journal*, 4 Aug. 1836; *Yeoman*, 26 June 1875; *TK*, 20 Jan. 1875. CORRECTION –

His mother was Amelia Sebastian, daughter of Judge Benjamin Sebastian, not Jude as stated therein. James Chambers and Amelia Sebastian were married in Jefferson County, probably in 1789, the bond being dated 30 Oct. 1789. *Jefferson County Book* I, p. 9

The author was thus encouraged to do further research on an apparently long-lived, vigorous and very interesting character: whose father had been killed in a duel in 1801 when he was 8 years old; who at age 15 was able to split rails for fencing at the rate of 100 rails a day; who by 19 was a volunteer for the United States military forces against Great Britain in the War of 1812; who then became a hat-seller in Louisville, and then (somewhat improbably) became a lawyer and judge and who was married three times and who had the 'energy' to father his last child Margaret (Maggie) White Chambers when he was 74 years old.

HIS YOUTH

His mother Amelia Sebastian came from a well-to do Kentucky legal family[15] (apparently with Spanish heritage). Aged 17 she first married a James Breckinridge from another leading Kentucky legal and political family in 1788. This union had produced one child named Catherine Breckinridge[17] born in 1788.

However this marriage did not succeed. No divorce papers or records are available and it is not impossible that any subsequent marriage was bigamous. In any event, within a year, in 1789, George's mother, Amelia Sebastian, married for a second time, this time to James Chambers of Tullynaskeagh, Ballee, County Down, and, from about 1783–4, of Bardstown, Kentucky. This appears to have been a happier marriage lasting until James Chambers' death after the duel with John Rowan on 3 February 1801.

SOLDIER IN THE WAR OF 1812

At 19 years of age George enlisted as a mounted cavalry soldier in the War of 1812 and fought against the British.[18] He was in James Hite's Company of the Kentucky Mounted Volunteer Militia (Calloway's Regiment) and appears to have joined up at a mustering or 'rendezvous' at Newport, Kentucky on 31 August 1813. He saw out the duration of the war in that regiment, seeing action both in modern day Ontario, Canada and in the modern U.S. state of Louisiana. To have owned and provisioned a horse and equipped oneself as a cavalry soldier in that era would have required finance and suggests that George may have had an income from the Sebastian family.

The War of 1812, fought between the United States and the United Kingdom, with their respective allies, from June 1812 to February 1815, arose from a British naval blockade to choke off neutral trade to France, which the U.S. contested was illegal under international law and the pressing of American merchant sailors into the Royal Navy. For the British it was an attempt to prevent supplies reaching Napoleonic France and the defence of Upper and Lower Canada from United States' expansion. When United States' forces invaded disputed territory in modern day Michigan, Britain in turn supplied arms to American Indians who raided American settlers on the frontier, hindering American expansion and provoking resentment in particular in Kentucky.[19] On 18 June 1812, President James Madison, declared war.

George served at the Battle of the Thames in 1813 at modern day Chatham, Ontario.[20] A small detachment of regulars from the 27th U.S. Infantry and five brigades of Kentucky militia led by Isaac Shelby, the then 63-year-old governor of Kentucky and 1,000 volunteer cavalry from Kentucky (of which George was one), soundly defeated their British opponents and Indian allies under Tecumseh.[21] George also served in the Kentucky Militia at the Battle of New Orleans in 1815 where U.S. forces were commanded by future President (and another inveterate duellist) General Andrew Jackson. The battle took place on 8 January 1815 (somewhat oddly, after peace had been declared) between the British, led by Major General Sir Edward Pakenham (himself of Anglo-Irish background) and the United States Army and state militias under Brevet Major General and later President Andrew Jackson (whose parents were themselves of Scots-Irish background). In later life George kept up his military connection and in 1874 just before his death attended military reunions, bearing the rank of General.

MARRIAGE(S) AND CHILDREN

On 15 June 1820, at the age of 26, George married a Miss Sarah Hickman, from a prominent Kentucky family. Through tragedy, George and Sarah were well suited: George's father was killed in a duel and when she was just 10 years old Sarah's father Paschal Hickman (then aged 35) was massacred and 'hacked apart' at the Battle of the River Raisin in January 1813 by Indians allied to the victorious British.

A PORTRAIT LOST

Sometime between their marriage on 15 June 1820 and 10 August 1827[22], a noted early U.S. portrait painter, Matthew Jouett (1788–1827), painted both George and Sarah Hickman. Jouett was of such skill and reputation he had previously painted both President Thomas Jefferson and General Lafayette. The image below is thought to be that of Sarah Hickman and remains in the ownership of George's direct descendants. Unfortunately the location of the portrait of George himself is now unknown.

Sarah Hickman

HAT-SELLER, POLITICIAN, LAWYER AND GLASSES WEARER

Two months after their marriage, on 7 August 1820, George and Sarah were residents of Louisville, Kentucky. There were 12 people in their household. Shockingly perhaps to modern sensibilities[23] these included eight 'free white persons' and four slaves (a man and woman aged 16–25 and two children). The latter were probably owned by George. Of these people, five were 'engaged in manufacturing'[24] George's ownership of slaves (common in Kentucky) continued into the late 1840s.

It appears that George's manufacturing activities related to hat-making which was a popular form of dress at the time and in which his slaves may have been engaged. An advert from a Louisville paper in 1834 shows that he was of an enterprising nature.

Fashionable Hat Manufactory,

SIGN OF THE GOLDEN HAT,

IMMEDIATELY opposite the Washington Hall, where can be had, wholesale or retail, HATS of superior quality, and of the latest fashion, on as reasonable terms as they can be furnished in the city, or elsewhere.

GEORGE W. CHAMBERS.

January 20   49

However George's military involvement continued. In 1835, the Journal of the Senate of the Commonwealth of Kentucky noted that: 'Robert Graham, to be General of the 29th Brigade, in place of G. W. Chambers, promoted'.[25] George had therefore continued to volunteer in the military and by July 1836 was appointed Major General of the 6th Division of Kentucky Volunteers.

LAWYER AND SPECTACLE WEARER

In the Federal Census of 1850 George was described as a 'lawyer and justice of the peace' and the value of his estate was about $12,000.[26] [27] He appears to have had a successful legal practice and judicial practice until the outbreak of the Civil War in early 1861. An advert in January 1851 indicates that he was both a lawyer and judge.

G. W. CHAMBERS,
ATTORNEY AT LAW AND MAGISTRATE.
OFFICE—Court Place, near east end Court House.   jan1dly

This legal work must have taken a toll on his eyesight, as *The Louisville Daily Courier* of Thursday 15 May 1851 noted that he had lost his spectacles and was offering a reward for their return.

LOST:
A PAIR OF GOLD SPECTACLES on Saturday last. Any one finding the same and
will deliver them to me at my residence on Main street, immediately opposite the Galt House, will not only confer a
great favor, but be liberally rewarded.
my14 d3 ·   G. W. CHAMBERS.

POLITICS AND THE IRISH FAMINE

His father was trained as a Presbyterian minister and then appears to have practised as a Episcopalian Vicar close to Chambersburg, Pennsylvania (en route to Kentucky). However George's own religious views and allegiances are unknown. It may well have been that his mother was a Roman Catholic and he would have been brought up in that faith. In the wake of the Irish famine and 'nativist' protests against Irish-Catholic immigration into the United States, George's own political affiliation appears to have been very liberal and strongly in favour of personal freedom of conscience and religion. This remains a touchstone of Presbyterianism. George appears to have been supportive of the new Irish arrivals and felt strongly-enough to defend in the press the disputed loyalty of Roman Catholic Irish emigrants, then flooding into Kentucky in great numbers. This was an area which, previously, had been a Scots-Irish Presbyterian and German Lutheran stronghold. In a long and interesting letter to the editors of the *Louisville Daily Courier* (22 June 1855), George stoutly defended religious liberty and emphasised the loyalty of newly-arrived Roman Catholics to the civil authorities of the United States. He also criticised 'no nothings' and other anti-Irish and anti-immigrant politicians as effectively religious bigots. The following excerpt gives some hint as to his beliefs:

> ... Though, in a word—for I have no time to say more—be his meaning and intention what it may, he knows full well that the church claims no such power as is ascribed to him, and that she, and she alone, is her own organ and expounder of her doctrines and principles. Therefore, any principle he may advance will be his *own*, and he alone responsible for it, as he himself publishes to the world, for he knows that the communication of approbation from the Bishops, which is published in the Journal was only in reference to his able defence of the *faith* of the Catholic Church, and nothing more; which, however, is what *outsiders* so little understand, that I am not surprised they do not comprehend it. But here follows ...

POLITICS, SLAVERY STATES RIGHTS AND THE CONFEDERACY

Although a staunch defender of liberty in religious matters, George appears to have taken a rather less liberal attitude to the issue of Federal Power and States' Rights and the continuity of slave-holding and its expansion in the approach to the Civil War. His first wife Sarah Hickman appears to have died sometime in the early 1850s. George (then at the advanced age of 67) married a Miss Margaret Harbour, aged 30, on 11 September 1860 in Holmes County, Mississippi, and started a second family. Aside from being a slave owner for some 30 years, George's second marriage to a much younger 'Southern Belle' from Mississippi in the cotton-growing Deep South of America, may have significantly coloured his opinion and bolstered his support for the Confederacy. Aside from marrying into a southern family, George, for intellectual reasons and perhaps pure stubbornness, seems to have favoured 'states rights' and to have opposed increased centralisation of power in Washington DC as perceived to be likely to be occurring under President-Elect Abraham Lincoln. George's views on the morals of slavery are unknown. However at a meeting of War of 1812 veterans in Louisville on 9 January 1861 – on the same day that Mississippi seceded – George proposed an overtly political toast (perhaps supportive of secession and the Confederacy) as follows.[28]

1st—The Declaration of Independence, 4th July, 1776—The Charter of Liberty of a great and growing nation of freemen.

2d—The memory of Washington and the heroes and sages[?] of the Revolution.

3d—The memory of Andrew Jackson, the Hero of New Orleans.

4th—The memory of Zachery Taylor the conqueror of Santa Anna at Buena Vista.

5th—The union of the States under the Constitution—*"Salus populi suprema est lex"*—The rights and interest of the people who are governed must be the supreme law of the land.

6th—The Star Spangled Banner, without submission or usurpation.

7th—The health and happiness of John J. Crittenden, the Patriot and Statesman—May God long preserve his life for the good of his country.

The following volunteer toasts were offered and drank with enthusiasm :

By Capt. Joyce—May the North come back to the Constitution, and the South stand up to it.

By Col. Thomas Anderson—Major Anderson, the Hero and Soldier of
Fort Moultrie.
By Major Levi—The memory of Ralph Farnham, the last survivor of
Bunker Hill.
By General Chambers—The Union with equal rights and privileges—
not otherwise.
By Capt. John Russell—J. J. Crittenden's resolutions or their equivalent
is what Kentucky desires. May he long live.

In any event, at the age of 67, George appears to have left Louisville for
the only extensive period of his life, and settled in Mississippi during
the years of the Civil War, only returning to Louisville in or about
1870. Although he would have been too old to fight himself, it is likely
that he was active in support of the Confederacy

RETURN TO KENTUCKY AND REDEMPTION?

In the census of 1870, George 76, was again living in Louisville, with
his wife Margaret Harbour (38, and 38 years his junior) and his three
children aged eight, four, and two. The Civil War (and/or a wife half
his age) had taken a toll: George's personal estate had dwindled from
$12,000 in 1850 to only $400 in 1870. Despite leaving Kentucky for
the Confederacy and backing the losing side in the Civil War, George
appears to have kept many friends and to have been much loved and
respected in Louisville. New York newspapers covered his death in the
following report.[29]
All the contemporary Louisville and southern newspapers produced
obituaries in glowing terms.[30]

GENERAL GEORGE W. CHAMBERS.

General George W. Chambers, one of the oldest
citizens of Kentucky, died a few days ago, aged
eighty-one years. General Chambers was born at
Bardstone, October 21, 1793. He served in the war
of 1812. While a young man he removed to Louisville, where he followed the business of a hatter,
but afterward studied law and was for over
twenty years County Judge. When troops were
called to go to Mexico, General Chambers
was senior Major General of the State,
and consequently entitled, under the State constitution, to command Kentucky's contribution to
the army for the Mexican war. President Polk,
however, refused to commission him, and his
friends say he did not regret it, as he considered
"the war a flagrantly unjust one in every point of
view, brought about by that Jacobin faction of
New York, Tammany democracy." When the
rebellion broke out he sympathized with it and
went South, returning broken in fortune.

Our readers were prepared for the announcement of the death of Gen. George W. Chambers, which occurred at his residence on
Twenty-third and Madison on Friday night,
January 8th—the sixtieth anniversary of the
battle of New Orleans, of which struggle he
was one of the few survivors. At the time of
his death, Gen. Chambers had reached the
ripe age of eighty-two years, having resided
for more than half a century in the city of
Louisville. No citizen bore a more irre-
proachable character—no stain ever marred
his good name.

Gen. Chambers was born in Bardstown,
where he grew up. When a mere boy he vol-
unteered in the army as a private, and made
a most gallant soldier. He was in the battle
of the Thames, and in the memorable expedi-
tion to Canada, enduring all the hardships,
privations and dangers incident to that campaign. He was also at the Battle of New Orleans; and all his time of service in the army
was a soldier distiguished for gallantry and
daring.—*Louisville Ledger*, 11th inst.

Gen. George W. Chambers, one of
the oldest citizens of Louisville, and
well known to nearly every inhabi-
tant, died at his residence, on the
corner of Twenty-fourth and Madison streets, on Friday night last, having reached the age of eighty-two
years.

A PORTRAIT FOUND?

Although the earlier Jouett portrait of George Washington Chambers has been lost, it was with much excitement that the author was provided by interested researchers in Kentucky with a selection of obituaries and, most remarkably, a contemporary portrait of George Washington Chambers. These were provided by interested researchers in Kentucky at The University of Louisville, Brandeis School of Law [31] and the University of Kentucky Law Library at Lexington, Kentucky.[32] George is depicted, perhaps just before his death in 1875, and certainly in his older years as follows.

It might be just wishful thinking on the part of the author (or purely coincidental) but there is some passing resemblance (given the separation of at least 4 generations) to the author's own grandfather William Lewis Chambers (3 Dec. 1916–17 Aug. 1991) at a similar age.

George Washington Chambers and
RIGHT: William Lewis Chambers

NOTES

1   Born 31 October 1793, Bardstown, Nelson County, Kentucky; died 8 January 1875, Louisville, Jefferson County, Kentucky.

2   Jonathan Chambers, 'From Ballee to Kentucky: the adventures of James Chambers', *Lecale Review*, no. 17 (2019) pp 74–9.

3   Tullynaskeagh Papers (held by the author).

4   Tullynaskeagh MMS (held by the author and available in scan). Jack Chambers pictured on right in picture with two Belgian soldiers and a Chambers Ambulance in Flanders in 1915.

5   Tullynaskeagh MMS (held by the author and available in scan). Jack Chambers' transcript written as a boy is deposited at the Linen Hall Library, Belfast (N156.94 929.2 CHAM (NB1218)).

6   Tullynaskeagh MMS (held by the author and available in scan). Jack incorrectly referred to the historian of 1858 as James Chambers who was probably the father or grandfather of the correct author Francis Chambers (22 June 1771–24 March 1862)

7   The author was not alone in his search and his thanks are extended to the late Frances Groves Mancusi-Ungaro (née Chambers), her daughter Diana and granddaughter Laura who are direct descendants of James and George Washington Chambers, for their assistance.

8   Public Record Office of Northern Ireland: https://www.nidirect.gov.uk/services/search-pronis-ecatalogue.

9   JSTOR: https://www.jstor.org; Google Book Archive: https://archive.org/details/googlebooks.

10 US archive: https://newspaperarchive.com/; UK and Ireland: https://www.britishnewspaperarchive.co.uk.

11 Kentucky Historical Society and Museums: https://history.ky.gov/resources.

12 Filson Historical Society: https://filsonhistorical.org/collections-resources.

13 My thanks to Diana Mancusi-Ungaro and Laura Saltarelli the direct descendants of Dr James Chambers and George Washington Chambers for this information

14 Courtesy of the Filson Historical Society, Louisville and available for free at https://www.werelate.org/wiki/Person:George_Chambers_(13).

15 Her father Benjamin Sebastian was a well-known Judge in the Kentucky Court of Appeals.

16 https://www.werelate.org/wiki/Person:Amelia_Sebastian_(1) and Catharine L Breckinridge 1788–1864 – Ancestry.

17 https://www.ancestry.co.uk/genealogy/records/catharine-l-breckinridge-24-318rjgm?geo_a=r&geo_s=au&geo_t=uk&geo_v=2.0.0&o_iid=41020&o_lid=41020&o_sch=Web+Property.

18 https://www.fold3.com.

19 Donald Hickey, *The War of 1812: A Forgotten Conflict (1989)*.

20 Also known as Battle of Moraviantown, **a** decisive U.S. victory over British and Indian forces at Chatham, Ontario, Canada.

21 After whom the US Civil War General William Tecumseh Sherman was named.

22 The death of the painter.

23 Kentucky was a border state and although slave-holding until 1st January 1863 it remained loyal to the Union in the Civil War of 1861–65 and did not secede. A star representing Kentucky was placed on both the flags of the Union and the Confederacy. Significant numbers of Kentuckians joined the Confederate Army and are now known as "The Orphan Brigade".

24 1820 U S Census; Census Place: Louisville, Jefferson, Kentucky; Page: 28; NARA Roll: M33_24; Image: 39.

25 Journal of the Senate of the Commonwealth of Kentucky, page 242 .

26 Jordan Dodd, 'Kentucky Marriages, 1802–1850', Ancestry.com (1997); original data: electronic transcription of marriage records held by the individual counties in Kentucky.

27 US$360,000 in contemporary currency.

28 *Louisville Daily Courier*, 9 Jan. 1861.

29 *New York Daily Herald*, 19 Jan. 1875.

30 *Louisville Ledger*, 11 Jan. 1875, and *New Orleans Bulletin*, 19 Jan. 1875.

31 Marcus Walker, Law School Archivist and Digital Collections Librarian.

32 Nicole Reynolds, Digital Collections Librarian.

33 Bobby Hanvey and Brian S. Turner, *Merely Players: Portraits from Northern Ireland* (1999).

The poor and distressed inhabitants of Belfast:
the Poor's Money Lists of 1753

IAN MONTGOMERY

During the seventeenth and eighteenth centuries a number of people bequeathed or donated money for the benefit of the poor of Belfast. This money was held in trust by the town Corporation which was charged with investing it and using the proceeds for the benefit of the poor. Three lists of payments from the fund for the year 1753, which are included in the Assembly Book of Belfast, held in the Public Record Office of Northern Ireland, constitute the only surviving records of people who benefited from the fund. They give a unique insight into the social structure of Belfast in the middle of the eighteenth century and contain information on people who are unlikely to feature in other records of the period.[1]

INTRODUCTION

Belfast has been well served with historical accounts, most of which focus on the period from the 1780s onwards when the town began to emerge as an important commercial and manufacturing centre. The growth of Victorian Belfast into one of the major industrial centres of the British Isles and the political and sectarian conflict of the twentieth century have seen a number of academic and popular works. The earlier history of the town is not so well served. In part, this is because early Belfast, while not quite the 'barbarous nook of Ireland' condemned by Milton, is not as well documented as the industrial city. George Benn, in his first attempt at a history of the town published in

1823, noted that '… there is not undoubtedly a town in the kingdom which has advanced to eminence with equal rapidity, or which has been so little distinguished in the ancient history of Ireland, and so much of the modern'.[2]

Benn's substantial history, greatly enlarged in 1877, made extensive use of the limited number of sources available. His work continues to be of value, not least because of the vast range of interesting and eclectic information that it contains, and has informed most later accounts.[3] Over the last 30 years more focused work by Jean Agnew, Raymond Gillespie, Ruairí Ó Baoill and others has expanded our understanding of the town's early history. These studies utilised a wider range of sources than Benn and his contemporaries, including leases, deeds, will abstracts and private correspondence. They have also benefited from the improvement in archaeological techniques and increasing interest in post-medieval archaeology which has improved our knowledge of the preindustrial town and its hinterland. Other disciplines such as historical geography have similarly shaped our understanding of the town and its inhabitants.[4]

There are relatively few surviving sources for seventeenth- and eighteenth-century Belfast which give information on the ordinary inhabitants of the town.[5] This is a particular problem for family historians. The registers of the Church of Ireland parish church survive from 1745 and a printed version is available.[6] Only a minority of Belfast's population, perhaps as little as 15 per cent, was connected to the established church, the majority being Presbyterians. The earliest surviving Presbyterian baptism or marriage records are those of the Third Congregation which date from *c.* 1723. There is also a 'Funeral Register' for First Presbyterian church for the period 1712–36. This is actually a record of the people who rented funeral garments from the church, many of whom came from outside of the town. A printed edition of this register is available.[7] There were only a few Roman Catholics living in Belfast and its hinterland at this period and there are no surviving Catholic registers before 1798.

Perhaps the most important source for the town's early history is the Town Book of Belfast. Ostensibly a record of the proceedings of the Corporation of Belfast from 1613 to the middle of the eighteenth century, in fact it contains a range of miscellaneous information about the town to 1816. The Victorian printed edition, with notes and additional material by Robert Young, was republished in 2008.[8] As well as recording the activities of the Corporation, the Town Book contains lists of cess or rate payers in the town, 1639–45 (around 350 names) and of freemen of Belfast (around 1,200 names), 1636–82 and 1723–96. Unfortunately, these are not indexed in the printed volume.[9] A list of people paying Hearth Money in Belfast in the 1660s has also been published.[10] While these sources are useful, they focus for the most part on the successful and prosperous people in the town. Nearly all the cess payers, freemen and those involved in the administration of the town were men and, if not necessarily wealthy, they had some standing in the community. The Poor's Money lists give us an insight into the lives of those who might otherwise have been forgotten.

THE POOR'S MONEY

Not a great deal is known about the Poor's Money and how the fund operated. There are some references in the Town Book of Belfast and the Assembly Book, which record the proceedings of the Belfast Corporation, 1613–1840. A more detailed account can be found in a report into the activities of the Corporation compiled by a Parliamentary Commission in 1835. However, this report focuses on the later years of the fund's operation as the Commissioners were principally interested in finding out what had happened to the money.[11] The Corporation had been established in 1613 when Sir Arthur Chichester was granted a charter for the settlement of Belfast. It consisted of a Sovereign (the equivalent of a Mayor) and 12 burgesses, all of whom were nominated by Chichester and his descendants, the earls of Donegall. Although the Corporation initially had a role in the administration of the town, it remained under the control of the Donegall family who effectively owned Belfast. The penal legislation of the early eighteenth-century restricted membership of the Corporation to members of the Established Church (Church of Ireland). In a town that was largely Presbyterian this excluded most of the population, including the prosperous merchant class. The Corporation continued in existence until abolished, as were most of the other Irish borough corporations, in 1840 but became increasingly irrelevant to the life of the town.[12]

The earliest known benefactor was Edward Holmes, a former Sovereign of Belfast, who bequeathed £40 in 1631 'for the future relief of the poor distressed inhabitants of the borough of Belfast'. The Sovereign proceeded to lend this money to various residents of the town, many of them connected with the Corporation. The interest from these investments was to be distributed annually to the poor by the Sovereign.[13] Both cash and credit were in very short supply in seventeenth- and eighteenth-century Ireland so the existence of the Poor's Money would have provided a useful source of working capital for local merchants and landowners. In addition, the high interest rates prevalent during the seventeenth century, up to 40 per cent in the early part of the century falling to 10 per cent by the 1680s, meant the Fund could yield a substantial income if managed properly.[14]

The downside of these arrangements was soon evident. The first account of the Poor's Money in the Town Book dates from 1647 and is concerned with the Corporation's attempts to recover outstanding interest payments. This continued to be a problem and in 1675 the then Sovereign, George McCartney, sought legal powers to compel those who held the money to furnish accounts and to provide securities for the capital.[15] In 1680 the Corporation ordered the names of those who had contributed to the fund be inscribed on a board which was to be placed in the parish church of Belfast. This board, which is now in Clifton House, was updated down to 1759 by which time the donations amounted to £1,186. The Parliamentary Commissioners found evidence of a couple of additional donations which brought the total up to £1256 by 1774 (see Appendix A below). They were also of the opinion that a much larger capital sum was available and that at least some of the interest received over the life of the fund had been added to the capital rather than paid to the poor.[16]

The fact that people living in Belfast continued to bequeath money to the fund until the later part of the eighteenth century suggests that it was still making provision for the poor people of the town. In 1752 an attempt was made by the newly created Belfast Charitable Society to raise funds by means of a lottery to build a poor house and hospital for the town. The lottery was not a success and the Poor House did not open until 1775, by which time the Society had been incorporated by Act of Parliament. The Charitable Society became the main source of support for the poor and destitute in the town from this date and from 1775 the Corporation began paying the annual interest of the Poor's Money to the Society. They refused however to transfer the capital of the Fund and the interest payments became irregular, leading eventually to legal action by the Charitable Society. The Parliamentary Commissioners concluded in 1835 that from the early nineteenth century there had been systematic abuse of the fund by members of the Corporation. The principal suspects were members of the May family who were related to the Earl of Donegall. The Charitable Society eventually received some of the money after prolonged legal proceedings but much of the fund was never recovered.[17]

PROVIDING FOR THE POOR

Provision for the poor and destitute was less developed in eighteenth century Ireland than in contemporary England or Scotland. In

England, the Elizabethan Poor, financed by a local poor rate, supported people in their home parish. This system was not extended to Ireland. Irish legislation, such as it was, focused on the control of vagrancy and the regulation of begging. In Ulster some parishes, possibly influenced by Scottish practice, collected money on a regular basis for distribution to the poor and issued badges to authorised beggars. In Belfast both the Presbyterian and Established churches raised money for the poor, although there were allegations that they only supported their own adherents. There are examples of *ad hoc* local arrangements in times of crisis: in the arctic winter of 1739/40 a door to door collection in Belfast raised money for people suffering from the severe weather. Apart from these crisis arrangements there was no formal system of support and the Poor's Money would have been an important source of financial assistance for the poor and destitute in Belfast.[18]

The first half of the eighteenth century was an era of economic depression in Belfast and the rest of Ulster. Between 1660 and 1710 Ulster had enjoyed a period of economic growth, punctuated by occasional harvest failures. The population had risen, particularly during the 1690s when there was an influx of people from Scotland driven by severe harvest failures and high rents. The number of households in Belfast increased fourfold between 1663 and 1725, with similar growth in other urban centres. From around 1710 however Ulster experienced a prolonged recession which lasted into the 1750s. A series of harvest failures caused distress and in some cases famine. The worst of these in 1741 may have resulted in the deaths of a larger proportion of the Irish population than did the Great Famine of 1847. While this famine had less effect in Ulster it still caused widespread devastation. One consequence of the economic downturn was increased emigration to North America, particularly of those recently arrived from Scotland.[19]

Belfast was also affected by the absence of the proprietorial family the earls of Donegall. The death of the third Earl in 1706 was followed by a fire which destroyed Belfast Castle, after which the family resided for the most part on their English estates. The fourth Earl proved incapable of managing his affairs and his family and trustees showed little interest in Belfast. Only relatively short-term leases were granted, leading to a lack of investment in the town. In addition, the family came into conflict with the merchant community over control of the town Corporation. This, and the effects of the Test Act of 1704 which effectively debarred Presbyterians from membership of the Corporation, resulted in the exclusion of most of the wealthiest residents from the government of the town.[20]

By 1753 the economic conditions in Belfast were recovering as the linen and provisions trades picked up across Ulster. The trustees of the Earl of Donegall obtained an Act of Parliament in 1752 which allowed them to grant extended leases, encouraging investment in the town. Work also began on new infrastructure projects such as the Lagan Navigation and the Brown Linen Hall. There were some setbacks to this recovery. The crises of 1756/7, attributed to harvest failures compounded by hoarding of grain, led to outbreaks of rioting in Belfast. The parish registers record a significant increase in deaths among the poorer members of society in these years. In response to this crisis a new poor relief system was created in the town, with money being levied from householders and distributed among the poor and destitute. By the spring of 1757 more than 600 people a month were being supported. The 1753 Poor's Money list therefore falls between two subsistence crises and gives an indication of the level of support provided in a relatively stable period.[21]

THE LISTS OF PERSONS

The lists of recipients of the Poor's Money are contained in a section of the Assembly Book which appears to have been bound in at a later date and is paginated separately from the rest of the volume. It consists of three alphabetical lists, along with a list of beggars and some additional names. The summary on page 12 mentions a 'Private List' which is not included in the volume. The lists contain the name of the recipient, in some cases an occupation or other identifier, the amount paid and what appears to be the name of the person who made the payment. The identity of these individuals is discussed below. In a few cases the pauper was paid directly. One individual, Francis Kirckly refused to accept the money. (He may be the Francis Kirkly who arranged the funeral of his child in April 1717.)[22] Another person, 'Widow

Johnston in the Falls' was marked as 'no charity', while others were removed from the list as dead.

The total amount paid to the poor, after the exclusion of a few claimants, was £112 6s. 6d. According to the official list of subscribers the fund at this stage amounted to £886, suggesting a pay out of nearly 13 per cent of the principle. However, the Parliamentary Commissioners estimated that by 1755 nearly £1,200 was available, making the expenditure just over 9 per cent. As the Corporation was apparently receiving 5 per cent interest on its investments at this time, this would appear to be a high rate of expenditure for a single year. It is however in line with the payment of £119 8s. 9d. from the fund to the Belfast Charitable Society in 1776 and the similar sums paid subsequently. This reinforces the theory that the capital available was greater than the list of donations would suggest.[23]

The total number of names recorded as receiving money, for themselves or their families, is 377. In addition, there were an unknown number of people in the 'Private list'. A survey of the town in 1757 gave the population as 8,549 living in 1779 houses. This suggests that less than 5 per cent of the population was receiving assistance. If each of the recipients represents one household, however, this would indicate that around 20 per cent of families were receiving some support from the fund. It should be noted that some of the recipients, such as the beggars, may have been homeless and others could have been living in multi occupancy houses, so that the proportion of families supported was probably somewhat lower.[24]

The three lists represent different levels of assistance given to the claimants. In the first list there are two relatively large payments of £1 2s. 9d. to 'Widow Anderson' and 'Robert Young son of John'. The rest of the list (46 people) received sums ranging from 18s. 3d. to 5s. 5d., with the majority getting between 7 and 11 shillings. (The average payment, excluding the two outliers, is 9s. 5d.) The second list contains 135 names with people receiving between 5s. 5d. and 7s. 7d., the average payment being just over 6 shillings. The 192 people in the third list, which included 11 beggars, received between 4s. 4d. and 1s. 1d., the average being 2s. 9d. There is a list of additional recipients receiving between 2 and 6 shillings. The precise amounts of money distributed to individuals may have been influenced by the amount and types of coinage available. The £1 2s. 9d. which Mrs Anderson and Robert Young received probably represented an English guinea coin worth 21 shillings sterling. The large number of payments of 5s. 5d. may have been in Spanish silver dollars which circulated at that value, while the frequency of amounts such as 2s. 2d., 3s. 3d., etc., probably reflects the use of English minted silver shillings which were worth 13 pence Irish.[25]

More than three quarters of the names in the lists are women, most of them widows. This reflects contemporary attitudes towards charity which considered widows, orphans, the elderly and the infirm as fit objects for support but not able-bodied men. The dangers to society of undiscriminating charity was a common theme in contemporary discourse. James Saurin, the Church of Ireland vicar of Belfast, in a sermon preached in Belfast on several occasions in the 1750s condemned:

> … the artfulness of those who living in idleness and sloth … and who counterfeiting misery and poverty deprive real objects of the bounty of their fellow creatures and apply to the encouraging of their idleness what was intended for the relief of the honest poor and the comfort of sickness and old-age.[26]

To be fair, Saurin in another sermon also condemned a society which was '… too ready to seek for any pretence to excuse our uncharitableness … [and] to lay the misfortunes of the poor at their own door.' Able bodied men would also have had more opportunities to support themselves by casual work. This is reflected in the record of pauper burials in the parish which were predominantly of women in the 1750s, except in the aftermath of the harvest failure of 1756/7 which saw a marked increase in the number of men described as 'poor'. This is probably the consequence of malnutrition resulting from food shortages making men on the margins of society more vulnerable to disease.[28]

As was normal in the eighteenth century (and much later) most of the women are identified by their husband's or father's names e.g. 'Erwin, widow of James a Carpenter', 'Gardner, daughter of Robert a Printer' or simply 'Anderson, widow'. This makes it difficult to find further information on individuals although some of the names can be matched with other sources. For instance, the 'Grub, widow of John a farmer' who received 8s. 1½d. is probably the Widow Grub, described as 'poor', who was buried in Shankill graveyard on 23 April 1758.[29] 'Ann Coats, alias Grove, widow', who received 18s. 3d. is slightly better documented. She was married to Richard Coats, a singing master, and their son Richard was baptised on 17 January 1745. On 1 April 1748, another Richard Coats was baptised, the son of the late Richard and Ann, otherwise Grove. A Richard Coats was buried in the churchyard of St George's on 10 September 1747, but it is not clear if this Richard is Ann's husband or her first-born son.[30]

As with all sources from this period there will be variations in the spelling of personal names, place names and descriptions of occupation. The 'Gaddis, widow of John a currier' was presumably the wife of the person described in the First Presbyterian funeral register on various occasions between 1723 and 1731 as 'John Geades, carier, Norstreat'; 'John Gades, corier'; 'John Gades, at North Geat'; and John Gaddas, Coriner'. On the first three occasions he was arranging the funerals of children or grandchildren, on the last on 6 November 1731 his wife appears to be arranging his funeral.[31]

In a few cases a specific disability is mentioned such as David Alexander 'a blind diaper weaver', Robert Hanna 'a sickly boy' and Jane Gordon 'lame carried on a barrow'. There was no specific provision for people with disabilities at this time and they would have relied on the support of their families or provided for themselves as best they could. One of the objectives of the poorhouse and hospital proposed in 1752 was the 'reception of infirm and diseased poor' but it was not until the nineteenth century that specialist provision was made for the blind or physically handicapped.[32]

Beggars are recorded separately at the end of the third list. There are only eleven names in this list, just over 3 per cent of the total number supported by the Fund. These people were probably the licensed or approved beggars in the town. Contemporary opinion saw 'rogues, vagabonds, sturdy beggars' as threat to society especially if they originated outside the relieving town or parish.

The Irish Parliament introduced legislation on several occasions to control vagrancy and at the beginning of the eighteenth century some

Ulster parishes issued badges to approved or licensed beggars in attempting to expel those from outside the parish. In Belfast, a bye law introduced in 1680 ordered that 'beggars who come into and secretly convey themselves into the town … may be diligently sought after and a speedy course taken to discharge the town of such.'[33] The Corporation also took steps to enforce this regulation. One of the people receiving money in 1753 was, perhaps ironically, the widow of John Doyle described as a 'Bang Beggar'. The term Bang Beggar was an alternative name for a beadle and was the civic official responsible for the control of vagrants. The office continued in Belfast into the 1780s by which time the Bang Beggar was responsible for bringing vagrants, by force if need be, to the Poor House.[34]

The relatively small amounts of money distributed by the Fund would not have been the sole means of support for the recipients. The average daily wage for a general labourer in Belfast in the first half of the eighteenth century fluctuated between five and eight pence per day. Skilled workers or craftsmen received between 12 and 19 pence.[35] At times of particular hardship, other types of support were necessary. During the Great Frost of January 1741, a house to house collection raised approximately £150 to provide additional support to around 850 people in Belfast. The harvest crises of 1756–7 saw the introduction of a more organised system of poor relief, funded by monthly payments made by householders in the town. This fund distributed money to between 400 and 600 people at the average rate of just over two shillings per fortnight during the early months of 1757. The scheme continued to operate until the Belfast Charitable Society began operations in 1774.[36]

Occupations, trades or professions are given for 176 of the people named in the list, either in respect of the person themselves or their former husband if a widow. This collection complements the lists compiled from the First Presbyterian funeral register and the Church of Ireland parish register and provides an insight into the economy of the town in the middle of the eighteenth century. Not surprisingly the largest single group are described as labourers (17). The labourers, along with the carmen, i.e. carters or carriers (13), porters (6) and huxters (hucksters) i.e. peddlers or hawkers (6), probably represented the most vulnerable socio-economic group. There are several trades and professions included in the list. These include shoemakers (11), tailors (5), butchers (5), carpenters (4) and glovers (4). From the late seventeenth century industries were developing on a small scale in the town, focused on the area between the modern Waring and High Streets. Among these was the manufacture of earthenware, including high quality delftware, leather making, sugar refining, paper making and printing. These industries are all represented in the Poor's Money lists.

The lists also include a significant number of weavers (12, plus a 'diaper weaver'). At this time weaving was a domestic industry, often undertaken to supplement household income and the production of fine diaper linens was becoming an important trade in east Ulster. The importance of the harbour and seaborne trade to the town is reflected by the number of sailors (12) in the lists, along with a boatman, three tidewaiters or customs officials and a gabbard man. The gabbards were small boats or lighters which ferried cargos and passengers between the larger ships anchored offshore and the quayside. The number of farmers (9) reflects the fact that Belfast was still a relatively small town with open country nearby and that Ireland was still an overwhelmingly agrarian society.[37]

There are also a small number of people on the lists whose occupations suggest that they should have been more financially secure. These include the widow of James Finney, a ship master. Finney's name appears in the papers of Alexander Stewart as the captain of a ship called the *George and William* trading between Belfast and the Baltic in the 1720s.[38] Mathew King, a shopkeeper and the widow of Robert Gordon, also a shopkeeper, are included, a reminder that misfortune, illness or the loss of a breadwinner could quickly reduce anyone to a state of dependency.

Three teachers are mentioned in the lists. The widows of John McLanachan, a mathematics master, and Robert Hay, a writing master, both received assistance. McLanachan may be the surveyor and map maker John Maclanachan who produced surveys of several estates in Ulster in the 1720s as well as one of the earliest maps of Belfast in 1715. The map is discussed by Raymond Gillespie in *Early Belfast* and reproduced in the *Historic Towns Atlas*.[39] Robert Hay or Heayes is mentioned in the First Presbyterian funeral register when he arranged the burials of his (presumably) first wife in 1714 and subsequently three children between 1719 and 1723. His address is given in the funeral register as the Market House, which was the main public building in Belfast, suggesting that he may have utilised the large upper room of the building, which was used as a court room or for public meetings, as a school. There is also a Janet Kennedy, described as a widow and schoolmistress. She, along with Eleanor Mullan and Sarah Allet who were described as 'washers', were the only women recorded as following any trade or profession.[40]

Perhaps the most intriguing entry is that for Mrs Fullerton, described as the widow of a 'Quack doctor'. Although the recognised medical profession used the term 'Quack' to disparage these practitioners, many of them prospered and grew rich. Fullerton was presumably not one of the lucky ones. Another medical professional is represented by the widow of Samuel Miller, a surgeon. Surgeons at this time had a lower social status than physicians and tended to be lumped together with apothecaries and wigmakers.[41]

While most of the people in the lists remain only names, the story of one of the recipients, Edward Hall 'late serjeant', is relatively well documented. Hall was elected one of the two Sergeants at Mace for the town in 1720. The Sergeants at Mace, elected at town assemblies, acted as town constables and assisted the Sovereign in the administration of the town receiving a small salary as well as fees. Hall was dismissed from his post in November 1744 due to his 'mismanagement in his office' and also because 'he is at present confined in jail at Carrickfergus for debt and … rendered incapable of doing his duty as Town serjeant'. In the ensuing election Clements Monepenny defeated Arthur Hall. Arthur may have been Edward's son. An Arthur Hall, son of Edward, was buried in the parish churchyard in September 1751. Edward Hall died in 1755.[42]

The names of the people who paid out the money to the claimants are given in Appendix C below. Some can be identified as sovereigns or burgesses of the town including Thomas Banks, John Duff, Margetson Saunders and William Byrtt (or Le Byrtt). James Blow (1676–1759) was a Scottish-born printer and paper-maker who established the first printing press in Belfast. He bequeathed money to the Poor's Fund and his son Daniel Blow took an active role in the Belfast Charitable Society. The Mctier was probably Samuel McTier (1689?–1773) a merchant who lived at Peter's Hill and who was the father of Samuel McTier the Belfast merchant and United Irishman. The elder McTier was also involved with the Belfast Charitable Society in its early years. Blow and McTier, along with John Greg, another Scottish born merchant, were in all probability Presbyterians and as such excluded from the Corporation. Their involvement in the work of the Poor's Fund shows that in practice the wealthy Presbyterian merchants played an important role in the life of the town at this period.[43]

The Poor's money lists provide a tantalising glimpse into life in the town of Belfast at an important juncture in its history. While the information on the individuals named is frustratingly brief, particularly for women, it can in some cases be put together with other sources to provide at least some record of their lives. For many of the names recorded, such as Mary Calbrath the 'lame beggar', it may be the only record of their existence.

APPENDIX A: LIST OF THE LEGACIES AND GIFTS MADE FOR THE USE OF THE POOR OF BELFAST.

This is based on a table, formerly in the parish church of Belfast and now held in Clifton House, which is reproduced in Strain's history of the Belfast Charitable Society, augmented with information from the Report of the Parliamentary Commissioners.[44]

NAME	DATE OF DEATH/DONATION	AMOUNT
Edward Holmes, burgess	June 1631	£40
Thomas Chaplin, yeoman	3 June 1659	£2
Thomas Waring, burgess	23 November 1665	£40
Nicholas Gardiner, chandler	2 July 1668	£10

NAME	DATE OF DEATH/DONATION	AMOUNT
John Ridgely, burgess	1 April 1669	£10
Hugh Doake, burgess	11 August 1669	£10
William Thorn, merchant	27 December 1670	£5
John Clugston, merchant	6 August 1671	£5
Thomas Kerron, yeoman	4 March 1672	£3
Arthur, Earl of Donegall	18 April 1674	£200
William Anderson, merchant	22 March 1675	£7
William Taylor, merchant	23 May 1676	£10
James Graham, butcher	1677	£1
Mrs Letice Andrews	20 March 1678	£3
Hugh Eccles, burgess	4 December 1680	£40
Letitia Countess of Donegall	(Gift) 1680	£100
James Chambers, merchant	31 March 1680	£100
Money raised from several causalities		£300
Mrs Jane Young	21 August 1755	£100
George Macartney, Esq	18 October 1757	£100
Mr James Blow	16 August 1759	£100
Total in 1759		£1,186

LATER DONATIONS

James Dobbin	1770	£50
Mrs Saunders	1774	£20
TOTAL		£1,256

APPENDIX B: TRADES OR OCCUPATIONS RECORDED IN THE POOR'S MONEY LISTS

Bailiff, Baker, Bang Beggar, Barber (x2), Boatman, Book Binder, Brewer, Butcher (x5), Butter Buyer, Cabinet maker, Carman (x13), Carpenter (x4), Chandler (x2), Chapman, Clothier, Coachman (x2), Coal measurer (x3), Comb maker, Cooper (x2), Curryer [Carrier], Diaper weaver, Dragoon, Farmer (x9), Fisher, Gabbard man, Gardner (x3), Glover (x4), Hatter (x3), Horse rider, Huxter (x5), Killman [Kiln man?], Labourer (x17), Linen draper, Mason, Mathematics master, Nailer (x2), Old soldier, Painter, Paper maker, Paver, Porter (x6), Potter, Printer, Pump maker, Quack doctor, Sadler, Sailor (x12), Sawyer (x3), School mistress, Sergeant, Sexton, Ship carpenter, Shipmaster, Shoemaker (x11), Shop keeper (x2), Slater (x2), Soldier, Sugar

Boiler, Surgeon, Tanner, Taylor (x5), Tidewaiter (x3), Washer (x2), Weaver (x12), Wheelwright, Wool comber, Writing master.

APPENDIX C: NAMES OF PERSONS MAKING PAYMENTS

T. Banks, J. Blow, W. Byrtt, J. Duff, J. Greg, T. Henderson, J. Hendry, M. Macartney, C. Maniger, C. Many, S. Mctier, Manipenny, J. Portis, M. Saunders, W. Simpson, J. Sims.

NOTES

1   PRONI, Belfast Corporation Papers, LA/7/2/AA/1/1.

2   George Benn, *History of the Town of Belfast with an Accurate Account of its Former and Present State* (Belfast, 1823), pp 3–4.

3   George Benn, *A History of the Town of Belfast from the Earliest Times to the Close of the Eighteenth Century* (2 vols, Belfast, 2008). This is a facsimile of the 1877–80 edition.

4   The main publications which have influenced this study are: Jean Agnew, *Belfast Merchant Families in the Seventeenth Century* (Dublin, 1996); Raymond Gillespie, *Early Belfast: the Origins and Growth of an Ulster Town to 1750* (Belfast, 2007); Raymond Gillespie and S. A. Royle, *Irish Historic Towns Atlas, no 12: Belfast, part 1 to 1840* (Dublin, 2003) and the articles by Ó Baoill, Macdonald, Gillespie and Connolly in S. J. Connolly (ed.), *Belfast 400: People, Place and History* (Liverpool, 2012).

5   Overviews of the sources for the early history of Belfast can be found in: William Roulston, *Researching Ulster Ancestors: the Essential Genealogical Guide to Early Modern Ulster, 1600–1800* (Belfast, 2018), pp 434–7, and Jean Agnew, 'Sources for the history of Belfast in the seventeenth and early eighteenth centuries', *Familia*, 2:8 (1992), pp 150–8.

6   Raymond Gillespie and Alison O'Keefe (eds), *Register of the Parish of Shankill, Belfast, 1745–1761* (Dublin, 2006).

7   Jean Agnew (ed.), *Funeral Register of the First Presbyterian Church of Belfast, 1712–36* (Belfast, 1995).

8   Robert M. Young (ed.), *The Town Book of the Corporation of Belfast, 1613–1816* (Newtownards, 2008). This is a facsimile of the 1892 edition.

9   I hope to publish these lists in the near future.

10   S. T. Carleton, *Heads and Hearths: the Hearth Money Rolls and Poll Tax Returns for Co. Antrim, 1660–1669* (Belfast, 1991), pp 36–8.

11   *First Report of the Commissioners Appointed to Inquire into the Municipal Corporations in Ireland.* H.C. 1835, XXVIII, *Appendix to the First Report*, Part 1, pp 695–731; the background to the report is discussed in Cornelius O'Leary, 'Belfast urban government in the age of reform', in David Harkness and Mary O'Dowd (eds), *The Town in Ireland* (Belfast, 1981), pp 187–202.

12   For an overview of the Corporation see: Ian Montgomery, 'The growth of a city: the Belfast Corporation and Council archive in PRONI', *Familia*, 31 (2015), pp 53–76.

13   Young (ed.), *Town Book*, pp 49–50.

14   Raymond Gillespie, *The Transformation of the Irish Economy, 1550–1700* (Dundalk, 1991), pp 54–7.

15   Young (ed.), *Town Book*, pp 49–50, 133–4.

16   The board is reproduced in R. W. M. Strain, *Belfast and its Charitable Society: a Story of Urban Social Development* (London, 1961), plate 2; Report of the Commissioners, pp 726–7.

17   Strain, *Charitable Society*, pp 89–92; *Report of the Commissioners*, pp 728–31.

18   David Dickson, 'In search of the old Irish Poor Law' in Rosalind Mitchison and Peter Roebuck (eds), *Economy and Society in Scotland and Ireland, 1500–1939* (Edinburgh, 1988), pp 149–59.

19   Raymond Gillespie, 'The early modern economy, 1600–1780' in Liam Kennedy and Philip Ollerenshaw (eds), *Ulster Since 1600: Politics, Economy and Society* (Oxford, 2013), pp 12–27; David Dickson, *Arctic Ireland: the Extraordinary Story of the Great Frost and Forgotten Famine of 1740–41* (Belfast, 1997).

20   Gillespie, *Early Belfast*, pp 128–62.

21   S. J. Connolly, 'Improving town, 1750–1820' in Connolly (ed.), *Belfast 400*, pp 161–197; Gillespie and O'Keefe, *Register*, pp 32–7.

22   Agnew (ed.), *Funeral Register*, p. 18.

23   Report of the Commissioners, p. 727; Strain, Charitable Society, p. 89.

24   Gillespie & O'Keefe, Register, p. 19.

25   Cormac Ó Gráda, *Ireland: a New Economic History, 1780–1939* (Oxford, 1994), pp 46–9.

26   Raymond Gillespie and Roibear Ó Gallachóir (eds), *Preaching in Belfast, 1747–72: a Selection of the Sermons of James Saurin* (Dublin, 2015), p. 205

27   Ibid., p 101

28   Gillespie and O'Keefe, *Register*, pp 36–7.

29   Ibid., p. 254.

30   Ibid., pp 64–5, 92, 101.

31   Agnew (ed.), *Funeral Register*, pp 27, 32, 35, 37.

32   Strain, *Charitable Society*, p. 20.

33   Young (ed.), *Town Book*, p. 146

34   Strain, *Charitable Society*, pp 69–70.

35   Liam Kennedy and Martin W. Dowling, 'Prices and wages in Ireland, 1700–1850', *Irish Economic and Social History*, 24 (1997), pp 92–3.

36   Dickson, *Arctic Ireland*, p. 18; Benn, *History* (2008), vol. 1, pp 596–7; Gillespie and O'Keefe, *Register*, p. 37.

37   Gillespie, *Early Belfast*, pp 98–9, 138–42, 156–8.

38   PRONI, Londonderry Estate Office Papers, D654/B/2/10–14.

39   See PRONI catalogue passim; Gillespie, *Early Belfast*, pp 128–62; Gillespie and Royle, *Atlas*, Map 7.

40   Agnew (ed.), *Funeral Register*, pp 16, 21, 26; Gillespie, *Early Belfast*, pp 100–01

41   James Kelly, 'Health for sale: mountebanks, doctors, printers and the supply of medication in eighteenth-century Ireland', *Proceedings of the Royal Irish Academy*, 108C, (2008), pp 75–113.

42 Report of the Commissioners, p. 701; Young (ed.), *Town Book*, pp 213, 215; Gillespie and O'Keefe, pp 159, 205.

43 Young (ed.), *Town Book*, pp 215–8, 233–45; Linde Lunney, 'Blow, James', in James McGuire and James Quinn (eds), *Dictionary of Irish Biography* (Cambridge, 2009); C. J. Woods, 'McTier, Samuel', ibid.; Strain, *Charitable Society*, passim.

44 Strain, *Charitable Society*, plate 2; *Report of the Commissioners*, pp 726–7.

Robert Jephson, 1794

The five lives of Robert Jephson[1]
1736–1803

BRETT HANNAM

If one were to imagine a group portrait that brought together a
selection of the finest minds of the mid-eighteenth century,
seated on the front row one might see Edmund Burke, Sir
Joshua Reynolds, Dr Johnson and David Garrick. Standing
behind in the second rank, perhaps would be found Richard
Brinsley Sheridan, James Boswell, Oliver Goldsmith and
Horace Walpole. And, although Robert Jephson knew each on
the list well and would have claimed to be counted among
them, today he finds no place alongside such luminaries.

Jephson was a man of many parts and in his five lives as a soldier,
courtier at Dublin Castle, member of the Irish parliament, satirist of
the literary establishment and successful playwright, his star burned
brightly, if not for long. Today, his numerous plays, poems and
pamphlets are all out of print and the story of his life can be found only
in the footnotes to the biographies of his better-known friends and

rivals. Nonetheless, a writer whose plays filled the theatres of two kingdoms for thirty years and whose publications sold in their thousands should not be entirely dismissed. This review of Jephson's life and work suggests that he could claim a place in our picture – albeit squeezed in at the end of the back row.

Robert Jephson was a descendant of Sir John Jephson, Major-General and member of Queen Elizabeth's parliament, who came to Ireland with the Earl of Essex, married an heiress and established the family at Mallow, Co. Cork. Jephson was the second son of Sir John's third son and thus well outside the line of inheritance for Mallow Castle, its 6,000 acres and pocket borough. Jephson's father was archdeacon of Cloyne and served under the philosopher Bishop George Berkley. Born in 1736, Robert was only seven when his father died. According to a relative, this was:

[…] in consequence of the pricking of an artery, leaving [his family] little upon which to depend. Their mother, however, with means very inadequate to such a purpose, contrived to educate them in a manner which enabled them to take a place in society to which they were better entitled by their birth and connections than by their fortune.[2]

Jephson went to a preparatory school in Dublin run by an enlightened divine, Dr Roger Forde. Here in 1749, Jephson first trod the boards, playing Cassius in a production of 'Julius Caesar' directed by the then-famous actor Charles Macklin. His schoolfellows included Edmond Malone, who would become a noted Shakespearean scholar and remain a lifelong friend.

Leaving Dublin, Robert studied for two years with a relative, Rev. William Reader, archdeacon of Cork. According to a nephew:

The Archdeacon was delighted with the engaging manners and lively genius of his young kinsman, but disturbed in his mind by his exuberant gait and the desultory fashion in which he addressed himself to his studies.[3]

Aged 15, Jephson entered Trinity College Dublin. His tutor, Rev. Dr Radcliff, thought Jephson intelligent, but idle. A story was told of how this led to Jephson being denied his rightful recognition.

An examination was held at which [prizes] were awarded to the most diligent students of literature, and a censure passed on those who had obviously been lax in their work. Dr Radcliff, painfully conscious of the fact that Robert had been anything but diligent, waited on the examiner afterwards to mitigate, if possible, the reprimand his pupil's idleness so clearly merited. 'Sir', replied the examiner, your application on behalf of Jephson has done him an injury. I had intended to give him a [prize], which, being meant as the reward of diligence, it would [now] be unjust to confer upon a confessed idler.[4]

Jephson left Trinity after two years without taking a degree.

While in Cork, Jephson had become friendly with the family of Sir Edward Barry. Barry was then the foremost doctor in Ireland. He became President of the Royal College of Physicians, a Fellow of the Royal Society, Regius Professor of Physick and Physician-General to the Army in Ireland. He published on medical subjects but also found time to write the first work in English on the history of wine and serve as a member of the Irish Parliament. Barry's son-in-law, Sir John Irwin, was an army officer and through his influence Jephson was able, in 1757, to obtain an Ensign's commission in the 70th Regiment of Foot. Jephson's family considered '... the profession of the army [...] better suited to his airy disposition than any of the other and graver walks of life.'[5]

Britain was at this time (1756–63) fighting the Seven Years' War, the first that can accurately be described as a world war, being fought in Europe, the Americas and India. The army expanded rapidly and Jephson transferred to a new regiment, the 90th, gaining promotion without purchase. Lt Col. Hugh Morgan raised his standard in Dublin in 1760 and Jephson was a lieutenant on the initial establishment. Following training, the novice unit moved to England where a contemporary account recorded that: '[t]he fine appearance of the 90th, Irish Light Infantry, lately come [...] from Ireland, [was] specially noticed'.[6] In March 1761, the 90th embarked from Portsmouth as part of an amphibious expeditionary force sent by Prime Minister William Pitt (the elder) to seize the small island of Belle Isle, off the south-west coast of Brittany. Belle Isle was of marginal strategic significance, but Pitt wished to humiliate the French army by beating it on home ground.

The campaign lasted six weeks and resulted in a British victory. Jephson's unit saw action: one of his fellow officers was killed, along with eight other ranks. Twenty-six were wounded. When the battle was done, Jephson travelled on leave to London and the home of Sir Edward Barry, who had recently moved to the capital. Soon, however, the 90th Regiment was directed to embark for the West Indies. Barry was alarmed by these orders, fearing that Jephson's health would not survive the unwholesome climate. He gave Jephson a certificate that enabled his young friend to retire aged 25 on half-pay with the rank of captain. This gave Jephson a small measure of independence: an income of £40 a year. Within a few months his former commanding officer had died of fever in Martinique[7] and the regiment was disbanded.

Barry had a house in Hanover Square and a wide acquaintance, including many intimately involved in politics and the theatre. Jephson entered the circle of David Garrick, by then the most famous actor in England, and through him came to know Sir Joshua Reynolds, Oliver Goldsmith and Dr Burney. He also met Thomas and Frances Sheridan, parents of the playwright Richard Brinsley Sheridan. It was in their house that James Boswell first met Jephson in 1762. Boswell records:

> I went to Sheridan's upon an invitation to drink tea and spend the evening and hear a reading of […] a new comedy written by Mrs Sheridan. […] I liked it much and was well entertained. Mrs Cholmondeley was there, also a Captain Jephthson, a lively little fellow […].[8]

Jephson and Boswell were not to meet again for another 26 years, by which time they had both forgotten this initial encounter.

Jephson's main concern at this time was to find permanent employment and he struck up a lasting friendship with a rich and successful politician, whose support and influence were to assist Jephson for the rest of his life. William Gerard Hamilton was known as 'single-speech Hamilton' on account of the excellence of his maiden address in Parliament and his opponents' claim that for the next 42 years he never spoke there again. In 1761, Hamilton was appointed Chief Secretary for Ireland. He took Edmund Burke to Dublin as his political fixer on a pension of £300, charged to the Irish establishment. Hamilton indulged in a very public affair with a friend's wife, argued with the viceroy, and returned to England in 1763. Hamilton and Burke then quarrelled and never spoke to each other again. Samuel Johnson worked briefly as Hamilton's secretary, but when he too resigned, Jephson took over.

Hamilton hoped to transfer Burke's £300 pension to Jephson, but news of the proposed assignment reached Dublin and prompted such opposition in parliament that the king revoked it and Jephson was again looking for paid work. He eventually found it through a combination of his wit and his connections. In 1766, Charles Townshend was the Chancellor of the Exchequer, while his brother George was about to take up the appointment of Lord Lieutenant of Ireland. During a night of drunken revelry, Jephson's impressions of notable personages so enthralled Charles that, in his cups, Townshend vowed to make the humourist his secretary. Once sober, he quickly changed his mind, but did recommend Jephson to his brother. Jephson had, however, already been introduced. The actor and dramatist John O'Keefe recorded:

> On one of the king's nights at Drury-lane, [...] Garrick said to [Lord Townshend], 'My Lord, here's [Jephson,] a young spark so plagues us behind the scenes, night after night, I wish you would take him with you over to your Ireland, or anywhere out of our way.[9]

Encouraging Townshend to find him a job was not the only kindness Jephson received from Garrick. The notoriously tight-fisted actor-manager lent him £500, which Jephson took ten years to repay.

While waiting for Lord Townshend to confirm his position, Jephson returned to his relatives in Dublin. Lack of funds and secure employment did not, however, prevent his marriage. Lady Hertford, wife of the then Viceroy, wrote to Horace Walpole to say:

> I pity Mr Jephson very much. [...] He has not a hundred a year in the world and is gone to England to marry a Miss Barry, who is ten or twelve years older than him, and who has no fortune.[10]

Jane Barry was the second daughter of Jephson's long-time friend, Sir Edward Barry. For whatever reason, her father did not provide Jane with a significant dowry and the newlyweds moved briefly to Boulogne, where the cost of living was lower than in England. However, in February 1767, Townshend installed Jephson in Dublin Castle as

Comptroller of the Household. When it cost at least £300 a year to live as a gentleman, the annual salary was a paltry £50, but within a few months, Jephson was promoted to the better-paid position he would hold for the next thirty years under thirteen successive Lords Lieutenant, that of Master of the Horse.

Lord George Townshend arrived in Dublin with the intention of bringing some discipline to the erratic politics of Ireland. Townshend was a soldier and approached the role of Viceroy with the same military intensity he had displayed when fighting alongside Cumberland at Culloden (1746) and Wolfe at Quebec (1759). He had two main objectives: to increase the contribution Ireland made to the defence of the Empire; and to break the power of the 'undertakers'[11], powerful aristocrats who managed Ireland on behalf of the King and who in exchange held extensive powers of patronage.

Jephson's first published work was *Considerations upon the Augmentation of the Army; Address'd to The Publick*, completed in 1768. The pamphlet set out Townshend's case for an increase in the size of the Irish army. Jephson makes a simple argument: despite the end of the Seven Years' War, France remains a threat and Ireland will always be a tempting object for invasion. As Jephson put it:

> Our Island is extensive and exposed everywhere. [...] How is it possible for a handful of Soldiers ... to be present at the same Instant in many Places? [...] Besides, a watchful Eye must be kept upon the People who surround us, lest their Rising should be as fatal as the landing of an Enemy.

Augmentation was eventually approved but was only one of a series of battles that Townshend had to fight against the Irish House of Commons. Defeats over the Loyal Address, the application of Poynings' Law and Money Bills led him to prorogue parliament. He came to realise that in order to assert the authority of the British government over the Irish undertakers, he would have to resort to the same corrupt and underhand tactics as his antagonists. Titles, jobs and pensions were dispersed to supporters and denied to opponents.

Townshend's political adversaries, including Henry Grattan and Henry Flood, used the newspaper *Freeman's Journal* as a vehicle to attack his policies, friends and character. A series of satirical letters lampooned

Townshend as 'Don Sancho', the despotic ruler of the fictitious but surprisingly Irish, 'Barataria'. Townshend did not humbly accept such mockery. He co-opted a rival newspaper – the *Dublin Mercury* – by giving it a lucrative monopoly to print the government's public proclamations and he used it to assault his critics. Jephson took over a column in the paper entitled 'The Batchelor' under the feebly punning by-line 'Jeoffrey Wagstaffe' (Shake-speare / Wag-staffe) and used it not just to rebut the charges from *Freeman's Journal*, but to launch fiery attacks on Townshend's adversaries. Grattan whined that Jephson was, 'taking personal invective to excess'[12] in articles that 'outraged, ridiculed and distorted'. The exchanges boosted the circulations of both papers and gained Jephson a reputation as a highly effective polemicist.

When Townshend left Ireland in 1772, having successfully brought the 'undertakers' to heel and established the pre-eminence of the Castle in Irish politics, he arranged for the next Viceroy to continue Jephson in his appointment and also enabled his loyal servant to take up a seat in the Irish House of Commons. Jephson remained an MP for the next 18 years, faithfully representing the interests of the Viceroys and the owners of the pocket boroughs for which he sat.

Jephson was a frequent speaker in the House and his delivery was widely admired. One commentator opined: 'His voice is excellent, clear, distinct, sonorous, and harmonious, extensive in compass, various in tones, and in all its gradations from its highest pitch to its deepest note melodiously attuned'.[13] However, the unswerving promotion of his employers' interests meant that few saw anything but obsequious toadying in his arguments. The same writer concluded:

> The matter of his speeches is commonly [...] poor, shallow [...] [and] inconclusive. [...] As he holds both a place and a pension under government, and is brought into the house by the influence of ministers; he is their willing and devoted adherent, prepared for every service [...].

In 1774 Jephson achieved an unqualified success when he spoke in support of a bill with the title 'For the better Encouragement of Persons professing the Popish Religion to become Protestants, and for the further Improvement of the Kingdom'. Jephson spoke with remarkable effect in favour of relaxing the Penal Laws and claimed in the published version 'The contents flew rapidly from the House to the people and became the principal topic of every conversation'.[14]

Jephson's arguments were similar to those of his erstwhile colleague Edmund Burke, first developed in the early 1760s when they shared Hamilton's house. Burke thought the Popery Laws in Ireland as 'one leading cause of the imbecility of the country'. Jephson described them as 'inconsistent with true religion and rectitude'. Burke wrote that they were 'unjust, impolitic and inefficacious'. Jephson similarly argued that they were:

> [...] unlike all other legal promulgations; not the bridle, but the spur to wickedness; tempting, not restraining the most dangerous passions; encouraging, not chastising the worst transgressions.

Jephson's salary of £300 a year was later increased to £600 and supplemented by his half-pay from the army, occasional payments from the Concordatum Money[15] and Fees of Honour payable to him by new peers and knights on their elevation. In consequence, his total emoluments compared very favourably to those of senior army officers. He was also provided with good-quality lodgings in Lower Castle Yard.

The position of Master of the Horse was in the personal gift of each Viceroy and 13 of them independently and successively decided that there was value in keeping him on. The duties of the post appear to have been somewhat loosely defined. Under Lord Townshend, they included attacking the Viceroy's enemies in print and supporting his policies in parliament. More mundanely, Jephson was responsible for the Viceroy's movements around the country, ensuring that horses and carriages were available when required. He seems to have had privileged access to his chiefs and, when he had earned their confidence, to have acted as their unofficial adviser. He was still engaged in sociable correspondence with some, such as Lord Dorset, long after they left Ireland. Another durable friendship was with Lady Louisa Conolly, one of the celebrated daughters of the Duke of Richmond and great-grand-daughter of Charles II. Lady Louisa lived at Castletown and wrote regularly to her sister, the Duchess of Leinster at Carton House. These letters show that the Jephsons were frequent and welcome visitors to both homes.

Jephson produced humorous verse to entertain his hosts and their guests. The titles of these capture the paradoxical mixture of formality

Robert Jephson *Esq.*
in the CHARACTER of MACBETH.

and frivolity, pomposity and light-heartedness that is a characteristic of much of Jephson's writing. The titles include: 'Inscription for a cottage at the seat of the Right Hon. Thomas Connolly, dedicated by his lady on Michaelmas Day'; and 'Extempore answer to an invitation from the late Mrs Gardiner to dance with her at a ball at her sister's, the Hon Mrs Beresford's, in 1778'.

At this time, there was a fashion for amateur dramatic productions. Initially, these took place at the great houses of the nobility. Louisa Connolly wrote of two such performances put on at Castletown: '[The] two plays were the prettiest things I ever saw, and incomparably well-acted. Mr Jephson and Mrs Gardiner, I think, are equal to any actors (Garrick excepted) I ever saw.'[16] Mrs Gardiner was the wife of the Hon. Luke Gardiner, MP for County Dublin and later 1st Viscount Mountjoy. His love of acting led him to erect his own temporary theatre-house and there produce 'Macbeth'. Jephson played the title role and Gardiner Macduff. According to the *Hibernian Journal*, Jephson's wife

Jane, as Lady Macbeth, sported '[…] gold ground silk, ornamented with artificial and silver flowers and with diamonds to the amount of 100,000 pounds'.[17]

Jephson suffered a grievous blow in 1787 when the Marquess of Buckingham discharged him from his position as Master of the Horse. Horace Walpole described Buckingham as an arrogant man with '[…] many disgusting qualities, […] pride, obstinacy and want of truth with a natural propensity to avarice'.[18] Lady Louisa Conolly recounts Jephson's side of the story:

> [Jephson] has met with a great disappointment in being turned out of his place. […] Lord Buckingham has shewn him a very mean sort of spite in this business, […] for he […] [said] Mr Jephson […] laughed at him […]… Now, the fact is that Mr Jephson did not laugh at him; on the contrary, [he] was rather partial to Lord Buckingham […] [However, nothing could move [Lord Buckingham's] inflexible temper, which, I understand, is very apparent upon all occasions where he has the power of oppressing; which is the case with the poor Jephsons, […] He is, I believe, a nasty sort of man.[19]

Jephson was somewhat disingenuous in claiming his innocence. Lord Cloncurry gave a different version of the story. According to him, Jephson:

> […] lost place and pension by an untimely exercise of his wit, when dining one day […]. The dinner was given to […] the Marquis of Buckingham, who happened to observe, in an unlucky mirror, the reflection of Jephson in the act of mimicking him. [Buckingham] immediately discharged him.[20]

Fortunately for Jephson, Lord Mornington interceded with Buckingham, asking him to reconsider. Buckingham replied curtly 'Your Mr. Jephson is a ——, I will not say what, but knowing him to be so, I may possibly keep him'.[21] Jephson was not immediately restored as Master of the Horse, but instead reverted to the lower-paid and lower-status position he had held twenty years earlier, Comptroller of the Household. He would not be fully reinstated until Buckingham had been replaced by the Earl of Westmoreland, two years later.

Jephson was capable of the most realistic, amusing and sometimes cruel impressions. Meeting him for the first time, Boswell described him as 'the best mimic in the world'.[22] Literary parody was similarly a key characteristic of Jephson's writing and his friends called him 'The Mortal Momus', the Greek mythological personification of satire and mockery; an image of the eternal critic, excoriating the weaknesses of men.

In 1771, Jephson published an elaborate lampoon that satirised two of Dublin's best-known men of letters: the Dublin printer George Faulkner and the solicitor and would-be poet Gorges Edmond Howard. Faulkner had been Jonathan Swift's publisher. Howard was prodigiously productive, but unblessed by talent. Jephson mocked him in his 'Epistle to G. E. Howard'. This takes the form of a laudatory poem with explanatory notes supposedly written by Faulkner and addressed to Howard. The notes are far longer than the poem and contain additional verse purportedly written by Howard. All these are wonderfully dreadful. The notes contain humorous fake advertisements for other books published by Faulkner, references to his dim-witted son and numerous shaggy-dog stories. The pamphlet was hugely popular, running into at least nine editions within a few months. Jephson followed it with another similarly successful satire that pretended to be Howard's riposte.

There is an element of mimicry in almost everything Jephson wrote. In addition to taking off Faulkner, his later 'Tour to Celbridge' was written in the orotund style of Dr Johnson and for the 'Confessions of Jean Baptiste Couteau' he adopted the persona of a rabid French revolutionary. A poem addressed to Francis Andrews, Provost of Trinity, mimicked Lord Townshend mimicking Horace. Not everyone appreciated the joke, particularly those who were the target of his satire. A rather po-faced critic laid out the case against him:

> Mimicry of personal defects, and ridicule of personal peculiarities, are [...] suited to the taste of the [...] vulgar [...]. They appertain much more to the buffoon than to the wit and are rather fitted to raise the broad laugh of Plautus than the correct smile of Terence.[23]

Other detractors were not slow to identify an imitative tendency, even in his serious works. The *Monthly Review* wrote:

> Mr Jephson [...], with talents perhaps for original excellence, has cramped those talents by the study and practice of dramatic mimicry, in which he must be allowed a proficiency. But this is poor ambition and unworthy of real genius![24]

It was as a dramatist that Jephson hoped his reputation would endure. During his lifetime this seemed very likely as his plays enjoyed both critical and commercial success. They were performed in London, Dublin and the major cities. For those unable to see their production on the stage, the texts could be bought and unscrupulous publishers issued pirated and inaccurate editions to compete with the authorised versions.

Jephson wrote his first tragedy, 'Braganza', in 1773, but faced significant difficulties in seeing the play produced. As a recently elected MP with a position at the Castle, he could not leave Dublin. He therefore had to rely on others to act as theatrical midwives. Horace Walpole said that Jephson was 'very happy in friends' and Irishmen based in London went to great lengths to help him. Edward Tighe was a rich lawyer, a member of the British Parliament and had served with Jephson under Townshend. When Jephson sent the first four acts of his play to Garrick in 1774, Tighe followed up with a series of letters urging Garrick to see it performed. Tighe concluded his entreaties with the plea 'Excuse my zeal, which is not for a plaything or a hobbyhorse, [but] for a work of great merit and a most ingenious friend'.[25] Arthur Murphy, a successful Irish writer and barrister, provided the play's prologue and Tighe persuaded Horace Walpole to write its epilogue. Walpole also wrote to his brother-in-law the Lord Chamberlain to obtain an expedited licence for its performance.

Before it was staged, Jephson's friends mounted a campaign to arouse interest and anticipation among its potential audience. It was reported that 'The Tragedy [has] been read by the Author's friends in most of the great families in London'.[26] Jephson himself read it to the Conollys and their guests at Castletown. In London, Edward Tighe read it at a meeting of the Bluestocking Society hosted by the Irish intellectual Elizabeth Vesey. When it premièred at Drury Lane, all the boxes were sold out for the first 15 nights. According to the theatre's prompter, 'No play was ever more attended to in the getting up, Mr Garrick spared no pains or expense, the Dresses are superb, the scenery quite in a new taste. It was received with very great applause'.[27] Horace Walpole described the audience's response, 'At the catastrophe in the fifth [act], they were transported; they clapped, shouted, huzzaed, cried bravo and thundered out applause.[28]

Also present with Garrick at the première were Lady Louisa Conolly, Edmund Burke, Samuel Johnson and Sir Joshua Reynolds. Reynolds sat in the orchestra pit as he was hard of hearing. When he turned to speak to his friends, he noticed that Garrick's eyes were suffused with tears. Burke was outraged by the scene in which a monk uses a poisoned communion wafer with murderous intent, saying that such dreadful modes of wickedness should not be divulged to the world. Samuel Johnson was, however, unimpressed, perhaps being envious of the play's reception. His own tragedy, 'Irene', had been booed on its first night and it galled Johnson that whereas Garrick had closed the play after a few performances, his friend hailed Braganza as 'the greatest effort of human genius'.[29] When Mrs Montagu, in an excess of admiration for 'Braganza' said that 'she trembled for Shakespeare', Johnson replied, 'When Shakespeare has got Jephson for a rival and Mrs Montagu for a defender, he is in a poor state indeed'.[30]

Johnson criticised the dramaturgy of Jephson's play, finding fault with its internal logic while Walpole thought that the production did not do the poetry justice. He wrote to the author, 'The immense applause which you drew from the audience was owing to yourself alone. [...] I will venture to say that Braganza will always charm more when read than when seen'.[31] *Freeman's Journal* agreed: 'As a poetical composition, the piece does honour to the writer. [...] As a dramatic author, we cannot think so highly of Mr Jephson as the general enthusiasm might warrant'.[32]

The play made £2,563 from its first 14 performances, of which Jephson received £474. He used this to pay off the outstanding balance of his 10-year-old loan from Garrick. 'Braganza' travelled to Dublin, Bath and Edinburgh and was reprinted nine times. Engravings were made of the actors in the characters of the main roles. Jephson sought to capitalise on this success and soon sent Garrick another tragedy, 'Vitellia', assuming it would be accepted. Garrick sent it straight back, writing:

> I not only read it myself to myself, but to some ladies and a gentleman of great taste in theatrical matters. They were ignorant of the author, but agreed that it was not at all calculated for success upon the stage. [...] Your reputation is, at present, high [...] and why you would venture to throw away your well-earned fame [...] I cannot conceive.[33]

Garrick's rejection embarrassed Jephson because he had already circulated the play widely among his friends and patrons. Worse, at Jephson's request, his brother-in-law Sir John Irwin had sought permission for Vitellia to be dedicated to King George III. Jephson wrote in despair that '[…] his Majesty was so gracious to give his permission, & I hear has since asked "where is the Tragedy?" This circumstance gives me concern [and] I certainly deserve some ridicule for my precipitancy'.[34]

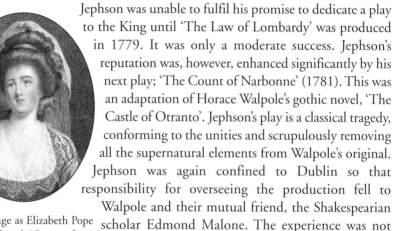

Jephson was unable to fulfil his promise to dedicate a play to the King until 'The Law of Lombardy' was produced in 1779. It was only a moderate success. Jephson's reputation was, however, enhanced significantly by his next play; 'The Count of Narbonne' (1781). This was an adaptation of Horace Walpole's gothic novel, 'The Castle of Otranto'. Jephson's play is a classical tragedy, conforming to the unities and scrupulously removing all the supernatural elements from Walpole's original. Jephson was again confined to Dublin so that responsibility for overseeing the production fell to Walpole and their mutual friend, the Shakespearian scholar Edmond Malone. The experience was not happy, and arguments arose over the date of the première and changes to the text. Jephson aggravated matters, sending a flurry of last-minute revisions and amendments from Dublin. Walpole wrote, 'I have been plagued about Mr Jephson's play [...] The author is dissatisfied, I had four sides last week, and tonight another letter of eight pages to scold me […]'.[35]

Miss Younge as Elizabeth Pope in Jephson's 'Count of Narbonne'

The play was an immediate success, continuing at Covent Garden for 21 nights. A press report noted: 'The play was received throughout with applause and in some parts of it with a vehemence we scarce ever remember'.[36] Walpole wrote: 'The Count of Narbonne was played last night with great applause and without a single murmur of disapprobation'.[37] 'The Count of Narbonne' continued to be revived, was translated and performed in French and anthologised throughout the nineteenth century. It was not, however, Jephson's most popular work. This was his comedy, 'The Hotel', first produced in 1783. It was adapted from Goldoni's Italian farce 'The Servant of Two Masters', a play the National Theatre has more recently presented worldwide as 'One Man, Two Guvnors'. 'The Hotel' clearly appealed to Dublin audiences as it was revived in each of the following 16 years and was still being performed there long after Jephson's death.

Jephson's later works enjoyed respectable, but not spectacular, success. A tragedy, 'Julia', was considered by some critics to be his best play but had only limited runs in London and Dublin. A comic opera, 'The Campaign', had an overture by Haydn and music by the popular composer Tenducci. It too was moderately successful. Jephson did not limit himself simply to writing for the stage or acting in semi-professional amateur productions. He also oversaw the professional production of his own plays, trained actors and, in 1779, made an audacious attempt to gain a monopoly over the theatre in Dublin.

Internecine competition between the Crow Street Theatre and the Theatres Royal in Capel Street and Smock Alley meant that none played to full houses, their managers fell into bankruptcy and the best actors fled to London. Jephson and the London actor-manager George Colman argued that the only way to address the situation was to pass a law that gave a monopoly to a single theatre. Colman had made a success of the Haymarket and believed he could do the same in Dublin, provided he had no competition. Jephson, as a Member of Parliament, had the required political connections to make such a plan feasible. A parliamentary bill to give effect to it was introduced in December 1779.

The proposal was criticised immediately. The owners of the existing theatres were naturally vehement in their opposition, claiming they would be ruined by the grant of a monopoly, while the Lord Mayor, who had the prerogative right to licence theatres in the city, also opposed the scheme. The *Hibernian Journal* did not hold back:

> The worst writer of tragedies [...] an upstart minion of the Castle, who has wriggled himself into Parliament by the Spanish Arts of Adulation, looks for an exclusive Act for regulating a playhouse in this city. [...] Surely neither Lords nor Commons, can [...] for the pecuniary advantage of a petty scribbler adopt [...] the measure of tyranny?[38]

Colman had not expected such a reaction and, in the words of his biographer 'found matters so deranged as obliged him to quit the design'.[39] Jephson had little choice but to withdraw his bill.

Jephson's last major work, over which he laboured for several years and hoped would earn him lasting fame, was 'Roman Portraits', a series of poems written in heroic verse which he intended would introduce and illustrate the qualities and virtues of the major characters of the Roman Republic and Empire. The poems themselves are augmented by substantial scholarly apparatus, replete with apposite quotations in Latin, Greek and French. Jephson continued his revisions up to and even after publication. A copy Jephson sent to a friend contains the author's lengthy manuscript additions to what were already extensive references and annotations. The work was produced in a handsome format with a fine binding and sold for a guinea. Jephson was disappointed that the publisher limited the edition to a mere 750 copies. The book was not well received. The *Critical Review* concluded that 'The poetry of this work is among the most insipid, prosaic and unmusical, which we ever perused'.[40] 'Roman Portraits' failed to sell and was not reprinted.

Jephson's health was rarely good. Letters from and about him are sprinkled with references to his afflictions. He once wrote to Lady Mountjoy:

> You may guess how ill it is with me […]. I have had a severe fit of the gout in both my feet— ... it is drawing teeth out of my left at this moment. In short, I have the pleasure of feeling as if my foot was well squeezed in an iron vice. ... I am carried about like a child of six weeks old. […] To add to my comfort my best servant has also got the gout, and poor Mrs. Jephson is worse than I am.[41]

In 1797 Jephson's wife Jane died. They had been married for 33 years and he was inconsolable. Described by Lady Conolly as 'a very pleasing woman', she had been the author's amanuensis, acted alongside him and maintained her own correspondence with Garrick, Tighe and others. Jephson published nothing after her death. In 1798, Jephson nearly lost a leg in an accident. Still Master of the Horse, he moved permanently from the Castle to his house in Blackrock. In 1802, he wrote: 'An unrelenting gout keeps me like an old Hulk moor'd to one Station. […] Time has left the mark of his hobnails very deeply on my anatomy'.[42]

Following the Act of Union, Jephson applied for compensation for the loss of his Fees of Honour. The claim was initially rejected because he failed to provide written proof that he had been Master of the Horse. Jephson quickly lodged an appeal supported by terse statements from a number of former Viceroys. However, he never saw the final decision of the Commissioner of Compensation. On 1 May 1803, Robert Jephson died of what was described as a 'paralytic disorder'. Jephson's heir was his nephew, Rev. John Jephson, to whom he left his house, library and most of his effects. The remainder were sold at public auction. They included 'Original caricatures of persons of celebrity during the Administration of Lord Townshend and his successor, few of which can be equalled in Ireland'.[43] The Blackrock house stands to this day and the Jephson coat of arms remains visible, embedded in the wall. Jephson's papers and library were dispersed on the death of his heir and vanished without trace.

Even Jephson's strongest advocates would not deny his grievous faults; he was pompous, proud and pretentious: a friend in need; a hired hack and a bought vote. In none of his five lives as soldier, courtier, politician, satirist and playwright did he achieve anything like pre-eminence, and it would be easy to describe him as an indifferent jack-of-all-trades. He joined the army as a long war ended; his employers dictated his politics and the targets of his satire are now of only the slightest interest. Most of all, he had the misfortune to be writing tragedy in an age of comedy.

Since his death, Jephson has been the subject of few scholarly studies: a Swiss doctoral thesis in 1913 and a short appreciation from Nebraska in 1930. Apart from occasional articles and footnotes, he has troubled neither the literary critics nor the theatre-going public. And yet, although he produced nothing that, for longevity, can be compared with Malone's *Shakespeare*, Gibbon's *Decline and Fall* or Johnson's *Dictionary*, Jephson's best work is not without value. Eighteenth-century actors, managers and audiences set exacting standards for tragedy. It was the most elevated form of drama. Written for a cultivated and educated audience, tragedy needed to affect audiences deeply; to engage both their intellect and emotions. But this standard set a high hurdle. Those that failed, failed quickly, taken off like Dr Johnson's 'Irene' while the jeers and catcalls still echoed through the green room.

Managers such as Garrick and Sheridan were rarely willing to bring a tragedy to the stage unless written by Shakespeare. For these reasons, fewer tragedies were performed than written and even fewer entered the repertoire. But Jephson's works did not fail. They were, by the standards of the day, wildly successful, pleasing both the pit and the box. His critics may have found fault, yet Jephson still found an audience of the brightest and best who valued and admired his work. For this, he deserves to be rescued from the *oubliette* of literary history and painted back into our picture of the eighteenth century.

NOTES

1 A version of this paper was delivered to the Belfast Literary Society on 2 November 2019.
2 Maurice Denham Jephson, *An Anglo-Irish Miscellany: Some Records of the Jephsons of Mallow* (1964), p. 301.
3 Ibid., p. 303.
4 Ibid., p. 304.
5 Ibid.
6 'The Siege and Capture of Belle-Isle, 1761', *Journal of the Royal United Services Institution*, 43:252 (1899), pp 161–83.
7 *The London Magazine*, vol. 40 (1761), p. 450.
8 *Boswell's London Journal 1762–1763*, ed. Frederick A. Pottle (2004 edn), p. 13, entry for 31 Dec. 1762.
9 John O'Keeffe, *Recollections of the Life of John O'Keeffe* (1826), p. 83.
10 W. S. Lewis (ed.), *The Yale Edition of Horace Walpole's Correspondence* (1937–83), vol. 39, p. 49.
11 So-called because they 'undertook' to discharge the King's business. As Thomas Bartlett, *Ireland. A History* (2010) p. 174, comments, 'For nearly five years Townshend struggled to implement his new system and by the time he left Ireland in late 1772 he could justly claim to have brought power back to the Castle … the "age of the undertakers" was over by 1772.'
12 *Baratariana*, 1st edn (1772), pp ix–x.
13 Falkland (John Robert Scott), *A Review of the Principal Characters of the Irish House of Commons* (1789), p. 107.
14 Robert Jephson, *The Speech Delivered by Robert Jephson, Esq; on the 11th of February 1774, in the Debate on the Committing Heads of a Bill, for 'the Better Encouragement of Persons Professing the Popish Religion to Become Protestants, and for the Further Improvement of the Kingdom'. John Foster, Esq; in the Chair* (1774) (http://name.umdl.umich.edu/004790100.0001.000).
15 A government petty cash fund.
16 Letter, Lady Louisa Conolly to the Duchess of Leinster, 8 Jan. 1775, in Brian Fitzgerald (ed.), *Correspondence of Emily, Duchess of Leinster* (1949).
17 *Hibernian Magazine*, Jan. 1778, p. 53.
18 Cited in Joseph Robins, *Champagne and Silver Buckles: The Viceregal Court at Dublin Castle, 1700–1922* (2001), p. 67.
19 Letter, Lady Louisa Conolly to Duchess of Leinster, Castletown, 29 Dec. 1787.

20 Baron Valentine Cloncurry, *Personal Recollections of the Life and Times: With Extracts from the Correspondence of Valentine Lord Cloncurry* (1849), p. 256.
21 Richard Plantagenet Temple Nugent Brydges Chandos Grenville Buckingham and Chandos, *Memoirs of the Court and Cabinets of George the Third: From Original Family Documents*, vol. 1 (1853), p. 333.
22 *Boswell's London Journal.*
23 Falkland, *Review of the Principal Characters of the Irish House of Commons.*
24 *The Monthly Review*, vol. 66 (1782), p. 64.
25 Cited in Jennie MacDonald, 'Working from Home: Playwright Robert Jephson's Theatrical Networking' in Ileana Baird (ed.), *Social Networks in the Long Eighteenth Century: Clubs, Literary Salons, Textual Coteries* (2014), pp 121–48
26 William Hopkins, cited in Robert Noyes, *The Neglected Muse, Restoration and Eighteenth-Century Tragedy in the Novel (1740–1780)* (1958), p. 174.
27 Ibid.
28 W. S. Lewis, Grover Cronin Jr and C. H. Bennett, (eds), *Horace Walpole's Correspondence with William Mason* (1955), vol. 1, p. 176.
29 Letter, Samuel Johnson to his sister Elizabeth, 23 Feb. 1775.
30 James Boswell, *The Life of Samuel Johnson, LL. D.: Including a Journal of a Tour to the Hebrides* (1835).
31 Letter, Horace Walpole to Robert Jephson, 24 Feb. 1775.
32 *Freeman's Journal*, 20 April 1775.
33 Letter, David Garrick to Robert Jephson, 18 Dec. 1775.
34 Letter, Robert Jephson to Lord Harcourt, 5 Oct. 1776.
35 Cited in Peter Martin, *Edmond Malone, Shakespearean Scholar: A Literary Biography* (1995), p. 70.
36 *Dublin Evening Post*, 29 Nov. 1781.
37 Letter, Horace Walpole to Henry Seymour Conway, 18 Nov. 1781.
38 *Hibernian Journal*, 27 Nov. 1779.
39 Cited in La Tourette Stockwell, *Dublin Theatres and Theatre Customs, 1637–1820* (1938).
40 The Critical Review, *Or, Annals of Literature* (1795), p. 286.
41 Letter, Robert Jephson to Lady Mountjoy, 13 July 1795.
42 Cited in Jephson, *An Anglo-Irish Miscellany.*
43 *Saunders's News-Letter*, 29 March 1805.

James Alexander Rentoul
1845–1919
a case study in Late Victorian Ulster Unionism[1]

PATRICK MAUME

James Alexander Rentoul, Conservative MP for East Down 1890–1902, is chiefly remembered as one of the few Ulster Unionist MPs of his generation to publish a memoir.[2]

Stray Thoughts and Memories (London: Leonard Parsons, 1921) appeared two years after Rentoul's death, and recounts his career from youth in Manorcunningham, County Donegal, where he spent a decade as a Presbyterian minister in succession to his father, through university education in the mid-Victorian Queen's Colleges, to transplantation to London and the English Bar, to parliament and finally the judicial bench. It is dominated by a series of anecdotes, often humorous and reflecting Rentoul's lifelong popularity as an after-dinner speaker. Rentoul concludes by advocating prohibition of the sale of alcoholic drink and by complaining that Sir Edward Carson's Ulster campaign against the 1912–14 Home Rule Bill had involved lawbreaking and threatened violence to an extent unknown during his own days in Ulster politics; his statement, that the persistence of Irish nationalism, and the abandonment of southern unionists (including those of his native Donegal) by their six-county brethren, had made him reconsider his lifelong opposition to Home Rule, roused the attention of some nationalist reviewers.

Recently, however, Rentoul has been presented in a darker aspect, as an advocate of the extinction of the Irish language whose attacks on its presence in the state curriculum foreshadow more recent controversies between Northern Irish unionists and nationalists over official recognition of the language. How liberal, then, was James Alexander Rentoul?

This article argues that while Rentoul understated the verbal violence and Orange flirtations of his early political career, he was a liberal unionist who genuinely believed Ireland's political and economic problems and religious divisions could only be pacified through Irish incorporation into a wider multi-national British identity and through economic and cultural modernisation founded on empire. The ways in which this glossed over the more intractable elements of Unionism and assured nationalists that they did not know what was good for them reflect problems which have dogged the liberal unionist project, from the Whig and Peelite reformism of the early Victorian era, through the constructive unionism of the 1880s and 1890s up to the O'Neillism of the 1960s and more recent integrationist and centrist restatements of unionism; but it was more complex than the simple façade for self-interest alleged by Rentoul's opponents.

James Alexander Rentoul was born at Errity House, Manorcunningham, County Donegal, on 7 August 1845, eldest son (of three sons and five daughters) of Alexander Rentoul, Presbyterian minister, and his wife Erminda (née Chittick).[3] The extended Rentoul family (of Huguenot and Scots descent) produced many Presbyterian ministers.[4] Erminda, a member of the Church of Ireland until her marriage, was descended from an old Donegal landed family, the Squires who, after a long period of extravagance and mismanagement, were sold up in the Encumbered Estates Court.[5] This family pedigree probably influenced Rentoul's later Conservatism. The writer Erminda Rentoul Esler was his sister, and her stories include interrogations of a lost Big House inheritance such as *The Wardlaws* (London, 1896).[6]

Rentoul was educated at local national schools[7] and at Cookstown Academy before spending a year at Queen's College Cork (1863–4). His father died unexpectedly in January 1864, when Rentoul was 17. The Second Ray congregation decided to employ substitute ministers until Rentoul qualified for ordination.[8] He transferred to Queen's College Belfast, graduating BA in 1866. He managed to spend some time in Brussels and Berlin (where he studied at the University of Berlin) to learn French and German, and gained the QCB senior scholarship in modern languages.[9] Rentoul then went to QCG to study law, winning several scholarships and making lasting friendships with contemporaries (including Catholics). After graduating LL.B. (1868) and LL.D. (1869) Rentoul decided on a career in the church, by his own account largely from pragmatic motives.[10] (He would have preferred to teach, but there were few openings in modern languages.)[11]

After studying divinity at Magee College, Derry and Assembly's College, Belfast Rentoul was licensed by Coleraine Presbytery in 1870 and ordained for Second Ray on 25 October 1871. Over the following ten years Rentoul provided for the upbringing and education of his younger siblings, several to university level. In hindsight, Rentoul thought he had not been a particularly effective Presbyterian minister, as he took little interest in dogma and hence did not provide the lengthy hair-splitting theological discourses expected by old-style Presbyterian congregations. (His favourite sister, Elizabeth, to whom he remained close, believed he underestimated his effectiveness in parochial work.)[12] Rentoul combined his pastoral responsibilities with cultivating a farm of just under 45 acres at Errity, near Manorcunningham; he later cited this as evidence that he understood the concerns of tenant farmers.

On 8 November 1881 Rentoul resigned from Ray and moved to London, where he took up a call to St Andrew's, Woolwich in south-eastern London. His three unmarried sisters moved with their mother to Belfast, where they opened a girls' school at The Lodge, Cliftonville on Fortwilliam Terrace in north Belfast. After her two sisters married Elizabeth became sole proprietor and headmistress of the school until its closure in 1918.[13] For many years she was a leading member of the Irish Temperance League; in 1914 she broke away from the ITL over its failure to censure sufficiently Unionist MPs who did not support restrictions on alcohol, and founded the prohibitionist Shamrock Temperance League.[14] Rentoul frequently visited the school and gave it as his address when in Belfast; he was deeply influenced by his sister's views on alcohol.[15]

On 27 April 1882 he married Florence Isabella Young (d. 1914), an Englishwoman who was Anglican until her marriage; they had two sons, of whom the elder, Gervase Squire Chittick Rentoul (1884–1946) was president of the Oxford Union 1906–07 and Conservative MP for

Lowestoft 1922–34. The younger son Mervyn Audley (b. 1888) probably died in infancy as he is not mentioned in his brother's memoir.[16] The sons' names are drawn from their Squire/Chittick ancestry (they claimed descent from the 7th Baron Audley, beheaded in 1497 for leading a rebellion against Henry VII; Gervaise Squire was Mayor of Derry during the 1689 siege).[17]

Rentoul resigned his charge on being called to the English Bar (17 November 1884), having won first place and a scholarship of 100 guineas in the Bar examinations. He remained a licensed minister and celebrated charity services (and preached sermons) in Belfast as late as 1889.[18] Rentoul was appointed QC in July 1895. He combined his legal practice and a Building Society directorship[19] with unpaid lecturing and campaigning for the Conservative mass organisation, the Primrose League and the chairmanship of the Borough of Woolwich Conservative Association (from 1885).[20] Rentoul claimed that during his political career he campaigned in about 300 constituencies, making a point of concentrating on marginals rather than safe seats. He was also a member of the (non-political) Oddfellows friendly society.[21]

Although the traditional association of non-Anglican Protestant churches with Liberalism often led commentators to assume that Rentoul was a member of the breakaway Liberal Unionist party who allied with the Conservatives in 1886 in opposition to Gladstonian Home Rule, he emphasised that as the son of an Orangeman he was a lifelong Conservative.[22] His political views included defence of the established status of the Church of England, on the grounds that its endowments allowed it to minister to impoverished areas inaccessible to the nonconformist churches (dependent on congregational contributions),[23] and that ecclesiastical disendowment contravened the rights of property; he believed disestablishment of the Church of Ireland did more harm than good[24], and opposed Welsh disestablishment by citing the traditional Presbyterian view that the state should recognise Christianity.[25]

On 16 September 1889 Rentoul lectured on 'The United British Empire: Its Greatness, Glory and Freedom' in the Ulster Hall, Belfast, scattering his oration with phrases from such verses as 'Rule Britannia' and 'Ye Mariners of England' and with statistics of trade and national income. While Rentoul begins with a homage to the empire's 'civilising mission' he principally emphasises self-interest, pointing out that the self-governing colonies were rich markets for British goods and outlets for surplus population, and that India served as 'a great farm for the mother country'. Rentoul argued that the remarkable achievements of the empire had only become possible through the political union of the home islands, which allowed the descendants of the sturdy victors at Bannockburn to join in mutual respect with the descendants of the defeated, and that while the empire was invulnerable to outside attack the 'Trojan horse' of Home Rule aimed at shattering it from within. (He denounced Irish Protestant Home Rulers as self-seeking opportunists.) He listed great Irishmen who had helped to build the empire, argued that the Scottish experience showed Ireland also could be reconciled to the union, and expressed the hope that Irish songs such as 'The wearing of the green' might one day be sung throughout Britain as was the case with their Scottish equivalents and with 'God Save the Queen.[26]

When moving the vote of thanks, both the Ulster Conservative organiser (and West Down MP) Lord Arthur Hill, who chaired the meeting, and the prominent Belfast Presbyterian cleric RJ Lynd predicted that Rentoul would soon enter parliament.[27] Almost immediately Hill offered Rentoul the East Down seat (heavily influenced by the Hill family) whose sitting MP wished to retire. Rentoul was initially reluctant to accept since taking on parliamentary duties so early in his legal career might damage his prospects at the Bar [28] and MPs were unpaid until 1911), and attributes this in part to the reluctance of many solicitors to brief a barrister MP.

Rentoul's recruitment was inspired by the need to strengthen Ulster Unionist debating power at Westminster.[29] This hope was not entirely fulfilled, although Lord Birkenhead – whom Rentoul treated acerbically in his memoirs – reportedly recalled him as one of the best speakers he ever heard.[30] Rentoul's selection also reflected a tendency to recruit lawyer MPs rather than silent landowners.[31] An early Rentoul speech on legislation concerning leaseholders' rights displayed a breath of knowledge which won admiration from legal and non-legal MPs.[32] In some respects Rentoul's debating style resembled that of the Unionist leader Edward Saunderson; he was physically imposing and unwilling to back down when challenged in debate.[33] Rentoul also resembled

Saunderson in being a self-conscious Irish humorist.[34] Rentoul retained his Irish accent,[35] but although he could be provocative his debating style owed more to the student debater's flyting, the after-dinner speaker's love of humorous anecdote, and perhaps kailyard deployment of humour as solvent of doctrinal gloom and rigidity[36], than to Saunderson's bitter and aggressive taunting of his nationalist opponents. His parliamentary contributions were mainly on the 1893 Home Rule Bill, on local government and educational issues, in support of land purchase by tenants and in defence of coercion legislation, arguing that the coercion legislation passed under Gladstone's second administration in 1880–85 had been more draconian than the subsequent Conservative coercion measures denounced by Gladstonians, and that the declining crime rates under the 1892-95 Liberal governments was not due to nationalist support for a Home Rule government, but to the ongoing effect of the coercion legislation which had been necessary to deal with:

> … men, who tarred the heads of girls, fired at people from behind hedges, mutilated cattle, and committed many other outrages; no Act could not be too strong for dealing with such crimes… crimes had been perpetrated in Ireland more disgraceful than had been committed in any other part of the Empire.[37]

Rentoul argued that provisions for pre-trial detention and interrogation under Conservative coercion legislation could not be described as an insult to Ireland, since similar provisions were a normal and longstanding feature of the Roman law-based Scottish legal system.[38] This was disingenuous, since in the debates on the 1893 Home Rule Bill Rentoul had tried to prohibit the Irish Parliament from replacing Common Law with a Roman law-based system because of the scope it would give nationalists to detain opponents.[39] As (for a period) the only Presbyterian Conservative representing an Irish seat, Rentoul also raised specific Presbyterian issues such as school endowments[40] and the taxation of Presbyterian manses where Anglican and Catholic parochial houses were exempt.[41]

Rentoul's unopposed return on 25 March 1890 was preceded by a speaking tour of the constituency in which Rentoul and Hill, accompanied by the South Belfast MP and Orange leader William Johnston, publicised the Orangeism of Rentoul's father and stated that while Rentoul was not an Orangeman he held Orange principles and would be willing to join the Order if his constituents so desired.[42] (Rentoul was never initiated, though he did sometimes address Orange meetings,[43] and after leaving Parliament repeatedly called for Orange demonstrations to be discontinued as unnecessarily provocations.)[44] The *Belfast Newsletter* noted that Rentoul began his tour at Ballynahinch, site of the decisive battle of the 1798 rebellion in County Down, and remarked that he would carry to Westminster his constituents' warning 'that one civil war within a century was more than enough; that the men of Down had fought their best and last battle in '98; and they object to an Irish Parliament because they would be compelled to draw the sword once more'.[45]

Although Rentoul was returned unopposed at every East Down election he contested, this underestimates the challenges he faced. Within a relatively short time of his election (probably at the 1892 general election) Hill tried to pressurise him into stepping down in favour of an aristocratic candidate. Rentoul defeated this by appealing to the constituency, remarking that tenant voters could no longer be coerced by the threat of eviction.[46] The episode left Rentoul with an abiding resentment of the snobbery and highhandedness of his former sponsors,[47] and his eulogy of Hill at an October 1894 meeting in West Down should probably be read as tongue-in-cheek.[48] (Hill's action may not have reflected simple snobbery; in 1891 Rentoul had clashed with the Irish Landowners' Convention for his independent actions on the Local Government Bill[49], and in a 22 March 1892 Commons debate on Irish national education William Johnston, who had campaigned for Rentoul in 1890, threatened him with de-selection for an allegedly lenient view of state support for Catholic education.[50] As a result of Johnston's accusation Rentoul had to produce at six constituency meetings written evidence that he was not a Catholic.)[51]

Rentoul was a strong advocate of 'constructive unionism', arguing that the strong Unionist government returned to power in 1895 must finally defeat Home Rule by addressing the material roots of Irish discontent.[52] He supported the Unionist government's 1896 Land Act – even nationalist amendments reducing the period between judicial rent revisions and reducing the ability of the landlord to proceed against a tenant in arrears – clashing with Edward Carson in the process.[53] He showed some sympathy for proposals by Arthur Balfour to establish a Catholic university in Dublin, though he stopped short of endorsing denominationalism because of constituency pressure.[54] He argued that he had benefited by attending interdenominational institutions in QCC and QCG, but that TCD and QCB were Anglican and Presbyterian in all but name and if a Catholic university was established QCB should become formally Presbyterian.[55] These views on university education, though shared by some Presbyterians associated with QCB, were unpopular among Ulster Protestants.[56]

Rentoul supported Alice Hart's promotion of Donegal cottage industries and technical education.[57] In 1891 and 1898 Rentoul opposed attempts to incorporate provisions for minority representation (such as cumulative voting and two-member constituencies) in Irish local government legislation; he argued on the basis of his LCC experience that such expedients were counter-productive and thought that the minority's best hope of securing re-election was by cultivating the respect of, and addressing common concerns with, their Catholic/nationalist neighbours.[58] Rentoul called on Ulster Unionists to set an example by electing suitable Catholics and avoiding discrimination in local government appointments. (He was praised for this by John Redmond, but widely criticised by unionists in his own constituency, stirred up by local newspapers.)[59] Rentoul was one of the few Ulster Unionist MPs to join nationalists in a campaign against the over-taxation of Ireland,[60] and supported nationalist proposals for relief to the congested districts of the West. (Nationalists protested, however, when Rentoul suggested that emigration must be part of the solution for the congested districts; when the Athlone-born London journalist and nationalist MP for a Liverpool constituency disagreed with him, Rentoul retorted, 'The honourable member and myself are both emigrants. We have both emigrated to our great advantage.')[61]

During 1896 and 1900 parliamentary debates on Irish education, Rentoul denounced the teaching of the Irish language in national schools, even where the population was Irish-speaking, as positively harmful to the pupils; he cited official neglect of Flemish in Belgium as an example to be followed, and advocated greater emphasis on modern languages such as French and German.[62] His equation of Anglophone schools for Irish-speaking pupils with language learning by immersion was rejected even by Chief Secretary Gerald Balfour.[63] Rentoul's statements were quoted in twenty-first century debates on language policy in Northern Ireland as exemplifying Ulster Unionist hostility to the Irish language.[64] (At least one contemporary unionist commentator saw Rentoul as an isolated figure expressing a personal opinion.)[65] Rentoul claimed that his opposition to the language was not politically motivated,[66] and given his acquaintance with impoverished Irish-speaking districts[67], his generally utilitarian outlook, and his own knowledge and love of modern languages,[68] it seems he genuinely believed the demise of the language would benefit Ireland. (In a lecture on the glories of Ireland delivered around the same time, he attributed Ireland's shortcomings – including inarticulacy, religious bigotry and political overenthusiasm – to geographical and cultural isolation, the latter partly attributable to the Irish language.)[69]

Rentoul was unopposed at the 1900 general election, but shortly thereafter entered into a public dispute with T. W. Russell who had lost his junior ministry after the government refused to accept his detailed scheme for compulsory land purchase. Rentoul believed Russell was engaged in a cynical exercise in demagoguery, and publicly denied his claim to have been sacked on the land issue.[70] When Russell published a letter from the Prime Minister confirming the reason for his departure from office, Rentoul refused to accept the general view that Russell had vindicated himself; he claimed that Russell's departure was due to his reckless political tactics, which spread division among unionists and damaged English support for compulsory purchase. In July 1901 parliamentary exchanges between Rentoul and Russell grew so heated that the Speaker intervened to restore order[71], and while addressing an English Conservative audience Rentoul called on British Conservatives to oppose compulsory sale if Russellites defeated sitting Ulster Unionists.[72] Rentoul was accused by both Russellites and Home Rulers of seeking a government appointment, but in his memoirs he describes his actions as a courageous defence of principle despite electoral damage.[73]

In November 1901 Rentoul was appointed a judge of the City of London Court and the Central Criminal Court. While appointment to any office of profit under the Crown normally vacated a parliamentary seat, Rentoul and his sympathisers maintained that his office was not a

Crown one because although the Crown made the appointment the salary was paid by the Corporation of the City of London.[74] Russellites and Nationalists joined in accusing him of being a place-hunter who had now got his reward for doing the government's dirty work by attacking Russell[75], with the Donegal Home Rule MP Swift MacNeill comparing his actions to Lord Castlereagh's role in passing the Union and predicting that at their first opportunity the electors of Down would reject Rentoul as they rejected Castlereagh in 1806.[76] After an extensive dispute, during which Rentoul appeared in the Commons at the beginning of the session but was advised by the Conservative leadership to withdraw without taking his seat, the Speaker decided that while the judgeship was compatible with a seat in parliament, a MP appointed to it must seek re-election.[77] After some indecision, Rentoul decided not to stand again, suggesting he feared defeat by a Russellite candidate.[78]

At the 1902 by-election (where Rentoul's failure to campaign was noted) the official Unionist was narrowly defeated by a Russellite.[79] In 1903 Rentoul declared his intention of contesting the seat again, partly in reaction to the emergence of James Craig as Unionist candidate.[80] (Craig's family wealth derived from a distillery; Rentoul had grown increasingly committed to temperance after witnessing alcoholic-related poverty in the East End of London and under the influence of his sister Elizabeth, and by the end of his life he was a prohibitionist.[81] Elizabeth Rentoul enlivened the occasion by composing and circulating scurrilous leaflets denouncing Craig and his supporters.[82] Rentoul withdrew, lacking local support; although he spoke of contesting another seat, this ended his parliamentary career.[83]

During his early career Rentoul had threatened violent resistance to Home Rule in terms which seem more than symbolic (e.g. during his 1890 election campaign: 'If Home Rule,' he said 'were granted to this country, I believe Ulster would rise and fight against it on the battlefield. You ask: Would you say it was right for Ulster to do that? I answer emphatically: Yes, I would … Home Rule can never exist in Ulster, no matter what Bill is passed, unless the men of Ulster are slaughtered by British bayonets to enforce it').[84] He later denied, however, that he, or any of his acquaintances, had meant to resort to violence. During a visit to Manorcunningham soon after the 1906 general election, Rentoul lectured a local Presbyterian and Church of Ireland audience on the prospect that Ireland would soon acquire a limited form of devolution (eventually embodied in the 1907 Irish Council Bill, abandoned after nationalists denounced it as insufficient). Rentoul denounced the slogan 'Ulster will fight and Ulster will be right' as 'a wicked and lying catchcry', praised the friendly relations between Donegal Catholics and Protestants, and advised his audience to acquiesce in devolution since Ireland would still be part of the Empire.[85] In 1911 he allowed the Home Rule MP Jeremiah McVeagh to publish his view that neither he nor any of his Irish-based Unionist relatives feared religious persecution under Home Rule.[86] As a member of the London-based Ulster Association (a social club founded pre-1900) he unsuccessfully opposed a September 1913 motion to add a political commitment to the Union to its constitution, although he stated that he was personally a Unionist.[87]

Rentoul's judicial career was relatively undistinguished, though his 1912 judgment that the legal unenforceability of gambling debts did not apply when payments were made by cheques (which he held were governed by the rules applying to bills of exchange) aroused considerable interest.[88] In 1903 he ruled that courts had no jurisdiction over disciplinary fines inflicted by trade unions on their own members.[89] On 7 March 1907 he was on the bench for the last case tried in the historic Old Bailey court building before its demolition.[90]

Rentoul was often outspoken when trying professional criminals or cases involving fraud; when faced with a bigamist who obtained money from numerous women through false promises of marriage, he expressed the hope that the suffragettes would soon change the law to make such offences punishable by flogging.[91] He described a wholesaler who sold meat which he knew to be unfit for human consumption as a murderer, and remarked that in some countries he would be lynched.[92] In his memoirs Rentoul defends flogging habitual offenders, but notes that he was as lenient as possible in cases of bigamy where there were no aggravating circumstances. (He attributed many such cases to the difficulties faced by the poor in obtaining divorces; as a Presbyterian he would have believed divorce and remarriage allowable in certain circumstances, whereas Catholicism and Anglicanism forbade it.)[93] In 1910 he complained that shopkeepers were insufficiently aware that telephones could be used to give them fraudulent orders.[94]

Rentoul's health declined in his last years, which were overshadowed by the death of his wife in 1914. In September 1911 he suffered a seizure in court[95] and in 1914 had a serious respiratory illness.[96] In 1915 he was censured by the Court of Appeal after accusing a barrister in open court of mishandling the defence of a soldier accused of larceny.[97] In 1919 the Court of Appeal reversed a conviction because Rentoul, summing up in a case involving two defendants, forgot to discuss one of them and used ambiguous language concerning the trustworthiness of accomplice evidence.[98] (The *Kerry News* gleefully reminded its nationalist readers that Rentoul had been 'one of the bitterest of Ulster MPs'.)[99] Rentoul admitted in his memoirs that he made a mistake, but complained that the denunciation of his conduct ignored similar mistakes made by senior judges (including the appeal judge who delivered the decision) and that a subsequent vote of no confidence in Rentoul by the Common Council of the City of London was inconsistent with judicial independence.[100] In February 1919 he was diagnosed as suffering from heart disease. After becoming bedridden, he formally retired on 2 July 1919[101] and died shortly before midnight on 12 August 1919 at his home in West Kensington.[102]

In the last months of his life Rentoul wrote and dictated recollections of his life and opinions; these were edited by his sister Elizabeth (sole beneficiary of his will, proved at £6,082)[103] and published in 1921 with a preface by his son Gervase.[104] They are anecdotal and focussed more on law than on parliamentary politics, but aroused additional interest for their statement that Rentoul's opposition to Home Rule might have been mistaken – a literal deathbed conversion. Rentoul states that he had genuinely believed Ireland was better off as part of the metropolitan power than as a detached provincial fragment, and that nationalists did not seriously want Home Rule and only put it forward as a means of gaining land purchase, but he was impressed by the persistence and strength of the demand for Home Rule and believed Ireland could not be held by transforming it into "an armed camp" as in 1919.[105] He praises John Redmond as a patriotic statesman genuinely loyal to the empire, and brackets him and George Wyndham as far-sighted leaders brought down by disloyal followers.[106] Carson and his associates are denounced for treasonable language and behaviour which helped to destabilise both Ireland and Europe, and Rentoul complains that claims by Ulster Unionists that they feared religious persecution under Home Rule were inconsistent with abandonment of Southern Unionists by accepting partition.[107]

Comparison of Rentoul's memoir with contemporary newspaper reportage shows that Rentoul played down some hardline or opportunistic aspects of his political career. In some respects he may have mellowed after the threat of immediate Home Rule receded with the Parnell split and the defeat of Gladstone's Home Rule Bill, but in others he could claim a record of moderation pre-existing his entry into parliament. He was a consistent utilitarian – sometimes, as with his views on language, a philistine driven by awareness of the difficulty of imbibing culture with a limited income and exiguous professional prospects – who believed that Irish nationalism could be defused by material reforms and by facilitating the pursuit by Irish Catholics of the educational and professional opportunities which the empire provided to talented outsiders such as himself. Alvin Jackson classes him among 'parliamentary West Britons' – Ulster Unionist MPs, often wholly or partly resident in Britain and principally active in the House of Commons, who found that by translating provincial unionism into broader terminology for a metropolitan audience, and trying to appeal to metropolitan opinion – and even to nationalists – by proposing limited reforms, forgot like Stewart Parker's fictionalised Henry Joy McCracken the bitterness of two men fighting over a field. It is a recurring tradition, whose achievements and limitations should not be overlooked.

NOTES

1   This paper derives from research on James Alexander Rentoul and Erminda Rentoul Esler undertaken for the Dictionary of Irish Biography. Thanks to Paul Bew, Andrew Charles, Derval Fitzgerald, Andrew Jackson and Gordon Lucy.

2   Lord Ernest Hamilton, *Forty Years On* (London, 1922) – see also Patrick Maume, "Borders: Lord Ernest Hamilton (1858–1939), race, religion and Ulster-Scots identity in the last decades of the Anglo-Irish Union" in Colin Younger (ed.) *Barriers and Borderlands* (Cambridge Scholars Publishing: Newcastle-on-Tyne, 2013) pp 110–126); Sir John Ross, *The Years of my Pilgrimage: some random reminiscences* (London, 1924); idem, *Pilgrim Scrip: some more random reminiscences* (London, 1927); Reginald Lucas, *Colonel*

Saunderson MP: a Memoir (London, 1908); Edward Marjoribanks and Ian Colvin, *The Life of Lord Carson* (3 vols, London, 1932–36); Aiken McClelland, *William Johnston of Ballykilbeg* (London, 1990); Alvin Jackson, *The Ulster Party* (Oxford, 1989); idem, *Colonel Edward Saunderson: Land and Loyalty in Victorian Ireland* (Oxford, 1995).

3   Erminda Rentoul, *A Record of the Family and Lineage of James Alexander Rentoul, LL.D., MP* (Belfast, 1890).

4   John W. Lockington, *The Rentouls: A Presbyterian Dynasty* (Belfast, 2016).

5   Erminda Rentoul, *A Record of the Family and Lineage of William Gervase Chittick* (Belfast, 1890).

6   Patrick Maume 'Education, love, loneliness, philanthropy: the ambivalences of Erminda Rentoul Esler' in Sinead Mooney and Kathryn Laing (eds), *Irish Women's Writing 1880–1920* (Brighton, 2020).

7   *Hansard*, HC Deb. 30 May 1892, vol. 5, cc259–261.

8   Rentoul, *Stray Thoughts and Memories*, pp 37–48.

9   *Belfast Newsletter*, 19 March 1890; Rentoul, *Stray Thoughts*, pp 49–65.

10   Rentoul, *Stray Thoughts*, p. 90.

11   Rentoul, *Stray Thoughts*, pp 88, 100.

12   Rentoul, *Stray Thoughts*, pp 93–105, pp 105–06n [note by Elizabeth].

13   *Irish Independent*, 17 April 1908; *Irish Times*, 13 Aug. 1883; *Belfast Newsletter*, 29 June, 29 Oct. 1918; Gervase Rentoul, *Sometimes I Think* (London, 1940), p. 15.

14   *Belfast Newsletter*, 28 Jan., 25 March 1914.

15   Gervase Rentoul, *Sometimes I Think*, p. 19.

16   Erminda Rentoul, *Record of the Family… of James Alexander Rentoul*; Gervase Rentoul, *This Is My Case* (London, 1945). A report of Rentoul being taken ill on the bench (*Cork Examiner*, 20 April 1911) states that his 'wife and son' were sent for. Gervase is the only son listed as attending Rentoul's funeral (*Irish Independent*, 18 Aug. 1919).

17   Erminda Rentoul, *Record of the Family… of William Gervase Chittick*, p. 6; Gervase Rentoul, *This is My Case*, p. 123.

18   *Belfast Newsletter*, 5 Sept. 1885, 7 Sept. 1889.

19   *Hansard*, HC Deb. 4 March 1891 vol. 351, c157.

20   *Belfast Newsletter*, 5 March 1886, 20 March 1889.

21   *Hansard*, HC Deb. 4 March 1891 vol. 351, cc157–158.

22   *Belfast Newsletter*, 17 Sept. 1889; Cork Examiner, 20 April 1892.

23   *Belfast Newsletter*, 5 Sept. 1885.

24   *Belfast Newsletter*, 22 April 1895.

25   Ibid.

26   *Belfast Newsletter*, 17 Sept. 1889.

27   Ibid.

28   Rentoul, *Stray Thoughts*, pp 130–31.

29   *Belfast Newsletter*, 20 March, 22 March 1890; *Leinster Leader*, 3 May 1890; *Irish Times*, 20 March 1890.

30   Gervase Rentoul, *Sometimes I Think*, pp 17–18.

31   Alvin Jackson, *The Ulster Party* (Oxford, 1989), pp 58–9.

32   *Irish Times*, 5 March 1891.

33 *Leinster Leader*, 27 July 1901. Rentoul praises Saunderson's debating style in *Belfast Newsletter*, 17 Sept. 1889.

34 Alvin Jackson, *Colonel Edward Saunderson: Land and Loyalty in Victorian Ireland* (Oxford, 1995). See also Patrick Maume, 'Music-Hall Unionism: Robert Martin and the politics of the Stage-Irishman', in Peter Gray (ed.), *Victoria's Ireland? Irishness and Britishness, 1837–1901* (Dublin, 2004), pp 69–80.

35 Rentoul, *Stray Thoughts*, p. 32.

36 Patrick Maume, 'Lady Microbe and the Kailyard Viceroy: The Aberdeen viceroyalty, welfare monarchy, and the politics of philanthropy', in Peter Gray and Olwen Purdue (eds), *The Irish Lord Lieutenancy, c. 1541–1922* (Dublin: UCD Press, 2012), pp 199–214.

37 *Hansard*, HC Deb. 8 May 1895, vol. 33, c734.

38 Ibid., cc735–738.

39 *Hansard*, HC Deb. 6 June 1893, vol. 13, cc377–378.

40 *Irish Times*, 9 Jan. 1891.

41 *Irish Times*, 21 March 1899.

42 *Belfast Newsletter*, 22 March 1890; *Weekly Irish Times*, 22 March 1890.

43 *Irish Times*, 18 April 1898.

44 *Ulster Herald*, 1 Sept. 1906; *Fermanagh Herald*, 8 Dec. 1906; Rentoul, *Stray Thoughts*.

45 *Belfast Newsletter*, 20 March 1890.

46 *Evening Herald*, 23 April 1892; Rentoul, *Stray Thoughts and Memories*, pp 26–7; Jackson *Ulster Party*, pp 219–21.

47 Hansard, HC Deb. 2 Feb 1893, vol. 8, c310.

48 *Belfast Newsletter*, 8 Oct. 1894.

49 *Hansard*, HC Deb. 23 May 1892, vol. 4, cc1592–1593; *Irish Times*, 3 Oct. 1891.

50 *Hansard*, HC Deb. 22 March 1892, vol. 2, c1494; *Irish Times*, 23 March 1892.

51 *Hansard*, HC Deb. 30 May 1892, vol. 5, cc260–261.

52 *Kerry Weekly Reporter*, 12 Oct. 1895.

53 *Irish Times*, 13 June, 22 July 1896.

54 *Belfast Newsletter*, 17 Sept., 19 Sept. 1889.

55 *Irish Times*, 24 June 1899.

56 Jackson, *Ulster Party*, pp 179–87.

57 *Irish Times*, 20 Jan. 1891.

58 *Westmeath Examiner*, 26 March 1898; *Cork Examiner*, 28 April 1898; *Hansard*, HC Deb. 27 April 1898, vol. 56, cc1290–1294; *Irish Times*, 18 April 1898.

59 *Hansard*, HC Deb. 11 July 1898, vol. 61, c572.

60 *Drogheda Independent*, 15 May 1897; *Irish Times*, 18 Feb. 1899; *Munster Express*, 17 Feb. 1900; Hansard, HC Deb. 9 Feb. 1900, vol. 78, cc1085–1086.

61 *Freeman's Journal*, 10 March 1897; *Irish Times*, 5 May 1898.

62 *Hansard*, HC Deb. 18 June 1896, vol. 41, c1423, 19 July 1900, vol. 86, cc511–512, 20 July 1900, vol. 86, cc691–700; *Freeman's Journal*, 22 May 1901; *Irish Times*, 20 July, 21 July 1900; *Irish Times*, 22 May 1901.

63 *Hansard*, HC Deb. 20 July 1900, vol. 86, cc705–709.

64 http://belfastmediagroup.com/so-whats-the-irish-for-deja-vu-then/ (last accessed 16 Oct. 2019); *Strabane Chronicle*, 15 Feb. 2017.

65 *Irish Times*, 21 July 1900.

66 Ibid.

67 Ibid.; *Hansard*, HC Deb. 20 July 1900, vol. 86, c700.

68 Gervase Rentoul, *This Is My Case*, pp 25–28 describes his father's sending him to France and Germany to learn their languages; his residence with a non-English speaking family in Berlin being seen as advantageous since it compelled learning by immersion.

69 *Ulster Herald*, 19 Oct. 1901.

70 Rentoul, *Stray Thoughts*, pp 114–15; *Freeman's Journal*, 29 Dec. 1900; *Irish Times*, 27 Dec. 1900.

71 *Leinster Leader*, 27 July 1901.

72 *Irish Times*, 22 Jan., 22 July 1901.

73 Rentoul, *Stray Thoughts*, pp 114–15.

74 *Freeman's Journal*, 4 Nov. 1901; *Irish Independent*, 4 Nov., 4 Dec. 1901, 18 Jan. 1902; *Cork Examiner*, 4 Nov., 30 Dec. 1901.

75 *Freeman's Journal*, 1 Nov. 1901; *Anglo-Celt*, 9 Nov. 1901; *Irish Independent*, 12 Dec. 1901;*Weekly Irish Times*, 9 Nov. 1901.

76 *Freeman's Journal*, 4 Nov. 1901.

77 *Irish Independent*, 18 Jan. 1902; *Freeman's Journal*, 21 Oct. 1907; *Weekly Irish Times*, 4 Jan. 1902, Irish Times, 11 Jan. 1902.

78 *Irish Times*, 18 Jan., 20 Jan., 24 Jan. 1902.

79 *Freeman's Journal*, 4 Feb. 1902.

80 *Kerry Evening Post*, 25 July 1903; *Irish Independent*, 5 Nov. 1903; *Weekly Irish Times*, 18 July, 29 Aug. 1903; *Irish Times*, 7 Sept. 1903; St John Ervine, *Craigavon: Ulsterman* (London, 1949), pp 126–127.

81 Rentoul, *Stray Thoughts and Memories*, pp 244–274; *Belfast Newsletter*, 19 June 1916.

82 Ervine, *Craigavon*, pp 126–127.

83 *Donegal News*, 5 March 1904.

84 *Scottish Liberal*, 4 April 1890, quoted *Irish Independent*, 12 Dec. 1901. See also *Hansard*, HC Deb. 19 April 1893, vol. 11, cc672, 680.

85 *Ulster Herald*, 1 Sept. 1906.

86 *Irish Independent*, 18 July 1911.

87 *Freeman's Journal*, 5 Sept. 1913; *Irish Independent*, 5 Sept. 1913; *Strabane Chronicle*, 13 Sept. 1913.

88 *Evening Herald*, 20 Nov. 1912; *Irish Independent*, 22 Nov. 1912.

89 *Drogheda Argus*, 1 Aug. 1903.

90 Rentoul, *Stray Thoughts*, p.184.

91 *Irish Times*, 5 July 1911.

92 *Skibbereen Eagle*, 20 July 1912.

93 Rentoul, *Stray Thoughts*, pp 179–181.

94 *Anglo-Celt*, 19 March 1910.

95 *Cork Examiner*, 20 April 1911.

96 *Irish Independent*, 3 Feb. 1914.

97 *Liberator*, 6 April 1915; *Kerryman*, 15 May 1915.

98 *Belfast Newsletter*, 25 Feb., 7 March 1919.

99 *Kerry News*, 7 March 1919.

100 Rentoul, *Stray Thoughts*, pp 184–8.

101 *Irish Times*, 3 July 1919.
102 *Cork Examiner*, 14 Aug. 1919; *Irish Independent*, 14 Aug. 1919; *Irish Times*, 14 Aug. 1919.
103 *Irish Independent*, 26 Nov. 1919.
104 *Cork Examiner*, 14 Aug. 1919; *Irish Independent*, 13 Dec. 1920; *Belfast Newsletter*, 9 April 1921; *Irish Times*, 27 May 1921.
105 *Irish Independent*, 28 March 1921; Rentoul, *Stray Thoughts*, pp 188–243; Paul Bew, *Ideology and the Irish Question: Ulster Unionists and Irish Nationalism 1912–1916* (Oxford, 1994), pp 37, 42–43, 105.
106 Rentoul, *Stray Thoughts*, pp 137–40, 236–40; for Wyndham and Rentoul, see also Gervase Rentoul, *This is my Case*, pp 42–3.
107 Rentoul, *Stray Thoughts*, pp 189–235.

Bulmer Hobson

an Ulster Quaker Nationalist, 1900–1916

SEAN WORGAN

John Bulmer Hobson (1883–1969) was an Irish Nationalist
and Quaker, who joined the Irish Republican Brotherhood
(IRB) in 1904.[1]

This organisation traditionally sought to achieve independence and
an Irish republic, independent of Britain, by physical force. While
Hobson was at the heart of efforts to reform the IRB and move it away
from physical force with his IRB colleague, Denis McCullough, there
nevertheless remains a contradiction here. It has plagued the study of
Hobson ever since by muddying the waters of historical understanding:
how could a Quaker, by their very definition peaceful, support physical
force in the way Hobson did. In my opinion this question has led
historians to downplay or ignore Hobson's Quakerism and concentrate
on his Nationalism instead; however, the two cannot be separated.

This article seeks to provide an explanation of the paradox of
Hobson's Quaker Nationalism by examining the latter through the
prism of his Quakerism. This is necessary since despite Marnie Hay's
2009 biography and other works on Hobson by figures like Des
Gunning and Roy Foster, the relationship between Hobson's
Nationalism and Quakerism remains, like the man, something of a
mystery.[2] Through this paper, a development of my Ph.D. thesis on
Hobson, I hope to redress that. Though the paper follows a rough
chronological timeline I have taken a thematic approach, concentrating
on particular aspects of Quakerism and what I see as the consummation
of the synthesis of Hobson's Quakerism and Nationalism in his

Defensive Warfare approach.[3] For this reason, events after and including 1908 are treated rather more briskly than would otherwise be the case. In the case of some, like the 1916 Easter Rising, I have examined them only from Hobson's point of view, i.e. how they played out in terms of his Quaker-Nationalist thought.

HOBSON'S EARLY YEARS

Hobson's early years were dominated by his Quakerism and his attendance of Friends' School, Lisburn. Despite this, Hobson says little in either his work, *Ireland Yesterday and Tomorrow* or his statements to the Bureau of Military History, about his Quakerism or his Quaker schooling, other than a few lines on the stir his subscription to Alice Milligan and Ethna Carberry's Nationalist newspaper, the *Shan Van Vocht*, created while a pupil there.[4] True, in the *History of Friends' School, Lisburn*, Hobson talks fondly of his old headmaster, Joseph Radley, but again there is nothing by him on Quakerism's spiritual or intellectual influence beyond this.[5] Hobson's sister, Florence, who also attended the Friends' School, on the girls' campus, only says her brother expressed his spirituality through 'his passionate desire for justice and hatred of all oppression'.[6] This tallies with Hobson's own assertion that it was from his father, a Gladstonian Home Ruler, that he inherited a natural urge to take the weaker side in every quarrel and to resent injustice of every kind'.[7]

Perhaps it is in Hobson's father that we find the first concrete link between Hobson's Quakerism and his Nationalism. Florence Hobson testified that their father 'was in my childhood the only Home Ruler in [the] Belfast Meeting and my young life was punctuated by '"Mr Gladstone's" Second Home Rule Bill'.[8] It must have been similar for Bulmer. That Hobson's family were Liberal is not surprising, for as Duncan Watts has noted: 'The two, Liberalism and Nonconformity, went hand in hand and where Dissent was strong, so also was the Liberal Party'.[9] Donald Read has echoed this and even gone so far as to state that the former Quaker, John Bright, 'as much as Gladstone, created the Gladstonian Liberal Party'.[10]

Liberalism and Quakerism were natural bedfellows since, as James Walvin suggests, 'Quaker feeling' is 'characterized by strong individualism', by what he calls an element of 'religious anarchism'.[11] Walvin notes that historically the Quakers had found it necessary to formulate a system of discipline to temper the individualism that Quakerism fostered. Only through this was individualism gradually brought to heel and subordinated to what was deemed the broader general good.[12] It is hardly surprising that in these circumstances Neville H. Newhouse described Hobson as a rugged individualist.[13]

However, it was Hobson's mother, Mary Ann Bulmer-Hobson, who seems to have had the greatest influence in fusing Hobson's Quakerism and Nationalism, not least because of her work in the social sphere, which chimed with William Penn's Quaker ideals: 'He never accepted the social system, with its sharp divisions of wealth and poverty, as a divine ordnance'.[14] Mary Ann Bulmer Hobson's work with the Belfast Board of Guardians in particular tallied with both Penn and her son's concern for the underdog. Mary Hobson arrived in Belfast some time after 1881, Quaker records showing that she and Hobson's father, Benjamin, were living in Carlow before that time.[15] She and Alice Milligan became friends and political colleagues through the Irish Women's Association (IWA). Mary Hobson noted the IWA grew out the earlier Belfast suffrage organisation: From this 'a band of women got together in Belfast, and started a new society, the Committee of which I was asked to join.[16]

Much of the impetus for Bulmer Hobson's later career stemmed from his involvement in the Irish Literary Revival and his attempts to bridge the sectarian divide. Both these aspects of Hobson's nationalism seem to have gained inspiration from Mary Hobson's involvement in the IWA. In a paper she delivered to the IWA in 1895, Mary Hobson noted: 'It is the duty of every woman to take an interest in the country in which she lived, to know something of its history, past and present ...'. This was part of Mary Hobson's belief that a knowledge of Ireland's history and literature could bridge its sectarian divide. Accordingly, she stated that the IWA's 'duty' lay in bridging 'the sectarian differences which have so much separated the people in the past, and making in the name of Irishmen and Irishwomen a title of honour in the land of their birth'.[17] Echoing the views of Theobald Wolfe Tone, with whom her son became so enamoured: '... To unite the whole people of Ireland, to abolish the memories of past dissentions and to substitute the common name of Irishman in place of the denominations of Protestant, Catholic and Dissenter – these were my means'.[18]

By bringing the two together, Mary Hobson was making the same case as her son later on, when he advocated the blending of Orange and Green through the recreation of the kind of Gaelic society that had existed in Ireland's past.[19] To achieve this Bulmer Hobson would advocate a social reconstruction, but even here he probably found the precedent in his mother's thinking. Mary Hobson's 1895 paper, 'The Social and Political Work of Women', stated that 'the aims of the IWA are not entirely political, but in large measure social'.[20] This was a reflection of her belief (passed on to her son) that sectarian differences would be removed through the socio-economic sphere.

While Mary Hobson was not thinking on the grand scale her son Bulmer would, it is significant that both her IWA programme and that of Hobson's Dungannon Club advocated using Boards of Guardians to achieve their social and political aims. Mary Hobson noted in her memoirs: 'the principal object' of the IWA 'was to bring together Catholic and Protestant women … Another activity, following on the heels of the "Irish Women's Association", was an effort to get women seats on the Board of Guardians.'[21] Mary Hobson envisaged IWA members as the public guardians of women and children less fortunate than themselves.[22] This fitted with her Quaker background and her son's, who had had his school fees paid by the Friends. This experience may help to explain the inclusion of the Board of Guardian's policy in Bulmer Hobson's later Dungannon Club Manifesto. While the policy was part of an overall push to win political independence through the capture of public boards as part of Arthur Griffith's (the founder of Sinn Féin) 'Hungarian policy', there was always more to it in Hobson's case. Like his mother, he saw the political side as secondary to the social. In this, Hobson must have aimed to go beyond Griffith's strategy of merely using the Boards to win political independence; he saw real independence as being achieved through social reconstruction, fusing his mother's Quaker social thinking with that of his Sinn Féin Nationalism.

DRINK AND NATIONALISM

In addition to Hobson's family, Quakerism in general exerted a formative influence on his Nationalist development. The Quakers' disdain for alcohol is well known and surely played a role in the young Hobson's joining of the Pioneer Branch of Cumann na nGaedheal in 1900, which combined teetotalism and Irish Nationalism in a way which must have chimed with Hobson's developing *weltanschauung*. Cumann na nGaedheal was an IRB front organisation but Hobson did not join the IRB until three years later, being sworn in by his Nationalist colleague Denis McCullough. In one way it was a natural step since McCullough had joined the Pioneer branch in order to find the kind of 'Irish-Ireland' movement he had first sought in joining the IRB. However, McCullough had been bitterly disappointed, finding middle-aged IRB figures debating politics in public houses; he found the Irish-Ireland movement he had been looking for in the Pioneer branch instead – as did Hobson.[23]

The Pioneer branch provided a kind of early blueprint for Hobson and McCullough's later work in reforming the IRB and diverting it from violence. However, it also provided an early demonstration to the young Hobson of how to combine Quaker and Nationalist principles. This is exactly what Hobson did in his later Defensive Warfare programme, combining teetotalism with resistance to British rule. On his American tour Hobson noted in 1907 how the example of Father Mathew, the apostle of temperance, had deprived the British of millions of pounds to run the country:

> For seven years he went about the country teaching people to be sober and when he started his propaganda there were 21,000 public houses in Ireland, and seven years later at the end of his mission, there were 13,000, and the English Government incidentally had lost millions and millions of money.[24]

From this Hobson advocated that, by abstaining from drink, the people could support the National movement by depriving the government of the tax it levied on drink:

> ... we are having a temperance movement, which is asking the people, not only for the sake of morality and religion, not only for

the sake of better social conditions in Ireland, but for the sake of depleting England's money revenues and keeping Irish money in Irish pockets, to decrease their consumption of drink.[25]

That he remained so wedded to the idea is testament that Hobson's Quakerism never left him, indeed, it continued to power his Nationalism.

RADLEY AND NEW LIGHTISM

Hobson's fusion of Quaker and Nationalist thought had a good deal to do with his study of Irish history as a boy, not least because of the apparent link between Hobson's Lisburn school and the United Irishmen rebellion of 1798. While the Friends' School had always sought to temper the anarchistic elements of Quakerism, the revolutionary atmosphere at the end of the eighteenth and beginning of the nineteenth century had made this increasingly difficult. In the early years of the nineteenth century the Friends' School had found it necessary to replace 39 of the Committee members appointed to run it in 1796, some because they had adopted New Light beliefs.[26] Despite being a Presbyterian movement, New Light posed a threat to the traditional forces of Quakerism. It did so because on a religious level it tapped into the Quaker idea of the individual's inner light. This rejected the idea of a priestly overseer, something which already gave Quakerism an anarchistic aspect.[27] New Light made this all the more dangerous because it acted as a transmission mechanism between religion and politics, many New Lighters, went on to become United Irishmen,[28] something that would have fired the impressionable young Hobson's mind, who was already fascinated by the whole United movement.

FOCUS ON YOUTH

Quakers had always sought to guarantee their future through their children, in particular by winning the battle for their hearts and minds: 'From the outset it had been appreciated that a way to ensure the survival of Quaker culture was through appropriate childcare and education'.[29] Once Hobson had nailed his colours to the Nationalist mast this Quaker strain of thought seems to have been the motivating factor behind Hobson's championing of the junior branch of the Gaelic

League and Gaelic Athletics Association (GAA). Famously, a 19-year-old Hobson resigned in 1901 in disgust at the GAA County Board's lack of interest in competitions for junior clubs. This was due to a dispute over the junior hurlers whom Hobson saw as having far more potential than the adults:

> To say that the players who had taken up hurling were inexpert is to put it too mildly – they were a positive danger and some of them had the marks for many years … I thought that if we were ever to have hurling teams that would compete with those in other counties we should concentrate on training the young boys and making first-class hurlers out of them.[30]

Hobson proposed at the Board's September meeting that there should be competitions between the junior clubs. To his great surprise, the County Board was 'just not interested'.[31] Annoyed, Hobson resigned as Secretary of the GAA.[32]

Unsurprisingly the next organisation Hobson founded was also for boys, Na Fianna Eireann, started in June 1902. Na Fianna Eireann's minute book recalls the first meeting of the Committee of the Fianna na Eireann, at the Catholic Boys' Hall, Falls Road, on 22 June was attended by nearly 300 boys.[33] The minutes record Hobson being elected president and chairman of the organisation and delivering 'a very neat little speech' laying out the aims of the League. They note that the chairman brought before the hurler's minds 'the necessity of forming such a league and that it will bind them closer together and be a means of spreading the game and doing a little towards the revival of the old Irish sport'. To ensure this, it was resolved that a delegate from each club attend the meeting of the Fianna Gaelic League to be held every Friday evening to transact general business.[34] By uniting hurling with the Gaelic language Hobson stressed to the boys that learning the Irish language was the more important activity of the two:

> He also reminds them that each one of them will have to learn the Irish language for this was the most important of the two because in learning to speak their own native tongue they would be doing a great, and noble, and exalted work for Ireland and [become] participators in the great Gaelic movement of today.[35]

Speaking the language would allow the boys to participate in the work of the Gaelic movement, which Hobson saw as vital to the development of Irish nationalism. Even at this stage it fed into ideas on Defensive Warfare Hobson had already started developing, which looked to create a self-contained republic, beyond the control of the British state. On this Hobson had earlier contributed an article on 'Defensive Warfare' to the *United Irishman's* 17 February 1900 edition.[36] While Hobson's Quakerism did not contribute directly to those Gaelic aspects that fed into his Nationalism, in its focus on youth was nevertheless important to even this side of Hobson's Nationalism.

Likewise, with Hobson's former headmaster, Joseph Radley, and *Ulad[h]* and the Ulster Literary Theatre (ULT).[37] The breadth of Radley's interests led him to bring many new influences into Hobson's school, including music, astronomy, literature and natural history.[38] Radley fought a prolonged battle with the Educational Committee over the introduction of music, and the purchase of a piano in particular, but it was his attitude towards the theatre that most ran counter to the Committee's traditional Quaker thinking. But Radley did not let this stop him and his wide interests created a pluralistic atmosphere, in which different fields of interest could emerge. In this respect, the atmosphere of the school was ideal for Hobson to nurture his Quaker nationalism. In other areas too Radley created a climate of tolerance at the Friends' school, Lisburn, in which the young Hobson's Nationalism could thrive.

QUIETISM AND POLITICS

Another Quaker influence on Hobson was 'quietism', which came much later in the north of Ireland than it did on the British mainland, 1800– *c*. 1900. It seems to have exerted a strong influence on Hobson's family and Hobson's Quaker Nationalism.[39] Frederick B. Tolles has noted Quietism gained particular support in England in the wake of the Affirmation Act of 1722:

> [This] finally gave English Quakers many of the privileges of citizenship they had hitherto lacked, including the right to sue in court and vote without impediment (though not to hold public office). [But] Curiously enough, the achievement of most

of the privileges of citizenship was followed by a widespread disinclination to use them'.[40]

The reason for this was because of a growing feeling among Quakers that politics tainted their religion. It is all the more difficult not to make the link between Hobson's Quakerism and his abstentionist Sinn Féin Nationalism (from the British Parliament) when one notes Tolles's observation on the link between worldliness and politics:

> The feeling grew that a good Quaker should have as little as possible to do with earthly government, that he must avoid temptations, the distractions, the compromises, the corruptions of political life, that he ought to maintain his religious testimonies with absolute purity, in isolation if need be, from the life of his time.[41]

The same rationale is evident in Hobson's Nationalism. There are numerous examples in his writing of how he thought British politics had corrupted Irishmen, particularly those belonging to the Irish Party whom he came to see as profiting from it. This was particularly apparent in Hobson's later articles for *The Gaelic American* on the Liberals' National Insurance Act. This was passed into law with the help of the Irish Parliamentary Party, and both the Irish National Foresters and the Ancient Order of Hibernians (AOH), which were linked to the Irish Party, benefited greatly from administering the scheme. In the AOH's case it set up an Insurance Section which became one of the largest in Ireland: it received government funds to build premises, which doubled up as AOH halls, further increasing the AOH's influence due to its importance for social activities in rural areas.[42] For Hobson the Insurance Act was typical of the way Westminster politics corrupted Irishmen's morals, as he noted at the time: 'The job hunters are the only class in the community for whom the Insurance Act is a godsend, and we have more than enough of them already.'[43]

Following on from this, Hobson took the Quietist view that Westminster politics, based as it was on party lines, compromised Ireland as a nation. This was because for both Hobson and the Quietists, compromise, a necessity in party politics, led to the corruption of ideals – Nationalism and Quakerism respectively. Attendance at Westminster was a 'violation of the national integrity' because:

> Compromise has eaten like a cancer into our political life; and that compromise must be made anathema in the eyes of the people … We are not concerned with the material affairs of a people – we are concerned with the existence of a nation. You can compromise on inessentials … but you cannot compromise on the question of whether they [a people] will live. … we are faced with the question of whether Ireland shall continue to exist as a nation – a separate and distinct nation – and on that question we cannot and will not admit of compromise.[44]

Quietism was equally a reaction to worldliness or materialism and one can again see parallels between Hobson's anti-materialist Nationalism and his Quaker background.

Given the coincidence of the timeframe between the end of Quietism in Ulster, around 1900, and Hobson's Nationalist years of prominence, it is difficult not to imagine one directly impinged on the other, not least when Hobson says, in his first 'Confession of Faith' in *Irish Freedom* that '… when adversity follows adversity that nation, though it has lost its wealth and material prosperity, usually finds its own soul.'[45] For Hobson, Ireland's faith was strengthened by the fact she had lost her wealth and prosperity, but through material loss and suffering she had gained spiritual strength. Further proof of this can be seen in Hobson's statement that:

> The faith of an Irish nationalist, then is different from the Imperialist creeds – different in this, that it sees that the destinies of men and of nations are things of to-morrow as well as things of to-day, and that it does not profit a man to gain the whole world and lose his soul.

Hobson was at pains to stress the difference between Irishmen and Englishmen, but it would surely have been more difficult to do so had both been Quaker, the source from which Hobson's dislike of worldliness or materialism first came. Hobson continued:

> … this is what nationality means to a country like Ireland—it means that instead of engaging in a mad and headlong rush for wealth, we have discovered that money and power and iron ships are not the only things worth having, that the nation like the individual has a soul, and that national action in its best and highest is the expression of that soul.[46]

How then to solve the problem of materialism in Ireland and at the same time advance the National cause?

QUAKER CIVIL AND SOCIAL SOLUTIONS

Hobson needed an alternative. Fortunately, he had other Quaker solutions to hand, this time provided by the influence of his cousin, the Guild Socialist, S. G. Hobson, and the American Quaker theologian, Rufus Jones. Jones's work, *Social Law in the Spiritual World* appeared in 1904 and seems to have complemented Hobson's. Jones's book outlined how 'Spiritual facts are facts are bound up with social facts, spiritual laws with social laws'.[48] This also lent itself to Hobson's Co-operative approach and S. G. Hobson's Guild Socialism. Like Bulmer Hobson, S. G. Hobson was a Quaker and had probably read Rufus Jones' influential text. As a Guild Socialist his approach would have been ideally suited to both his cousin, Bulmer's, and Rufus Jones's of developing the kind of social institutions the latter's book envisaged.[49]

Bulmer Hobson must have seen such an approach as crucial to building up the social economy. This was because unlike state socialism, Guild Socialism looked to manufacturing in the workshop, rather than the factory. This was precisely the kind of manufacturing Hobson saw as being compatible with the development of the social economy, which he developed through the nineteenth-century Nationalist, James Fintan Lalor. Griffith's Hungarian Policy might do as a stop-gap in the meantime but for Griffith the extra-parliamentary means, like councils, district and regional, were only a means to the end of re-establishing an Irish Parliament. For Hobson, with his hatred of party politics, the means was the end. Fortunately, Hobson's policy of developing a social economy provided a workable alternative which could function as an alternative. In this, Bulmer Hobson was again able to draw on Quaker thought, via Irish nationalism.

Before moving on to this however, it is interesting that Hobson's two projects of 1908, both with the Socialist-Nationalist, Constance Markiewicz, complemented his overall Quaker-inspired Defensive Warfare programme, particularly in its social purpose. At Belcamp Park in the north Dublin suburb of Finglas Hobson and Markiewicz set up what could be described as the second attempt to establish a national social order in Ireland (Hobson had described the Owenite attempt at Sir John Valdaleur's Ralahine property as the first).[50] In the same year both revived Hobson's Fianna, which Hobson equally saw as linked to his social project project (though perhaps not Markiewicz), the Fianna living and staffing the commune. In this and Defensive Warfare's light Hobson opposed resolutions at the Fianna's 1915 Ard Fheis (gathering, convention) that would have put 'the government of the Fianna' into the hands of 'half a dozen Fianna officers'. Interestingly, Hobson thought 'there was a civil side in the Fianna which was of even greater importance than the military one'.[51]

Hobson was able to employ the Young Irelander of the 1840s and later, James Fintan Lalor's, system of resisting British rule in Ireland. This would work in conjunction with Quaker business methods and what can only be described as 'inclusive dealing'. This would allow Hobson to build up his own 'social economy' on Quaker-Lalorian lines, but first Hobson would have to reduce the existing social economy, before putting his own in place. Hobson outlined how this would work on his 1907 east-coast American tour:

> It is necessary for the further continuance of the Irish people that the system should be broken up, and we are confident that there is enough independent and National spirit in the people of Ireland that they will break it up, and they are starting to break it up at the present time.[52]

This had been tried before and successfully during the Tithe War of the 1830s, a series of agrarian disturbances in Ireland during the 1830s over the collection of the tithe, an annual tax payable to the Anglican church of one tenth of the produce of the land. Before Lalor set down his Defensive Warfare strategy (which Hobson developed further), his father Patt had already applied an earlier version of it during the Tithe War by adopting the idea of 'exclusive dealing' from the Quakers. As opponents of the link between church and state, the Quakers had long resisted paying the Tithe, so it made sense for the Catholics to join forces with them to resist this tax. Patt Lalor helped to lead the resistance, later telling the House of Lords' Committee on Tithes: 'there was every facility to avoid the payment of tithes, if the people were only unanimous, and acted peaceably, as the society called the Quakers did'.[53]

It is therefore possible to see a line of continuity running from the Quakers to the Land League via Patt and James Fintan Lalor, and once again it points to the Quaker influence on Hobson's Nationalism.

As a Sinn Féiner, Hobson envisaged building on this through James Fintan Lalor's example. Through the Dungannon Club Hobson looked to implement both Patt and James Fintan Lalor's 'Defensive Warfare' policy, building ironically on the worldly know-how of Quaker business acumen. As the basis for Hobson's counter-state, the Dungannon League branches' Co-operative work played a particularly important role. As part of this, Hobson seems to have developed the traditional nonconformist link between Co-operatism and governance. The Fabian, Beatrice Webb, noted around the time that: 'It is difficult to over-estimate the debt which the English democracy owes to the magnificent training given by Protestant dissent to the art of self-government'.[54] The same point may be made about Hobson's use of Quaker methods of business in his approach to co-operation and other economic approaches within the social economy.

That Webb also identifies co-operatives as leading, in some cases, to what was almost a 'state within a state' further explains the fusing of the IRB and Dissenting tradition within Hobson's programme.[55] If we factor in Sinn Féin's local Boards policy (which operated at both district and county level) it is easy to see just how important the Co-operative scheme was to Hobson's overall plan. Such a plan would obviously call down the wrath of the British at some point, and it is notable there was a further fusing of Dissenting and IRB tradition as provision against this. As part of the Co-operative effort Dissenters had developed strong benefit societies and Hobson's Dungannon Club colleage, Patrick McCartan outlined to his boss in Philadelphia, Joseph McGarrity, how these featured as part of Hobson's scheme: 'There will be a beneficial fund. Imprisonment renders one worthy of benefits'.[56] Hobson first outlined his scheme in full in *The Republic* and then in *The Peasant* and *Defensive Warfare*, but it is clear McCartan was already aware of the details in 1906.[57] In *The Republic* Hobson noted:

> … we cannot expect many men who have women and children
> depending on them to leave these defenceless and unprovided for,
> or dependent on the charity of the more fortunate of their

countrymen. And even those who are practically independent need to have some fund on which they can fall back, to enable them to start afresh after they escape from the clutches of 'the Law'.[58]

This was a way of ensuring men (and women) would continue to build up the national life in the social sphere. But it was also important to give those doing it the necessary technical expertise.

QUAKER BUSINESS SOLUTIONS AND EDUCATION

In trying to improve the Raiffeisen banks (an idea imported from Germany by the Irish Co-operative Society) Hobson sought to improve on them using a Quaker business model of providing expert advice with the loan. He advocated a co-operative successor that would both advise and educate Irish farmers. Expanding on the idea of co-operative banking, Hobson wrote: 'Our co-operative bank must not only lend, but teach its members how to use the loan; its aid must be educational as well as monetary …'.[59] He further noted:

> The [Co-operative] society should … be as much educational as financial in its operations, aiming at keeping its members abreast of the latest developments in scientific agriculture. This would ensure that loans would be used to the best possible advantage, and obviate the possibility of money, already too scarce, not being used for the best and greatest possible production.[60]

In combining the functions of both finance and technical advice Hobson seems to have had the Quakers in mind, and is noteworthy that the Dungannon League drew heavily on such Dissenting ideas in operating its Co-operatives and the alternative 'Department of Agriculture' which proceeded from it. Writing about this aspect of the Quaker business model, James Walvin has noted: 'The Society of Friends provided institutional help in that it served as a regulator to activity'.[61] The beauty of this approach was that it allowed Hobson to create one overarching body that combined the role of the Raiffeisen banks and the Council for Technical Instruction into one Nationalist organisation. In many ways this was an improvement on what had gone before since it allowed for the same kind of economic regulation as the Quakers had exercised but crucially enabled economic resources to be concentrated in and directed toward certain ends. Nevertheless, the real advantage for Hobson was political since he intended to use the co-operatives to achieve a widespread reintroduction of tillage – the growing of crops, as opposed to pasture farming with cattle. The advantage of tillage was that it would repopulate the land, something that was vital if Hobson was to create the kind of social economy he saw as necessary to win independence.

As the Dungannon Club, and later the Sinn Féin League, sought to proffer technical advice to farmers, so it also sought to give the children of Ireland a technical grounding. This chimed with the Constructive Unionist approach of Horace Plunkett who had previously identified 'two glaring weaknesses' in the Irish administration: there was no single department to deal with the myriad of problems of Irish agriculture, neither was there proper provision for technical or vocational education within the school system.[62] While the first had been solved with the foundation of the Irish Department of Agriculture (though Hobson could never have admitted it), the second remained a problem.

Since the Dungannon League's programme sought to assert Irish independence through the 'social economy', it was crucial that the social economy functioned effectively – in other words, was productive. However, Hobson believed that the state of education in Ireland prevented this:

> … we have a population rendered unfit and ineffective by the educational facilities that they receive. This is done of deliberate design, and generation after generation the minds of the children of Ireland are atrophied by the English Board that controls education in this country. Our people are made non productive in their own country …[63]

To solve the problem Hobson again turned to Quakerism. Hobson's own schooling recognised the vital link between industry and education. The school's recognition of the link between education and the local economy came in the form of the science examination, which was in animal physiology.[64] For this reason it comes as little surprise Hobson makes the point in *Defensive Warfare*, noting: 'The "National" Board of education was founded to prevent the children of Ireland getting an effective education or being productive workers in their own country.'[65] For Hobson the particular problem was that:

In an agricultural country it has not taught them to be good agriculturalists but rather to despise agriculture. In commercial centres it has never prepared them for commerce or fitted them for industry. The minds of the children of Ireland are atrophied by this English board, they are made non productive in their own land …[66]

The Dungannon League looked to build on the solution outlined in the Dungannon Club Manifesto: that local boards could bypass the National Board of Education, whose system had 'left Ireland's children unfit for citizenship and hopelessly handicapped in the world.'[67] Hobson noted: 'In addition to their helping to build our industries they can combat the ruinous educational regime at present in operation.'[68] Under the heading of *Local Government*, the Dungannon Club Manifesto noted that the County and Local Elective Boards could:

… found or subsidise schools throughout the country that will teach our children to be citizens of the Irish nation. It is in their power to levy a special rate for educational purposes sufficient to found and support the schools; and they can establish libraries and build reading-rooms in every village throughout Ireland.[69]

What Hobson envisaged was the Sinn Féin movement and its supporters using the County and Elective Boards to set up a decentralised alternative to the National Board's centrally-controlled provision. In this way Nationalists would subvert government control of education. Sinn Féin might also take advantage of the earlier Conservative government's Technical Education Act of 1890, which provided for local authorities to levy a special rate for educational purposes. This enabled authorities to raise the rate for the specific purpose of providing technical education, but had been largely ignored in Ireland (in 1893 the Belfast Technical School was still a private institution).[70] Accordingly, Hobson stated of the technical schools: 'They must be modified to suit the present commercial requirements in Ireland, and must supplement the work of the primary schools, but the remedying of them is in our own hands'[71].

As well as technical schools Hobson may well have had in mind a role for the voluntary schools, not least because of the example of Quaker voluntary schools in meeting the country's industrial needs. Hobson would have been well aware of this tradition through Brookfield

Agricultural School, the sister institution to his own school in Lisburn.[72] Brookfield's approach remained consistent with William Penn's educational principles 'that boys should be taught the rudiments of construction and agriculture, and girls taught to spin, sew, garden, preserve'.[73] This could be easily adapted to the kind of social economy Hobson wished to create and it seems likely Hobson had it in mind when he wrote:

> The spread of education through the voluntary school, such as is found in hundreds of centres in Ireland ... may be made of greater effect in moulding the mind of the people than the foreign controlled schools. They can remedy many of the defects resulting from the latter and be in reality the educative force in the nation, until such time as the State School, by the break-up of the foreign Government, is restored to popular control.[74]

Given that Hobson had left the Friends School as a fully-fledged Nationalist it seems likely his Quaker schooling provided him with the model for the kind of patriotic, techno-savvy institution he had in mind.

PHYSICAL FORCE

By now it should be clear that Hobson was not thinking so much on physical force lines to rid Ireland of the British presence as creating alternative structures to the state, which could subvert it, making its presence irrelevant. This is not, however, to say that Hobson was not willing to use force in certain cases. Hobson later claimed that he resigned from the Society of Friends when he started organising the Volunteers 'because membership was incompatible with the work on which I was engaged'.[75] Hobson's friend, the journalist, William Glynn, also noted that 'Bulmer resigned from membership of the Lisburn monthly meeting in 1914, judging this to be incompatible with any form of military activity'.[76] Yet Hobson saw the Volunteers, like the Fianna, as having a more important civic than military purpose, although if provoked that would change. Ralph Bossence has noted:

> Hobson did not object to armed action on traditional Quaker principles – he had organised the Howth gun-running [to supply the Irish volunteers with arms] – but he held with MacNeill [the Volunteers' Chief of Staff], that the Irish Volunteers should be used

if there were an attack by the British Government or in resistance to Conscription.[77]

For the above reasons Hobson had no problem with the use of physical force, it merely had to be justified. This is further proved by the fact Hobson was instrumental starting the Volunteers in November 1913 and organising their landing of arms at Howth in July 1914.[78]

It is unclear when exactly in 1914 Hobson tendered his resignation (if he did in that year). However, it was not accepted until 14 October 1915, which begs the question why did Hobson wait until 1914 to resign, especially when his work with the Irish Volunteers (an extra-parliamentary eighteenth-century style militia) was tailing off due to his fall from grace with the IRB from June 1914 because of his acceptance of John Redmond's (the Irish Party leader) nominees onto the Volunteers' Provisional Committee. Hobson's views had emerged from his earlier flirtation with Lalor and Defensive Warfare; however, Hobson's ideas on the use of force went back even further again and were shaped in the first instance by his Quakerism. Two months before the launching of the Dungannon Club in 1905 there appeared an article on war in Standish O'Grady's *All Ireland Review*, written by 'a member of the Society of Friends': this was surely Hobson's take on the new organisation's strategy:

> I was greatly interested in your attacks on the Peace question [sic], and was very near writing you a letter on the subject at the time, because I consider the line taken almost exactly represents the true position of the early Quakers in reference to the subject. In fact, you seem to have arrived at an almost identical doctrine by a quite independent process of evolution.[79]

If the writer was Hobson, and it seems probable it was, this passage sheds valuable light on Hobson's reconciliation of a theoretical physical force position with Quakerism. In line with the 'member of the Society of Friends' statement of the 'true position' of the early Quakers in reference to the peace question, Christopher Hill states:

> The first official declaration of absolute pacifism in all circumstances was made by the Quakers in January 1661, after a number of the Friends had been arrested in the aftermath of Venner's unsuccessful Fifth Monarchist revolt.[80] It was intended

to protect Quakers especially against charges of sedition, but it also marks the beginning of an absolute refusal to accept civil or military office.[81]

Such a position would have allowed Hobson to reconcile his IRB membership with Quakerism in the service of Irish nationalism. And it should be remembered that Hobson's forebears were from this earlier Quaker stock:

> My people came over here in the Cromwellian settlement ... and have been here since. They settled ... between Portadown and Dungannon ... My grandfather was small farmer not far from Lurgan. I was born in Belfast myself where my father was in business. Our family has had a long connection with the Society of Friends. Two of the three brothers who came over at the beginning joined the Society of Friends and the association was handed down from father to son.[82]

What aided the process of integrating Hobson's Quakerism and Nationalism further was the primary importance, then and now, of the inward guide or inner light. The 'inward guide', or 'inner light' as it is known to Quakers, was 'that of God in every man'. For Quakers this links the individual to God and acts as a guide in all things, including war and the Quaker Peace Testimony. A. Neave Brayshaw notes of the Quaker Peace Testimony:

> The Quaker testimony concerning war ... is based on the conception of "that of God in every man" to which the Christian in the presence of evil is called to make appeal, following out a line of thought and conduct which, involving suffering as it may do is ... the most likely to reach the inward witness and so change the evil mind into the right mind.[83]

Hobson applied the logic of the Peace Testimony to Ireland's situation. His Defensive Warfare strategy was designed to avoid the need for violence, which appealed to those Nationalists who opposed violence; at the same time, Hobson could also appeal to the IRB since the Peace Testimony did not proscribe war for the attainment of national safety.

Even William Penn recognised the need to qualify the orthodoxy of the Friends' teaching on non-violence, tolerating the setting up of a defensive militia in Pennsylvania.[84] As a Quaker Hobson would have known about Penn's Holy Experiment and that it only failed because Pennsylvania had found itself at war with the Delaware and Shawnee Indians. Although the Quaker Peace Testimony (or Principle) allowed for defensive warfare, the war had nevertheless resulted in many of the Friends stepping down from office due to their consciences or inner lights. With so many capable administrators removed from government in this way the Holy Experiment could not continue. What caused Penn's Holy Experiment such problems were not his own beliefs, which allowed for the conduct of a defensive war, but those of his colleagues, which did not. Hobson, working with non-Quakers, experienced no such problem.[85] Hobson's own inner light had permitted him to join the IRB on the basis of his Defensive Warfare programme; working with men like McCullough he could be equally sure that they would not abandon his scheme on the basis of conscientious objection.

Indeed, Hobson had the opposite problem and often had to take a harder line than he would actually have liked, particularly in America where he was fundraising and had to exaggerate the programme. Hobson noted: 'Unfortunately, at this present time it is a physical impossibility for the Irish nation, so weakened as are they, to attempt revolution.'[86] However, what Hobson sounded like and what he actually thought were not always the same. In America and at IRB gatherings Hobson's tone was dictated by the nature of his audience and, since these were invariably more militant than he or his colleagues, Hobson adjusted his tone accordingly. Yet Hobson sought to employ the same Defensive Warfare strategy throughout, that of Lalor's passive resistance. Through historical association and the careful use of rhetoric, Hobson went about convincing his audience of the merits of this approach. In the same speech he noted:

> And when I speak of passive resistance let no one misunderstand me. As Fintan Lalor pointed out in 1848, the only difference between active and passive resistance is the difference between acting on the aggressive and acting on the defensive. And when we say to our people that we will have a passive resistance movement in Ireland, it means that that movement will be one of genuine resistance, which will be one of the people acting on the defensive, simply and solely because they are not, unfortunately at the present time, strong enough to assume the aggressive.[87]

Hobson's speeches and writings on Defensive Warfare attribute his strategy to James Fintan Lalor, but this is not the whole story since it fails to take account of the crossover between Quaker thinking and Lalor's ideas, in particular how Hobson built on Frederick Lucas' work. Like Hobson, Lucas was a Quaker and, although he later converted to Catholicism, it was Quakerism that shaped him most, not least the Quaker Peace Testimony, which helped shape his relations with Young Ireland. Lucas' early biographer, Christopher Riethmuller, has noted that having come under their influence Lucas tried to induce members of the Young Ireland party to 'abandon their schemes'. By this Riethmuller was referring to their plans for the 1848 uprising, but whereas Lucas had come under the influence of Young Ireland, Hobson had been influenced by their successors, the IRB, and where Lucas had tried to deter an uprising by Young Ireland in 1848, Hobson would attempt to do the same thing with the IRB in 1916. Although Hobson could not prevent the 1916 Rising, he did everything in his power to stop it, including using his position in the Volunteers to countermand Pearce's (the leader of the Rising) orders mobilising them.

While both Lucas and Hobson would have felt uncomfortable about the use of violence due to the Quaker Peace testimony, it is notable that both chose to work for an alternative from the inside, using their relations with Young Ireland and the IRB respectively to argue against the use of violence. Many years after the 1916 Rising Hobson explained the logic of his position to the Bureau of Military History. He told them that the IRB's constitution:

> specifically forbade an insurrection such had taken place in 1867 when there was no public support, no adequate organisation and no chance of success. In swearing in men into the I.R.B. I was often asked if there was any assurance that their oath of obedience would not land them in a futile insurrection, and I frequently had to assure men that the Constitution specifically forbade such a development.[88]

Essentially, this kind of thinking was why Hobson opposed the 1916 Easter Rising. It ran counter to his whole Quaker-Nationalist Defensive Warfare programme. As Hobson stated:

[Patrick] Pearse had always had a curious belief in the necessity of a periodical blood sacrifice … On the other hand, I and those who thought with me wanted to build up a real strength in Ireland, which would be sufficiently powerful to wrest control of the country from the British Government …[89]

Hobson tried everything he could to prevent the Easter Rising, not because he was unpatriotic or lacking in Nationalism but because by his own Quaker Inner Light it was the right thing to do – just as applying Quaker thinking and techniques to Nationalism to gain independence was. It was the same across his Nationalist beliefs.

CONCLUSION

From his family and everyday Quaker values Hobson's Nationalism was steeped in Quaker principles. Whether this was temperance, or a focus on youth, or the abnegation of politics it is impossible to imagine Hobson's particular brand of Quakerism existing without the Quaker influence. True, Hobson's Nationalism was not completely dependent on his Quakerism, for instance the Pioneer branch of Cumann na nGaedheal, but the way it blended together was. Given Hobson's prominence on the advanced Nationalist scene up to 1914 one has to conclude that Quaker influence on advanced Irish nationalism was profound. Had Hobson not fallen from grace with the IRB from 1914, Irish independence may have been achieved on the basis of Quakerism.

NOTES

1   Bulmer Hobson, IRB and *Irish Freedom*, 17 Oct. 1947 (National Archives of Ireland, Bureau of Military History (henceforth NAI, BMH), WS 30), p. 2.
2   Des Gunning, 'Bulmer Hobson, "the Most Dangerous Man in Ireland"', *History Ireland*, 10.1 (Spring 2002). For Marnie Hay's work, see Marnie Hay, *Bulmer Hobson and the Nationalist Movement in Twentieth-Century Ireland* (Manchester, 2009) and *Na Fianna Éireann and the Irish Revolution, 1909–23: Scouting for Rebels* (Manchester, 2019) in particular.
3   I have not italicised Defensive Warfare in many cases because the strategy predated and surpassed the more limited one set out in Hobson's pamphlet, *Defensive Warfare: A Handbook for Irish Nationalist* (Belfast, 1909). See my thesis, Sean Worgan, 'Bulmer Hobson: An Ulster Nationalist, 1902–1908', Keele University (2011).
4   Bulmer Hobson, *Ireland Yesterday and Tomorrow* (Tralee, 1968), p. 2.

5   See Neville H. Newhouse, *History of Friends' School* (Lurgan, 1974), p. 81.

6   Florence Patterson (née Hobson) to William Glynn, 10 Aug. 1969 (Friend's House Library, Dublin, Box 3A, No. 85).

7   Bulmer Hobson, quoted in Hay, *Bulmer Hobson*, pp 33–4.

8   Florence Patterson (née Hobson) to William Glynn, 21 May 1972 (Friend's House Library, Dublin, Box 3A, No. 85).

9   Duncan Watts, *Whigs, Radicals and Liberals 1815-1914* (London, 1995), p. 8.

10   Ibid., p. 6.

11   James Walvin, *The Quakers: Money and Morals* (London, 1998), p. 25.

12   Ibid., p. 26.

13   Newhouse, *History of Friends' School*, p. 81.

14   M.E. Hirst, *The Quakers in Peace and War* (London, 1923), p. 155.

15   Minutes of the Lisburn Monthly Meeting, Entry 176, 14 Nov. 1881 and 15 Dec. 1881, Entry 575, 17 Dec. 1881, Friends Archive, Lisburn.

16   Mary Ann Bulmer Hobson, *Memoirs of Six Generations* (Belfast, 1947), p. 69.

17   Catherine Morris, 'From the Margins: Alice Milligan and the Irish Cultural Revival, 1888–1905', Ph.D. thesis, University of Aberdeen (1999), pp 72–3.

18   Quoted in T.A. Jackson, *Ireland Her Own: An Outline History of the Irish Struggle* (London, 1971), p. 117.

19   See my thesis, Worgan, 'Bulmer Hobson'.

20   Ibid., p. 73.

21   Bulmer Hobson, *Memoirs of Six Generations*, p. 69.

22   Morris, *From the Margins*, p. 73.

23   Owen McGee, *The IRB: The Irish Republican Brotherhood, From the Land League to Sinn Fein* (Dublin, 2005) p. 291.

24   'Bulmer Hobson's Speech, Aims, Methods and Workings of the Sinn Fein Movement', *The Gaelic American*, 23 Feb. 1907.

25   Ibid.

26   Newhouse, *History of Friends' School*, p. 32.

27   Walvin, *The Quakers*, p. 25.

28   See Ian McBride, Scripture Politics, Ulster Presbyterians and Irish Radicalism in the Late Eighteenth Century (Oxford, 1998).

29   James Walvin, *The Quakers: Money and Morals* (London, 1998), p. 36.

30   Hobson, *Ireland Yesterday and Tomorrow*, p. 15.

31   Ibid.

32   Hobson, General Statement, 26 Jan. 1948 (NAI, BMH, WS 82), pp 1–2. Hobson, *Ireland Yesterday and Tomorrow*, pp 3, 15. *United Irishman*, 14 Sept. 1901, p. 5.

33   Fianna Eireann Minutes, 22 June 1902 (National Library of Ireland, henceforth NLI, Ms 12, 176, Bulmer Hobson Papers).

34   Ibid.

35   Ibid.

36   Matthew Kelly, *The Fenian Ideal and Irish Nationalism, 1882–1916* (Oxford, 2006), p. 135.

37   The journal of the ULT.

38   Ibid., p. 76. Radley was responsible for setting up the School Literary and Natural History Society.

39   W. King Baker, *A Quaker Warrior: Life of William Hobson* (London, 1913), pp 56, 58.

40   Frederick B. Tolles, *Quakers and the Atlantic Culture* (New York 1960), p. 44.

41   Ibid.

42   Patrick Maume, *The Long Gestation: Irish National Life 1891–1918* (Dublin, 1999), p. 125.

43   Bulmer Hobson, 'English Connection a Growing Danger', *The Gaelic American*, 26 Oct. 1912.

44   Fergus MacLeda [Bulmer Hobson], 'The Confession of Faith of an Irish Nationalist I', *Irish Freedom*, Jan. 1911. For an explanation of how we know Fergus MacLeda was Hobson's pseudonym see my thesis, Worgan, 'Bulmer Hobson', appendix I.

45   Fergus MacLeda (Bulmer Hobson), 'The Confession of Faith of an Irish Nationalist I', *Irish Freedom*, Dec. 1910.

46   Ibid.

47   Ibid.

48   Rufus M. Jones, *Social Law in the Spiritual World: Studies in the Human and Divine Inter Relationship* (London, 1904), p. 20.

49   See S. G. Hobson, *National Guilds: An Inquiry into the Wage System, and the Way Out* (London, 1919), Third Edition and S. G. Hobson, *National Guilds and the State* (London, 1920).

50   'A History of Ralahine', *Irish Freedom*, Oct. 1912, p. 2. For a more in depth analysis of both communal projects and their link, see Sean Worgan, 'Anarcho-Nationalism and *Irish Freedom*', *Saothar*, 44 (Irish Labour History Journal), pp 73–88.

51   Eamon Martin, Witness Statement, 1 Oct. 1951 (NAI, BMH, WS 591). 'Fianna Congress, Honorary Officers Abolished, Headquarters' Staff Appointed', *Fianna*, Aug. 1915. pp 6–7.

52   'Bulmer Hobson's Speech: Aims, Methods and Workings of the Sinn Fein Movement', *The Gaelic American*, 23 Feb. 1907.

53   David N. Buckley, *James Fintan Lalor: Radical* (Cork, 1990), p. 11.

54   Beatrice Webb, *The Co-operative Movement in Great Britain* (Aldershot, 1987), p. 37.

55   Ibid., pp 170, 204. Webb also notes that these co-operatives were responsible to a central body, just as Hobson's were to the Dungannon Club's Executive.

56   McCartan to McGarrity, 23 Dec. 1905 (NLI, Ms 17 457, McGarrity Papers).

57   Bulmer Hobson, 'The English Government and Irish National Movements', *The Republic*, 31 Jan. 1907. Also, Hobson, *Defensive Warfare*, pp 59–60.

58   Ibid.

59   Bulmer Hobson, 'On Tillage Societies', *The Peasant*, 15 June 1907.

60   Ibid. The 'best and greatest possible production' through tillage.

61   Walvin, *The Quakers*, p. 72. Like Hobson, later on this institutional help was allied to cheap loans, including to farmers.

62   Trevor West, *Horace Plunkett: Co-operation and Politics, An Irish Biography* (Gerrards Cross, 1986), p. 43.

63   Curoi MacDare [Bulmer Hobson], 'On Organisation II', *The Republic*, 2 May 1907, and Hobson, *Defensive Warfare*, p. 11. It appears Hobson took this passage in *Defensive Warfare* from 'On Organisation II'. Both contain the same

section beginning with the words 'The minds of the children of Ireland are atrophied by this English board …', paragraph one, p. 11, *Defensive Warfare*, and paragraph six of 'On Organisation II'.

64 Newhouse, *History of Friends' School*, p. 69. 203 Walvin, *The Quakers*, p. 41.

65 Hobson, *Defensive Warfare*, p. 10.

66 Ibid., p. 11. Hobson continued this theme throughout his Nationalist career, quoting the *Irish Times* in his *Gaelic American* column in 1913, he noted: 'We have surely suffered too long a system of education which seems to be designed for the purpose of making the youth of Ireland absolutely unfit for life in an agricultural community.' Bulmer Hobson, 'How England Dwarfs Irish Education', *The Gaelic American*, 14 June 1913.

67 In the section 'The Building Up of Ireland Intellectually'. 'Dungannon Club Manifesto', in Hobson, *Ireland Yesterday and Tomorrow*, Appendix I, p. 94. Hobson makes the same point in *Defensive Warfare*, p. 11, and in 'On Organisation II'.

68 'Dungannon Club Manifesto', in Hobson, *Ireland Yesterday and Tomorrow*, Appendix I, p. 97.

69 Ibid.

70 West, *Horace Plunkett*, p. 43.

71 Hobson, *Defensive Warfare*, p. 52.

72 While Hobson's own schooling may have been less typical in this respect due to Joseph Radley's introduction of languages and music, it too recognised the vital link between industry and education. During the 1890's, when Hobson attended the school, the syllabus included chemistry, magnetism, physiology, and drawing, all of which could be used to practical effect in local industries. The school's ultimate recognition of the link between education and the local economy came in the form of the science examination, which was in animal physiology. Newhouse, *History of Friends' School*, p. 69

73 Walvin, *The Quakers*, p. 41.

74 Hobson, *Defensive Warfare*, pp 51–2.

75 Seán O Lúing, 'Talking to Bulmer Hobson', *Irish Times*, 6 May 1961 (Eoin McNeill Papers, UCDA. LAI/F/367). William Glynn, 'Bulmer Hobson', *The Friend*, 12 Jan. 1973, p. 41. 7 Hobson's resignation was accepted on the 14 Oct. 1915 (minutes of the Lisburn Monthly Meeting, 14 Oct. 1915, Friends Archive, Lisburn). Sandra King's book states that Hobson resigned his membership of the Friends in 1914, 'lest his associations would compromise the Society'. However, this is based on Hobson's own testimony from Ireland Yesterday and Tomorrow, a book written over fifty years after the event and containing several inaccuracies on dates. King, *History of the Society of Friends*, p. 40. Glynn, 'Bulmer Hobson', p. 41.

76 William Glynn, 'Bulmer Hobson', *The Friend*, 12 Jan. 1973, p. 41.

77 Ralph Bossence, 13 Oct. 1969 (Friend's House Library, Dublin, Box 3A, No. 85).

78 See Bulmer Hobson, Statement on The Formation of the Irish Volunteers 1913, 11 Nov. 1947 (NAI, BMH, WS 51), p. 2. For a discussion of this episode see Hay, *Bulmer Hobson and the Nationalist Movement in Twentieth-Century Ireland*, pp 135–8.

79   'War: By a Member of the Society of Friends', *All Ireland Review*, 7 Jan. 1905.

80   A radical English Civil War Puritan grouping, who wished to facilitate the Fifth Monarchy, Christ's kingdom on Earth. Some Quakers were associated with them.

81   Christopher Hill, *The World Turned Upside Down: Radical ideas During the English Revolution* (London, 1991), p. 241.

82   Seán O Lúing, 'Talking to Bulmer Hobson', *Irish Times*, 6 May 1961 (Eoin McNeill Papers, UCDA. LAI/F/367).

83   A. Neave Brayshaw, *The Quakers: Their Story and Message* (York, 1982), p. 131.

84   Ibid.

85   Ibid., pp 369–75.

86   'Bulmer Hobson's Speech: Aims, Methods and Workings of the Sinn Fein Movement'.

87   Ibid.

88   Bulmer Hobson, Statement on IRB and *Irish Freedom*, 17 Oct. 1947 (NAI, BMH, WS 30), pp 1–2.

89   Bulmer Hobson Witness Statement on The Rising, 17 Dec. 1947 (NAI, BMH, WS 81), p. 10.

The Manor of St John the Baptist and the 1718 County Londonderry migration

ANDREW KANE

In 1718 Rev. William Boyd of Macosquin Presbyterian
congregation travelled from County Londonderry to
Boston, Massachusetts to present a 319-signature petition
to Governor Samuel Shute seeking his 'encouragement'
for the establishment of a new settlement of Scots-Irish
in the New World.

The ensuing migrations were led by Boyd's clerical neighbours, Rev.
James McGregor of Aghadowey and Rev. James Woodside of
Dunboe. The leaders of the migration were thus from three adjoining
(still largely Presbyterian) parishes on the western bank of the River
Bann, opposite Coleraine town. Although no academic analysis of the
origins of the rank and file migrants has been completed to date, we are
entitled to make a *prima facie* assumption that many of them came from
this small area. The estate of the Merchant Tailors' Company (the Manor
of St John the Baptist) lies in the centre of this 'hotspot' and is largely
coterminous with the civil parish of Macosquin/Camus-juxta-Bann. My
study examines the surviving records from when the estate was first
valued in 1613 to determine variations in the surnames of lessees and
the value of property before and after the migration of 1718. The
principal purpose is to see what can be learned about the migrants and
their reasons for leaving. As a genealogical resource I have traced when
a family first appears in (and disappears from) the estate records as well
as associated locations.

In the county of Londonderry the historian is relatively blessed by the fact that it was granted to 12 of the London livery companies in the Plantation. The landlord was therefore both an absentee and a corporate body, ensuring that detailed records were required and held in duplicate in both London and Ulster. Unfortunately paperwork has proved to be highly flammable, both here and in London, but the duplication of records at least doubles their chances of survival.

The 12 great guilds of London had been persuaded by James I to undertake the plantation of County Coleraine, with the forests of Glenconkeyne and Killetra (to provide timber for building) added from County Tyrone, the Liberties of the Town of Coleraine from County Antrim, and the Liberties of the City of Derry (re-chartered as 'Londonderry' in 1613) from County Donegal. This new county of Londonderry was then divided between the 12 companies (or guilds). These 12 estates were created manors in 1618 covering only 57 per cent of the county area[1], a fact often overlooked in dealing with the records. The (Anglican) Church of Ireland held 23 per cent, Irish gentlemen 10 per cent and Sir Thomas Phillips's manors of Limavady and Moyola 4 per cent. The remaining 6 per cent at Coleraine and Londonderry was retained by the Irish Society (the subcommittee of London Corporation formed by the companies to oversee the Plantation).

The displayed map shows the location of the Manor of St John the Baptist in the Bann Valley and its relationship to its neighbours. In this period the London companies leased their entire estates for a fixed term to one individual who acted as 'lord of the manor' and sublet the estate. Most individual farmers living on the land had no lease with the London company that actually owned it, except in the case of freeholders, six of whom were allocated townlands on each manor. The neighbouring manors, with details of their leasing arrangements, were as follows:

CLOTHWORKERS (**Killowen**) This manor borders St John the Baptist to the north and was in the hands of the same head lessees from 1663 to 1805 – the Jackson family of Jackson Hall, now the location of County Hall in Coleraine. The previous head tenant was a Scottish laird, Sir Robert McClelland, who also leased the neighbouring Manor of Freemore. A 51-year head lease was granted to William Jackson in 1664 at £100 p.a. and a fine (or lease premium) of £1,000.

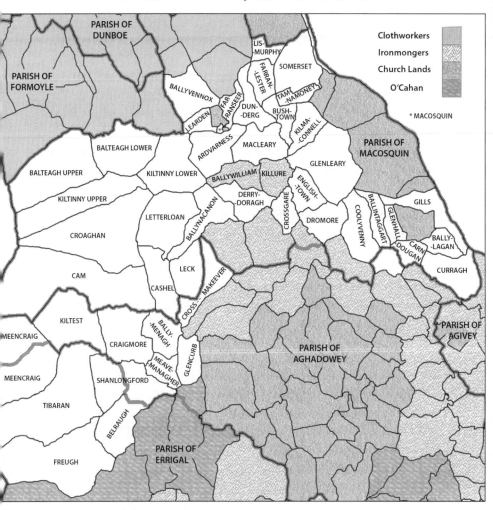

FREEMORE (**Haberdashers**) This manor borders St John the Baptist to the west and was never actually administered by the company who assigned (not leased) their interest to two members, Freeman and Moore (hence the name 'Freemore') in 1611 before the estate was formally conveyed. The Beresford family (now marquesses of Waterford, of whom more later) had effective control of the manor from 1614 as part owners and attained sole outright ownership in 1674 at a cost of £1,200. The manor was leased to Sir Robert McClelland from 1617 to 1658 before being absorbed into the larger Beresford (later Waterford) estates.

LIZARD (**Ironmongers**) This manor borders St John the Baptist to the south and was in the hands of the Canning family as head lessees from 1614 to 1726. A lease granted for 41 years in 1658 at £270 p.a. with a £500 fine was followed by a 21-year lease granted in 1705 at £250 p.a. with a fine of £1,900.[2] In preparation for the ending of this lease the company sent Isaac Pyke to survey the manor. He produced a full list of 215 tenants on the estate by townland. This list does not just include the chief tenant for each townland as given in earlier documents, but gives all farmers renting land across the entire manor, excluding freeholds.

COLERAINE (**Irish Society**) The Manor of St John the Baptist is bordered on the east by the River Bann as it flows past the Earl of Antrim's lands and the town of Coleraine. The town and parish of Coleraine were in the hands of the Irish Society itself and excellent documentation survives for the letting of their property. Thirty-year leases were issued in 1662[3] and again in 1692[4] for the town tenements and all land in the parish. The 1692 leases were in effect at the time of the 1718 migration, with a rent roll dated 1700 and the bids for re-letting in 1733 giving us further details of changes in occupation during the term of those leases.[5] Twelve members of Coleraine Corporation (out of 36) were disenfranchised in November 1704 under the Test Act of that year which effectively barred Dissenters from holding public office.[6] This demonstrates the high percentage of affluent Presbyterians in the Coleraine area at the time. In all 141 tenants are listed in the records during our period.

MERCERS (**Kilrea**) This manor lies upstream of the Ironmonger's Manor of Lizard and, on the expiry of the previous lease to William Jackson (41 years at £300 p.a. and £500 fine), was let in 1714 to John McMullan of Dublin for another 41 years at £450 p.a. plus a fine of £6,000. As with his neighbour Henry Lecky ten years later, the large fine payable by McMullan caused him financial problems which meant he sub-let his lands on long (39-year) leases with large fines to improve cash flow. From these leases 100 tenants of the estate are identified in 1714–16, with tenements in the town of Kilrea or leasing whole townlands.[7]

LISNEYCOURT (Vintners) This manor borders the Mercers' estate and was leased as a whole to John Clotworthy, Lord Massereene, in 1673. William Connolly obtained the interest in this lease on Massereene's death in 1714 and, after protracted negotiations, purchased the freehold of the manor from the Vintners for £15,000 in 1737. The rental income of the manor reported by Connolly in 1718 was £594 p.a.[8]

LIMAVADY (Connolly) The Manor of Limavady was granted to Sir Thomas Phillips and adjoins the Manor of Freemore to the west. It was sold to William Conolly by William Phillips in 1696 for £1,800. Connolly's rental of 1718[9] lists 122 tenants in the town and surrounding townlands producing an income of £604 7s.

CHURCH LANDS As stated above, 23 per cent of the total area of County Londonderry was allocated to the Church of Ireland, (usually) one townland per parish as glebe land and the remainder for the support of the bishop and other diocesan officials. Within the area of my study the Bishop's lands were let in 3 large groups: (1) the entire parish of Tamlaghtard (Magilligan – 40 townlands) let to William Gage in 1622; (2) 21 townlands in Dunboe parish let to the Beresford family; and (3) 52 townlands in the baronies of Coleraine and Loughinsholin let to Edward Rowley in 1636 on a 60-year lease. This lease was renewed for a further 61-year term in 1696 by Arthur Langford as trustee for his minor grandson, Hercules Rowley. There are rent rolls for the Rowley lands in 1693[10] (50 tenants) and the Gage lands in 1718[11] (60 tenants). The head rents on these estates also increased significantly during our period, Gage was paying £160 p.a. in 1688 and £200 p.a. (25 per cent increase) in 1718.

BALLYMONEY (Dunluce) The eastern bank of the River Bann downstream of Kilrea (except the parish of Coleraine) falls into the estates of the Earl of Antrim and, in particular, his Manor of Dunluce ('the Route'). Ballymoney is the chief town of the manor and a rental of the town listing 143 tenants was prepared in 1734.[12] Following the Restoration in 1660, the Earl created a large number of 41-year leases for townlands (normally groups of townlands) from 1664 which fell due for renewal in the early eighteenth century. One hundred and fifty-one townland leases (often in groups) were granted in Dunluce barony in the period 1695–1718, usually to gentlemen of substantial means.[13]

THE MANOR OF ST JOHN THE BAPTIST

The manor contained 18,700 acres over 32 townlands in the parish of Camus-juxta-Bann (Macosquin) as well as ten townlands in Aghadowey, five in Errigal and one in Dunboe. The manor, like that of the other 11 companies, was valued by townland in 1613 by the representatives of the Irish Society at £333 per annum.[14] The company initially leased the Manor for 51 years at £150 p.a. plus a fine of £500 to Valentine Hartopp, who assigned it to Ralph (or Randolph) Wall in 1621. Wall suffered financial problems from the outset and the Company appointed Robert Goodwin as steward in 1626 to look after its interests on the ground. Despite this, Wall retained the manor in 1639 under Royal Commissioners following the sequestration of the companies' estates in the Court of Star Chamber. At this time the revenue of the whole Manor was £508 10s.[15] When the company was restored to its estates, Michael Beresford (of Waterford family) acted as their agent in Macosquin until the 1618 lease expired and during his tenure 'Pender's Census' of c. 1659[16] gives 340 inhabitants on the townlands within the manor. These are presumed to be adults – male and female – over the age of 15 who were liable for the poll tax. This compares with a population of 5,830 in the 1831 census[17] and a valuation of £7,046 in the rates valuation of the same year. In 1668 a new lease was granted to Colonel John Gorges, a Cromwellian army officer who had settled at 'Crahan' on the manor and was MP for Londonderry._

The new head lease was also for a term of 61 years. When this expired in 1729, the manor was sold outright to William Richardson for £20,640, whereupon rents rose sharply to £1,264 10s. (1735[18]) illustrating that local conditions matched the received wisdom that rapidly rising rents were a major problem in the early eighteenth century and that the new regime only came into operation here 11 years after Rev. William Boyd made his initial voyage. From the foregoing survey it can de demonstrated that only a percentage of actual residents are recorded on these estates in the period, consisting mostly of those renting a townland and/or living in the main town/village on each manor. However the American literature[19] would suggest that this is exactly the class of person who did in fact emigrate in 1718.

Despite the English origins of the Macosquin landlords and their head lessees, there is considerable evidence of Scots as tenants on the manor in the first half of the seventeenth century. Members of the following families mustered on the Manor in 1631: Hamilton, Kirkpatrick, McLeod, Blair, Knox, Rennie, Houston, Reid, Spiers, Liggett, Creighton, Sanderson and Dunlop.[20] In 1639 leases were granted to the following Scots: Fullerton, Fulton, Craig, Kirkpatrick, Reid, Houston, Campbell and Smith (could be English but Presbyterian – see below).

Until the 1670s, Macosquin Presbyterians were part of Aghadowey congregation and, even as a separate body, were mostly served by the Aghadowey minister until 1701.[21] The Route Presbytery minutes record a dispute between Macosquin congregation and Rev James McGregor – of 1718 fame – over £15 owed to him for work in that parish. This suggests that Presbyterians were not numerous or prosperous enough to support their own minister in Macosquin during the period following 1690. Dominick Heyland of Castleroe, who acted as agent for his nephew, Hercules Rowley, and later inherited the Rowley interest in local church lands, was a prominent member of Macosquin Presbyterian congregation, although his grandson Robert became Church of Ireland rector of Coleraine in 1769. This, together with the sprinkling of Irish/Gaelic names among the contemporary Presbyterian records, shows that the migration was an event which is part of our shared history, and not restricted to one religious or national tradition. This is borne out by the report by Bolton that the 1718 migrants had the (Anglican) Book of Common Prayer among their possessions on arrival in Boston.

The Heyland family had been in Castleroe since at least 1638 when Dominick's father, Nicholas, was appointed to the Coleraine Corporation. The Synod of Ulster minutes record the following families in the congregation between 1694 and 1715: Boyd, Craig, Fulton, Hemphill, Heyland, Mills, Moore, Morrison, Smith and Workman. Four of these families (Heyland, Craig, Fulton and Smith) can be traced back in the manor records to the 1630s; Boyds, Moores and Hemphills appear in Macosquin parish in the 1663 Hearth Money rolls[22]; with

Morrison families in neighbouring Aghadowey and Dunboe parishes and the Mills family in Coleraine. Only the Workmans appear to be recent 'blow-ins' to the area.

The Scots-Irish narrative that is often narrated is of a generation born in Scotland, growing up in Ulster and moving on to the New World. Again the evidence from the local records does not bear this out as being generally applicable. T. H. Mullin quotes Professor Oscar Cargill of New Jersey as stating his ancestor David Cargill came to Ireland in the late 1680s due to religious persecution in his native Scotland; however, a John Cargill appears at Ballinrees in (northern) Aghadowey parish on the 1663 Hearth Money rolls. While David may in fact have come to Ulster at that time, his family were well established here a generation before he appears as leaseholder of that same townland in 1693. It is also possible that the family story carried down through the generations is inaccurate and both David and his children, including Rev. James McGregor's wife, were Ulster-born and -bred.

A comparison of family names on the Shute petition, Nutfield land grants and local records shows the following position. Of the 108 different surnames in the Nutfield land grants in 1722, 65 occur on the rent roll of the Manor of St John the Baptist or a neighbouring estate before 1718. Twenty of those are on the manor itself and nine of those who had leases in 1695 are no longer tenants by 1735. The nine are listed in Table 2.

Of more interest is the list of signatories to the Shute petition. We have no way of knowing how many of the petitioners actually travelled in 1718 or where they came from in Ulster. The most readily identifiable group are the clergy – nine ministers of the word of God ('Verbi Dei Minister'] and three Masters of Arts are listed in Table 3. None of these can be shown to have travelled in 1718 and the three clergymen who definitely made the journey – Boyd, McGregor and Woodside – did not sign the petition. The signatories represented all the congregations in north-east County Antrim with the notable exception of Rev. Robert McBride of Ballymoney.

Three hundred and nineteen people signed the petition, including Andrew McFadden from Macosquin and Alexander McGregor, possibly the brother of Rev James McGregor who farmed at Moynock near Kilrea on the Manor of Mercers. We know McFadden did emigrate to Maine and that McGregor did not – as the family can be traced forward in the Mercers' records and I have met his descendants. Of the 151 different surnames on the petition, 118 are in the local rent rolls or Route Presbytery minutes in the years leading up to the migration – 29 are in the rentals of the Manor of St John the Baptist alone. Thirteen additional surnames appear on the Manor's 1735 rent roll who could be petitioners who did not migrate or close relatives of petitioners – see Tables 4 and 5.

A few examples of signatories who could link to Macosquin will suffice to illustrate the findings. ANDREW MCFADDEN – not named in manor records, but his widow in Maine wrote that their home had been on Fullerton's land at Somerset on the Bann. He is stated to have travelled with the Dunboe party who did not travel on to Nutfield with their Aghadowey brethren, so it is possible that other Macosquin residents also migrated to different parts of New England. JOSEPH BEVERLAND – William Beverland rented Coolyvenny in 1639 and John Beverland rented neighbouring Ballintaggart in 1695. The family does not appear in the manor rental of 1735 (or in Nutfield in 1722) and may have moved on, died out or fallen on hard times. If Joseph the petitioner was of this family, his signature could be an early sign that the family was looking to build their future elsewhere. JAMES MCCARROLL – the McCarroll name only appears on the Manor of St John the Baptist in the rent rolls I have examined, where James had leased Ballyvennox in 1695. This makes it more likely that he was the James McKerrell who signed the petition. Again his absence from the 1735 rental is suggestive but not conclusive. McCarroll does not appear in the Nutfield land grants.

CASE STUDY: THE CRAIGS OF CROSSGARE

Crossgare is a small townland of 109 acres on the boundaries between Macosquin and Aghadowey parishes and the Manors of Lizard and St John the Baptist. It is the site of the Secession Presbyterian congregation for Macosquin parish formed in 1787 and adjoins Englishtown (formerly Kilconogher) townland where the Synod of Ulster Presbyterian church for Macosquin was built in 1705. It was leased to James Craig in 1639 for 21 years at £15 10s. James Craig appears on the Hearth Money roll for Macosquin parish in 1663 so presumably was among the four people (over 15) recorded in the townland in Pender's Census of *c.* 1659. By 1695 Hugh Craig was paying £10 p.a. to lease Crossgare from Colonel Gorges but had negotiated a reduction in rent between 1689 and 1694 due to the disruption of the Williamite War. Hugh also acted as ruling elder of Macosquin Presbyterian congregation in 1715. By 1735 Robert Craig was renting Crossgare from the Richardson family at £20 p.a. In 1718 Robert, David, John and James Craig were among the 319 signatories of the Shute petition and David, John and James appear in the list of lot holders in Nutfield (later Londonderry, New Hampshire) in 1722. David Craig also appears in the session book of Aghadowey Presbyterian congregation in the years immediately before the migration so we cannot tell if the petitioner and/or migrant are from our Crossgare family. However, it looks like Robert Craig may have considered moving and signed the petition, but remained behind in spite of the doubling of the Crossgare rent. In 1831 the population was 142 people living in 28 families. The Craigs were not among them.

CONCLUSION

Of course, the appearance of a particular name in records in the Bann Valley cannot be tied to an individual of the same name in New England without further evidence. The Ulster records can, however, show how long a family name was established in the Bann Valley and give an indication of the financial status of (at least some) members of that family prior to 1718. What the records clearly indicate are that the idea of a large number of 21-year leases made in the immediate post-revolution period in the 1690s on terms favourable to the tenant and which were expiring around 1718 when the market favoured the landlords, is an over simplification. The existing rent rolls on the estates along the Bann Valley show few farmers were direct tenants of the manors and so the majority were presumably under-tenants at will. In addition the renewals of the head leases of the London companies were based on fixed terms commencing from the re-grant of their estates under the Commonwealth in 1658, rather than the Williamite settlement of the 1690s. As we see from the rentals of the Manor of St John the Baptist, pre-revolutionary leases continued in effect with tenants given temporary reductions due to the disruption of the war.

Of the 'manors' (including Bishop's lands – not technically a manor) in the Lower Bann valley, only the Irish Society, Clothworkers, Ironmongers and Mercers re-let their estates wholesale in the 30-year period between 1696 and 1726. The spiralling costs of renewal fines (lease premiums) or outright purchases meant that head lessees sought to mitigate their up-front costs by issuing leases with fines to their own subtenants. The longer the lease term, the higher the fine/premium that could be asked, so long (21 years or more) leases generally ran from the granting of the head lease, therefore only a minority of agricultural land is likely to have changed lease terms between 1696 and 1726. That is not to say that sub-tenants on yearly tenancies did not see a sharp rent rise, but the narrative of the widespread expiry of Williamite leases leading to the 1718 migration cannot be demonstrated by the local estate records.

This runs counter to Joseph Marriott's advice to the Clothworkers' Company and the Merchant Taylors' Company (as joint proprietors of the Manor of Clothworkers) in August 1718 that 'one reason they give for their going is the raising of the rent of the land to such a high rate that they cannot support their families thereon with the greatest industry'. A few months before this, Marriott had commented that on Jackson's lands several farms had been raised to double and in a few instances even treble their value since 1690.[23]

POSTSCRIPT

Government concern at the ongoing large-scale Presbyterian migration from Ulster to America led to the commissioning of a report to the Irish Privy Council by two Presbyterian ministers, Francis Iredell and Robert Craghead, in 1728. They found the principal cause to be poverty due to high rents (partially due to increased competition for land from Roman Catholics) and insecurity of tenure. Other factors cited by Presbyterian ministers as influencing emigrants included: unscrupulous tithe collection by middlemen, especially where the rector was not resident; arbitrary proceedings in manor and sheriffs' courts; the Sacramental Test Act of 1704 barring Dissenters from public office; other penal legislation regarding Presbyterian marriages, schools and Meetinghouses; recent corn shortage. Interestingly, the commissioners state that in their enquiries they only heard of one clergyman contemplating emigration and it was clearly in the interests of remaining clergy for their congregations to stay in Ulster to pay their stipends. This is at odds with the 1718 situation where nine serving ministers signed the Shute petition, three more led the migration and Rev. James McGregor gave the following reasons for leaving in a sermon on the eve of his departure:

> To avoid oppression and cruel bondage; To shun persecution and designed ruin; To withdraw from the communion of idolaters; and to have an opportunity of worshipping God, according to the dictates of conscience and the rules of his inspired Word.

TABLE 1

MANOR	LOCATION	OWNER	HEAD LEASES	TERM
Freemore	Artikelly	Haberdashers	sold 1611 & 1674	Perpetuity
St John the Baptist	Macosquin	Merchant Tailors	1668 & 1729	Perpetuity
Clothworkers	Killowen	Clothworkers	1664 & 1705	51 years
Lizard	Agivey	Ironmongers	1658, 1705 & 1726	41 years
Mercers	Kilrea	Mercers	1658 & 1714	41 years
Lisneycourt	Bellaghy	Vintners	1673 & 1737	Perpetuity
Coleraine	Coleraine	Irish Society	1692 & 1734	21 years
Limavady	Limavady	Phillips family	sold 1696	Perpetuity
Dunluce	Ballymoney	Earl of Antrim	1664 (B'money 1714)	41 years
Rowley	Aghadowey etc	Bishop of Derry	1636 & 1696	60 years

TABLE 2

SURNAME	1695 LESSEE	TOWNLAND	1722 GRANTEE	LOT NO.
Blair	John	Coolyvenny	John	33, 157 & 158
Blair	sons of Mrs	Ballylagan	James	32
Campbell	George	Balteagh	William	25
Clark	Forrest	Farranseer	Matthew, James & John	various
Fulton	Thomas	Macleary	Samuel	2
Gray	Thomas	Ballynacanon	John	16, 132 & 147
McAllister	Patrick	Dunderg	David	159
McLaughlin	blank	Glenleary	James	blank
McNeill	blank	Freugh	Alexander, John & James	35, 105 & 115
Mitchell	John	Ballyvennox	John	31, 39 & 138
Mitchell	Thomas	Tamnamoney	see above	see above

TABLE 3

James Tate VDM	Minister of Killeshandra (Cavan) 1705–29
Thomas Cobham VDM	Minister of Clough (Co. Antrim) 1718–32
Robert Nelson VDM	Minister of 1st Kilraughts 1702–12
William Leech VDM	Minister of 1st Ballymena 1698–1738
Robert Higginbotham VDM	Minister of 1st Coleraine 1710–70
John Porter VDM	Minster of Bushmills 1713–38
Henry Neill VDM	Minister of Ballyrashane 1709–45
Thomas Elder VDM	Minister of Ballyrashane 1700–04
James Thomson VDM	Minister of Ballywillan 1718–47
Alexander Dunlop MA	Not ordained in Ulster
Archibald McCook MA	Not ordained in Ulster
Samuel Wilson MA	Not ordained in Ulster

TABLE 4

MANOR	DATE(S) COVERED	LESSEES	PETITIONER SURNAMES
Clothworkers	1664	36	28
Freemore	1684	20	4
Coleraine	1692	141	17
Rowley	1693	50	15
St John the Baptist	1695	55	29
Dunluce	1695–1718	151	24
Mercers	1714	100	17
Ballymoney Town	1714	143	30
Limavady	1718	122	25
Gage	1718	60	11
Lisneycourt	1718	104	15
Lizard	1725	215	50
Route Presbytery	1694–1719	n/a	48
Aghadowey Session Book	1702–25	226	76
St John the Baptist	1735	52	13
No local estates	(all above)	n/a	25

...

...

...

...

NOTES

1 T. W. Moody, *The Londonderry Plantation, 1609–41* (Belfast, 1939), App. G.
2 J. S. Curl, *The Londonderry Plantation, 1609–1914* (Chichester, 1986), p. 358.
3 London Metropolitan Archives (LMA), CLA/049/EM/03/001.
4 LMA CLA/049/EM/03/002.
5 PRONI MIC9A/6.
6 PRONI T3380/1.
7 https://www.familysearch.org/search/film/007763683?cat=185720.
8 PRONI, D2094/21.
9 PRONI, T2825/C/11.
10 Trinity College Dublin (TCD), MS 1995-2008/271.
11 PRONI, D673/4A.
12 PRONI, T394/1.
13 Ian Montgomery, 'Tenants on the estates of the earls of Antrim', *Directory of Irish Family History Research*, no. 23 (2000) and no. 36 (2013).
14 T. W. Moody, 'Schedules of the lands in Ulster allotted to the London livery companies, 1613', *Analecta Hibernica*, 8 (1938), pp 299–311.
15 http://www.greatparchmentbook.org and PRONI, T724/1.
16 Seamus Pender (ed.), *A Census of Ireland circa 1659* (Dublin, 1939), pp 141–4. In actual fact, the 'census' probably dates from 1660–61.
17 http://www.census.nationalarchives.ie/pages/1831/Londonderry/Coleraine/Macosquin.
18 PRONI, T656/1, p. 40.
19 Charles K. Bolton, *Scotch Irish Pioneers in Ulster and America* (Boston, 1910); Rev. Edward L. Parker, *The History of Londonderry, Comprising the Towns of Derry and Londonderry, N.H.* (Boston, 1851); and George F. Willey *Willey's Book of Nutfield* (Derry NH, 1895).
20 R. J. Hunter (ed.), *Men and Arms: the Ulster Settlers c. 1630* (Belfast, 2012).
21 T. H. Mullin, *Aghadowey: a Parish and its Linen Industry* (1972), pp 44–8.
22 http://www.billmacafee.com/17centurydatabases.htm.
23 R. J. Dickson, *Ulster Emigration to Colonial America, 1718–1775* (Belfast, 2016), p. 29.
24 'Protestant Emigration, 8 March 1728/9, PRONI, T808/15261 (http://www.dippam.ac.uk/ied/records/34892).
25 Parker, *History of Londonderry*, p. 34.

John Makgee of Dumfries and his descendants in Tyrone:

a Catholic Plantation family

BILL MCGEE

WILLIAM ROULSTON

Old Leckpatrick graveyard is located just north of the
village of Ballymagorry in County Tyrone. The busy A5
road passes close to the edge of the graveyard, but probably
few of the thousands of people who travel on that highway
are aware that this ancient burial ground contains one of
the oldest marked graves in Northern Ireland. Though now
largely overgrown and not easy to find, this fine carved
stone has a coat of arms featuring what we now know to be
three leopards' heads. The inscription in false relief runs
around the edge of the stone in Roman capitals and reads:
'Here is the burial place of John Maghee who deseased
26 February 1617 and his family.' Above the coat of arms is
a hand holding a dagger and above that hand is
a Celtic cross.

A question frequently asked by those with Scots-Irish/Ulster-Scots
roots is: 'How can I find where my ancestors lived in Scotland?'
Certainly it is possible to identify the home place of most of the Scottish
grantees of land in Ulster in the early seventeenth century. However,
tracing the 'ordinary' settlers back to a parish or farmstead in Scotland
is not easy. No official lists of those making the journey across the North
Channel survive and only rarely do Irish sources from the early

seventeenth century provide a place of origin in Scotland. Nonetheless, finding the Scottish roots of a family that moved to Ulster in the early 1600s is not always an impossible task. Persistence, hard graft and determination, the belief that there is always one more book to read, one more document to review, one more archive to visit, and allowing, of course, for serendipitous discoveries, mean that it might, just might, be possible to find that link. This article tells the story of John Makgee, following his life from Dumfries in Scotland to Ulster, and demonstrates how his son David became one of the most influential figures in the Plantation settlement around Strabane. A comprehensive history of the family in Scotland will have to wait for another generation of genealogists but it is our belief that the Makgee family of Dumfries were a junior branch of the family in Balmaghie.[1]

JOHN (E) MAKGEE IN SCOTLAND

On Friday, 8 February 1574 26-year-old John Makgee, son of David Makgee, burgess of Dumfries, was examined in Edinburgh by Alexander Colvill, Abbot of Culross, and William Douglas of Quhittinghame, members of the Lords of Council. The purpose of the examination was to determine John's fitness to be a notary public. At the conclusion of the examination he was declared to be a notary public, with a note being made there were at that time very few notaries around New Abbey.[2] Thus begins this story and the public career of a man with deeply held religious convictions which were to pit him against the religious and political tides of the time and ultimately lead him to leave Scotland for sanctuary in Ireland.

Members of the McGhie family had been prominent in Dumfries since at least the early sixteenth century. In 1509 a David McGhie was a chaplain of St Michael's Church in Dumfries.[3] There are subsequent records of a David McGhie's notary public work in 1539, 1550, 1576 and 1578.[4] In 1564 the Clerk of the Commissariat of Dumfries was David McGhie.[5] By 1580, John McGhie held this position.[6] In 1568 and 1580 David McGhie purchased land in Dumfries; in the 1580 transaction he was referred to as a burgess.[7] In 1591 he was still a burgess and notary public.[8] This lengthy record of over 80 years suggests that there were at least two men named David McGhie, one probably the father of the other, and the younger David probably father to John Makgee. Apart from the records of his examination to become a notary public, the earliest records found for this John Makgee are from March 1580 when he was both a witness to and a signatory to a feu charter by Gilbert Broun, perpetual commendator of the monastery of Sweetheart in Newabbey, near Dumfries.[9] Gilbert Broun was a very prominent figure in early seventeenth-century Dumfries. He was accused of single-handedly keeping almost the whole south-west of Scotland in 'ignorance and idolatry'. Due to his efforts, Dumfries was said to have become the seat of excommunicated 'papists' and Jesuits.[10]

In 1581 both John and David were called as witnesses in a court case involving deforcement.[11] In 1583 both of them were denounced as rebels for not bearing witness in a court case.[12] As late as 1606 John was still a notary public in Dumfries.[13] It was in 1601 that the records began to demonstrate John's difficulties resulting from his adherence to his Roman Catholic faith in the face of the Reformation. He was on the wrong side, or at least the losing side, of contemporary Scottish history and it would upend his life and the lives of all those who followed him. Had he adapted to the tide of history and converted to Protestantism this paper would have a very different nature.

In November 1601 John McGhie was among a long list of inhabitants of Dumfries called to answer for 'their Popish proclivities'. The charges against him were: hearing Mass and profaning the sacraments, aiding Jesuits and seminary priests, and trafficking 'Papists'. All were forbidden by various Acts of Parliament and Privy Council. When the king was informed that those charged had not only aided Jesuits but also had been with them at Mass, they were called upon to answer in the matter before James VI and Council on 17 December under pain of rebellion.[14] Many of the defendants appeared but John got a certificate from the bailies and council of Dumfries stating that 'disease and infirmitie' precluded his personal appearance. A reading of the charges makes it clear that the defendants were accused of hearing mass and aiding both John Hammiltoun and Gilbert Browne, Abbot of New Abbey (Sweetheart Abbey), around seven miles west of Dumfries. Browne was charged with not only saying Mass but baptising 'sindrie bairns.' Trial was set for 14 January next but the outcome of the case is not known. Whatever happened, it is clear it did not deter John.

Events between 1601 and 1606 are unclear, but by 31 January 1606, John 'McGie' (also spelled John McKie in the document), had been excommunicated and appeared before the Privy Council in Edinburgh. He declared he was not presently resolved to subscribe to the Confession of Faith and asked for additional time to resolve the matter. He was granted until 1 March, providing that in the interim he conferred with the brethren of Nithsdale, kept himself as a private man, and practiced no public calling. He was thereafter to subscribe to the Confession of Faith and the articles of religion presently confessed within the realm. He was to adjure 'papistry', and thereafter appear on two Sundays in the place of public repentance in the church of Dumfries. There he was to confess he had done wrong, and that it was his own fault that he had been so long excommunicated. Thereafter the minister of Dumfries would absolve him.[15]

This also failed to deter John. And on 28 March 1606 the ministers of Dumfries filed a complaint before the Privy Council against 'Johne MckGie, excommunicate'. It was complained that at no point since John's 31 January appearance in Edinburgh had he satisfied the Kirk as he was directed. But instead, after continual 'driftes and delayes', he absolutely refused to do anything. Moreover, he stated his intention to stay in the country to the discontentment of the Kirk, notwithstanding any remedies of law.[16] Next was a complaint by the Presbytery of Dumfries in 1606 that John McGie, Commissary Clerk of Dumfries, had refused to 'adjure papistry' under pain of rebellion, had declared that he was not resolved to subscribe, had continued his clerkship of the court and had declared he would continue in the country to their discontentment.[17] For his defiance he was denounced a rebel. The statement that he had declared he would continue in the country to the discontentment of the Commissioners suggests he had been threatened with banishment. At the same time there were accusations against William Douglas, Earl of Angus, for at numerous times during 1606, committing the offense of 'disregarding the excommunication of Johne McGie, sometime Commissary Clerk of Dumfries and instead treating him with great kindness, familiaritie and friendschip, as if no such sentence had been pronounced against him.'[18]

The final and ultimately most serious clashes with the Crown and the Reformation began in 1607. The reformers had successfully petitioned parliament for the authority to pull down the abbeys, which they regarded as symbols of the abuses of the old Church. But the progress of the Reformation was slow to take hold in those regions where Catholicism was strongly entrenched and in certain enclaves in the south-west, such as Dumfries, Mass continued to be said in spite of it being a punishable offence. In June 1607 members of the king's guard were sent to apprehend the defiant Gilbert Broun, Abbot of New Abbey. When the guard attempted to apprehend Broun, 'Johnne McGhie, sometime Commissary Clerk of Dumfries, Johnne Maxwell, called Robert's Jock with convocatioun of a grite nowmer of the rude and ignorant people of the Newabbay' armed with staves, muskets and hagbuts came to the guard in 'a tumultuous and unseamelie maner' and 'directlie and avowedlie withstood and resisted the apprehensioun of the said Mr. Gilbert, and consequentlie the executioun of his Majesteis commissioun granted to that effect.'[19] The offenders were called to answer the charges but evidently failed to appear.

In 1608 Johnne McGhie, Johnne Maxwell, Thomas Turnoure (called 'Thome of the Play'), Mungo Grassie (or Grecy) in New Abbey, Richard Broun, son of Abbot Gilbert Broun, and John Broun of Lochill were denounced rebels.[20] In time the authorities would be more successful and eventually Broun's front door would be knocked down by John Spottiswood and a 'grite number of bookis, copes, imageis and uther popische trasche' found in his chambers were burned in the streets of Dumfries. Abbot Broun was then warded in Blackness castle. Upon his release he left Scotland for good, dying in Paris in about 1612, at the reputed age of one hundred.[21]

FLIGHT TO IRELAND

Burke's Peerage states John left Scotland and settled in Strabane in 1610. On 5 December 1610[22] an entry in James Cunningham's protocol book states 'James Cunyngham as procurator for John McGhie infefts Janet Reddick in liferent and David McGhie their natural son in fee in a tenement in Friar's Rennick occupied by Richard Moir and belonging to the said John McGhie'. Witnesses included several burgesses of Dumfries, including James, Patrick and John Young, plus Edward Horner, husband of John's cousin Margaret Makgee.[23] A procurator (agent) was required when someone was not present to conduct business, therefore requiring an agent; John, it seems, had gone to Ireland.

We do not know of any siblings for John but it appears that he had cousins named Helen, Margaret and William. Margaret married Edward Horner, a burgess of Dumfries, and died in 1647.[24] William died before 18 August 1596. Besides son David, John had daughters Jean and Isabella, both of whom were described as being natural daughters, just as David was later mentioned as a natural son.[25] We know nothing of Jean and little of Isabella. As they were referred to as natural rather than legal children it would seem that John and Janet Reddick were not married when these children were born, at least not in the eyes of the authorities. What became of John's cousins or of his daughters Jean and Isabella is not known, although we do know that Isabella was married and in 1622 she was in Strabane, County Tyrone, where she signed inherited property over to her brother David.[26] We do not know whether his wife, Janet Reddick, went with him to Ireland. John's gravestone says that buried with him is his family. So it is entirely possible that his wife and daughters are interred there with him.

It seems that John eventually found living in Scotland no longer tenable and that he went to County Tyrone and settled among the Scottish settlers, a proportion of them his co-religionists, in and around Strabane and just across the river in Lifford, County Donegal. By the end of the 1500s a significant Scottish settlement had developed in the vicinity of Strabane, arising in part from the marriage in the late 1560s of the chief of the O'Neills, Turlough Luineach, and Lady Agnes Campbell. After the commencement of the Plantation these earlier arrivals were tolerated or encouraged by Protestant James Hamilton, the first Earl of Abercorn, and his Catholic brother Sir George, both of whom received substantial grants of land in the area in 1610, and began to introduce Scottish settlers of their own. John McGhie needed a safe place to settle beyond the reach of both English and Scottish authorities, an area where the Reformation had gained no traction. Settling in Ulster created a match of both needs and opportunity. It is not clear whether John McGhie knew the Hamiltons while living in Scotland.

We know little about John once he settled in Tyrone. He died on 26 February 1617 and, as noted at the beginning of this article, was buried with his family in the Old Leckpatrick graveyard, a few miles north of

Strabane. We know the John who lies buried in Old Leckpatrick is the same man as the one we have been examining due to a service of heir dated 22 October 1617, in which property in Dumfries belonging to the late John Makghie, notary and Clerk of the Commissary Court in Dumfries who died February 1617 is transferred to his natural son David and to a sasine (a legal document recording the transfer of property – land or buildings – into new ownership) in which the date and place of death are given.[27]

As noted already, Sir George Hamilton, younger brother of the first Earl of Abercorn, was a major landowner in the Strabane area in the early 1600s and a devout Catholic. Under his patronage a settlement of Scottish Catholics developed in and around Strabane. In 1630 the number of Catholic settlers so alarmed the Earl of Cork that he warned that the Crown's policy of planting civilisation and Protestantism in Ulster had not had the expected impact. By giving estates to Sir George Hamilton and other Catholics the result had been far from encouraging Protestantism. Rather it had 'drawn thither Papists'.[28] A few months earlier the Protestant bishop of Derry had warned the Lord Chancellor of Ireland: 'Since he got part of the Earl of Abercorn's grant of the Barony of Strabane, Sir George Hamilton has done his best to plant Popery there, and has brought over priests and Jesuits from Scotland.'[29] The bishop also wrote to Claud, Master of Abercorn (second son of the first Earl of Abercorn and heir of his lands at Strabane):

> I hear that, though your father was given land at Strabane in order to maintain the reformed religion, the place is become the sink into which all the corrupt humours purged out of Scotland run. Idolatrous Popish masses are daily celebrated. As your Church is heretical and your Pope an anti-Christ, I think it my duty to oppose you, but, before appealing to the higher authorities, I write to ask you to come and see me in order that I may convince you that you are in the wrong. Meantime the Provost of Strabane is to arrest the two Papists McSwyne and Blackney. You will resist him at your peril.[30]

The bishop further warned the authorities:

> Sir George Hamilton, who is otherwise a courteous and civil gentleman, has tried to draw people to Popery. Claude Hamilton, Master of Abercorn, would be a hopeful young gentleman were he

not poisoned with Popery, but countenances Papists so much that there will be a revolt in Strabane if any more of the Scotch Papists come there. The Archbishop of Glasgow has sent to me (the Bishop of Derry) hoping that I will not harbor in my diocese Papists who have been expelled from Scotland.[31]

DAVID MACGHEE

We know that John's son David was born before 1610, probably around 1600, and that he was in Ireland by 1622, where he is listed among a group of Scottish settlers on the lands of Sir George Hamilton. Listed with him is John Browne, perhaps a man from the family of Abbot Gilbert Broun and possibly the man of that name who was denounced as a rebel along with David's father John in 1608.[32] What little we know of David personally comes almost entirely from his will (see Appendix), in which are named his wife Catherine and several but not all of their children. Catherine's maiden name was probably Browne. From an Exchequer Bill of 26 Jan 1676 and reply of 28 November 1676, it seems likely she was a member of the same Browne family which came from Dumfries to Strabane about the same time as John McGhie.[33] James MacGhee, son of David and Catherine, was a witness to John Browne's nuncupative will in which Catherine was left the house in Strabane and where she and her children lived. It is clear from the records that David was a Catholic, a man of considerable talents, and that he rose to a position of prominence in Tyrone.

He was agent of the Abercorn estate, a position to which he was appointed following the death of a previous agent, William Lynne in 1625.[34] As such he exercised great control over business matters including leases, farming and relations with tenants. By 1628 he also held the office of seneschal of the manor of Strabane which was inherited by the first Earl of Abercorn's son Claud (known as the Master of Abercorn and later as Lord Strabane). As the official in charge of the manor court he was the key figure in resolving legal disputes between tenants and adjudicating minor criminal offences. He was to retain these positions until his death in 1678.[35] Since the Hamiltons were often absentee landlords, David was one of the most influential figures in the area. He received a grant of denization in 1631, which gave him the same legal rights in Ireland as an English subject.[36]

There are numerous records of David's activities on behalf of and with the Hamiltons. Two of them, evidence of land acquisitions, are of particular interest and may well explain the names of two of David's sons, George and Claude. According to the Civil Survey of 1654–56, he received the townland of Balliburney, also known as Holy Hill, in Leckpatrick parish from Sir George Hamilton in fee farm (i.e. in perpetuity); on this occasion he is called David 'Marghee' and described as a 'Scottish Papist'.[37] Also in the Civil Survey he is listed as David 'Marghue', holding the townland of Drumnaboy in neighboring Camus-juxta-Mourne parish from Claud Hamilton, Lord Strabane.[38] It was not uncommon at that time to name children after benefactors and it seems probable that David named his sons George and Claude for these Hamilton landlords. As far as can be determined, neither name was used in the family before that time.

Further evidence that the relationship between David MacGhee and Sir George Hamilton was a strong one may be found in two other land transactions and David's will. By orders dated 26 February 1669 [1670] and 12 May 1673, Sir George Hamilton of Nenagh (another son of the first Earl of Abercorn) appointed James Hamilton of Crewe (Crew) and David McGhee of Strabane, gent., his attorneys to execute estates pursuant to his orders, including to Jane, Lady Strabane, widow of Claud Hamilton, and to his daughters and younger sons.[39] Also, as part of an indenture between Sir George Hamilton of Nenagh and Patrick Hamilton, Sir George appointed David Macghee and James Macghee as his executors and refers to them as his 'beloveds in Christ'.[40] Finally, in David's will it will be seen that David forgave a substantial debt of £150 owed by Sir George Hamilton of Nenagh. Between 1654 and 1660 little is known of David's activities, though as discussed below there is evidence he was in County Clare for at least part of that time. In addition, there are records of a land transaction in 1661 in which David was named as seneschal to the Hamiltons and that James Macghee was authorised to assist him.[41] In his will David is referred to as 'of Loghmony.' Also, he was referred to as 'of Loghony' when he was recorded as being a member of a Chancery inquisition jury in 1638.[42]

THE CHILDREN OF DAVID MACGHEE AND CATHERINE BROWN

In his nuncupative (unwritten) will of 9 October 1678 David lists his wife Catherine, his eldest son George and George's sons David and Toby, sons John and James, and an unnamed daughter ((other sources suggest Elizabeth) married to Alexander Browne (who had a daughter named Mary Browne, married to John Rea). We also learn from the will that James was or was about to be married to Marianna Leighton. Not mentioned in the will are sons Andrew and Claude. A transcription of the will is found in the Appendix. In his will David says that his eldest son George is to inherit his property at Holy Hill after the death of David's widow Catherine. Catherine evidently died within the next five years for in 1683 George, by then known as Captain George, mortgaged the property to Gordon O'Neill of Crowe in Ardeka parish (probably Crew in Ardstraw parish).[43] Gordon O'Neill was the son of Sir Phelim O'Neill, one of the principal instigators of the 1641 uprising, and the widow of Lord Strabane. On 20 July 1683 Captain George sold the property to Rev. John Sinclair and on 23 July 1683 O'Neill likewise transferred his interest to Sinclair.[44]

George Macghee attended the Scots College at Douai (now a city in northern France), entering on 22 September 1637 at the age of 15. The reference claims Glasgow as his place of birth and that his parents were 'Davida and Catharina'. The reason for his being born in Glasgow is a mystery but it may be connected to the fact that the power base for the Hamilton family to which George's family was connected was Renfrewshire. We know he also studied rhetoric and philosophy at a seminary in Paris and following his studies went to Ireland about 1641.[45] Although it is recorded that George was among those students who left to fight for Charles I, no records have been found of George's military activities during the 1640s.[46] On 11 December 1680 he was referred to as being 'of Galway' but in June 1681 he was in Balliburney, or Holy Hill.[47] The same reference documents that his wife was named Helena and that he was settling his estate on Helena, then after her death to her eldest son David. It also mentions the existence of other unnamed living sons and daughters. We do not know when Captain George died or where he is buried, nor do we know where or when Helena died. In a very interesting petition of Captain George Magee to Charles II, written some time between 1670 and 1678, there are further references to his financial difficulties and a connection of those difficulties to something called the Salisbury plot. He also states he has been responsible for the maintenance of his aging parents and mentions he had 13 or 14 children.[48]

In his 1678 will, David directed that his son James should receive all of his tenements in and about the town of Strabane that had previously been transferred to James and his wife, Marianna Leighton. He also left him a bond of £65 which was owed by James Hamilton of Eliston, a Tyrone landowner who was a member of the wider Abercorn connection. In addition, James was left his mother's house once she had passed away. On 15 November 1680 the fourth Earl of Abercorn granted lands to James in 'Liskylymigin' (probably now Lisky, Camus parish) at an annual rent of £20.[49] In 1688, King James II appointed James Magee one of 23 burgesses of the 'Jacobite' corporation of Strabane. Though James has been styled MD in later publications, there is no evidence that he practiced medicine. However, his son George was a well-known apothecary who became one of the leading residents of Strabane in the first half of the 1700s.[50]

David McGhee had two sons not mentioned in his unwritten will of 1678. Since that will constitutes such a great portion of our knowledge of David, Claude and Andrew would have escaped our attention altogether but for a familial commitment to education for they too studied at Douai.[51] According to Tom McInally, Claude, who was 11 years younger than his brother George, left university at Douai at age 15 to become a soldier in August 1649.[52] McInally also states that it is likely both George and Claude joined the French army following their return from abroad, although no corroborating evidence for this has been found. Claude married Grace Norton and died in August 1668 in Moybracken, County Clare.[53] What became of Grace is unknown. Andrew, listed as the brother of George and Claude, entered university in Rome and when he left in 1655 he undertook missionary work in Scotland as a Jesuit. McInally states that he died in December 1690, while serving the Church in Rome.[54] Gordon states that Andrew was the rector of the Scots College in Rome when he died after many years of service.[55] As in other aspects of the lives of these McGhees, the fact that George and his two brothers Claude and Andrew were educated abroad illustrates the human side of historical conditions at a time when it was illegal to receive a Catholic education in Scotland.

In his 1678 will David mentions a son-in-law, Alexander Browne, who was married to his daughter (unnamed in the will, but probably Elizabeth). Although the name Browne is certainly a familiar one within this Macghee family, we know nothing further of Alexander and his wife beyond the statement in the will that they had a daughter, Mary Browne, who was married to John Rea.[56] It seems they also had a son, Valentine, about whom nothing is known other than that he, too, was educated abroad at Paris and Douai. Listed among the students of the Scots College at Douai is Valentinus Browne, a Scottish Catholic born in Tipperary in 1658 to Alexander Bruno and Elizabeth Maghie.[57] If correctly identified, Elizabeth and Alexander were part of what appears to have been a familial exodus from Ulster during the Cromwellian period. It appears that not only did David leave Tyrone, but that his sons John and James and his daughter Elizabeth Browne were also displaced.

THE COUNTY CLARE CONNECTION

John Macghee is mentioned only briefly in his father's will, which states that he is to be left £30. Beyond this the only references to John are indirect. We do not know the name of his wife. Some things do seem clear, however, from records associated with the Cromwellian land settlement in Ireland in the 1650s. Under the plan, those who had participated in the first stages of the rebellion, or had participated in the killing of civilians, or who failed to surrender within 28 days, were exempt from pardon. All other Catholic landowners would be subject to partial forfeiture, depending on the extent of their delinquency. Further, they were required to move across the River Shannon into the province of Connacht or County Clare. The programme was immediately beset by problems and confusion and by 1659 it had been abandoned. Nonetheless, John Macghee and his family were caught up in this scheme and moved to County Clare, which would indicate that he was not known to be an active participant in hostilities, but was instead an 'innocent Papist'.

On 15 March 1655 Col. Henry Ingoldesby leased to John Macghee, gent., of Knockbeach, County Clare, various lands in the barony of

Bunratty in that county.[58] The lease was for 99 years or the lives of the said John, his unnamed wife, and James Macghee his brother. The rent was three shillings per acre, with a provision for paying proportionately more if the three cartrons (a unit of land measurement) of Tullyglasse were found, on further survey, to contain more than 75 acres. The tenant was to pay all taxes and country charges, build within seven years a decent and sufficient house after the English manner, quick-set within 15 years the fences and enclosures, plant within seven years an orchard of 300 trees, and to plant every ten years 300 ash, oak, birch, or other suitable trees.[59] Just over a year later, in July 1656, John resigned the lease in favour of his father and mother, David and Catherine Magee.[60] It seems very unlikely that John and James were descendants of anyone else other than the David MacGhee and Catherine Browne discussed above. Based upon this it seems that John's parents had chosen to or had been forced to leave Strabane. This would explain the long gap in records of David's activities in Tyrone during the years after the 1641 rising.

The so-called 'Census of 1659' (in actual fact an abstract of the poll tax returns of 1660–61) provides further evidence of family's connection with County Clare. Three Magees are listed as 'tituladoes' (a term that seems to mean title-holder) in Tomgreany parish, which adjoins Feakle parish.[61] They were George Magee, John Magee and David Magee, all styled 'gents'. George Magee's townland was not specified, but John Magee was listed in Ballyvanane and David Magee in Scariff. In George Magee's townland there were 55 poll tax payers, all Irish, while in Ballyvanane there were 44, again all Irish, and in Scariff there were only 11, once again all Irish. We have no way of determining how many family members accompanied these Magees to County Clare.[62]

The lead author of this article, Bill McGee, hopes that it will stimulate thoughtful comments. He would be pleased to hear from anyone with suggestions or refutations and can be emailed at wiscbmcgee@gmail.com.

APPENDIX: TRANSCRIPTION OF THE WILL OF DAVID MACGHEE

Memorandum that on or about the ninth day of October one thousand six hundred seventy eight David Macghee of Loghmonye in the County of Tyrone deceased did in the presence of the undernamed witnesses declare his last will and testament nuncupative in the words following or words to the like effect (viz). He left Catherine Magee his wife all his yearly rent out of Loghmonye, Dromneboy and the houses and acres in and about Strabane during her natural life. ITEM he left her sole administration of his last will and testament, ITEM He left his eldest son George Macghee after the death of the said Catherine his mother whatever yearly rents should accrue out of his lands in Loghmonye, Dromneboy, Holyhill and Kenarhane and the house in towne which now James Hamilton the merch:t hath. But left noe power to him to sell or dispose of any part of the above said lands or tenements from his eldest son and heir but to depend upon his said son and his heires. ITEM Whereas George Hamilton of Nenagh in the county of Tipperary, Gent., Knt. and Barntt. was endue him by bond one hundred and fifty odd pounds for principall debt the interest whereof bill the time of his death he ordered to be forgiven to the said Sr. George always provided that his said son should not be forced to sue the said Sr. George or his heirs of which sums he ordered his son John Macghee thirty pounds sterl [ing] and to his son in law Alexander Browne thirty pounds sterl more and to his grandchild Mary Browne wife of John Reane ten pounds sterl for all the residue of the said sums or bond he left equally to be divided to his said son George and his two sons David and Tobye ITEM He left his son James Macghee all his tenements and acres in and about the town of Strabane that was bound over to the said James his wife upon their marriage and also he left the said James a bond of sixty five pounds which James Hamilton of Eliston, Esq. was endue him with any other little penny debts that was endue him ITEM He left his foresaid wife the house wherein she dwells and furnishings thereof during her life and then to his said son James being present then Ja: Macghee Marianna Lighton.

NOTES

1   For a current scholarly discussion of these very early McGees and related families, see a recent article by Alan Milliken in the October 2018 issue of the *Transactions of the Dumfriesshire and Galloway Natural History and Antiquarian Society* titled 'Michael McGorth and the Clan Afren'. Dumfries and Balmaghie are separated by about 21 miles.

2   Registration of Notaries, NP2/2, 8 March 1574, National Records of Scotland.

3 Robert Edgar, *Introduction to a History of Dumfries* (1915), p. 138; *Registrum Magni Sigilli, 1432–1513*, no. 3335.

4 *Protocol Book of Mark Carruthers, 1531–1561*, ed. R. C. Reid (1956), p. 30; 'Protocol Book of Herbert Anderson, 1541–1550', *Transactions of the Dumfries and Galloway Natural History and Antiquarian Society*, 3rd series, vol. 2, no. 97; Acts and Decreets, 1578–81, R. C. Reid Collection, Ewart Library, Dumfries, vol. 155, p. 41; Extract of Wills and Testaments, from Edinburgh Testaments, R. C. Reid Collection, Ewart Library, Dumfries, vol. 6, F179.

5 Edgar, *Introduction to a History of Dumfries*, p. 241.

6 Philip Hamilton Grierson, 'Sheriff Court Book of Dumfries 1577–1583', *Transactions of the Dumfries and Galloway Natural History and Antiquarian Society*, 3rd series, vol. 12 (1926), pp 163, 216. Register of the Privy Seal of Scotland, PS1/69 f. 61, 22 Feb. 1596, National Records of Scotland.

7 Protocol Book of Herbert Cunningham 1561–74, R. C. Reid Collection, Ewart Library, Dumfries, vol. 129, no. 131; Edgar, *An Introduction to the History of Dumfries*, p. 13.

8 Deeds Collected from Register House, R. C. Reid Collection, Ewart Library, Dumfries, vol. 157, p. 104.

9 A. E. Truckell, 'Three Sweetheart Abbey Charters', *Transactions of the Dumfries and Galloway Natural History and Antiquarian Society*, 3rd series, vol. 37 (1958–9), pp 171–2; Broun's protocol book recording his activities as a notary is not in the Ewart collection in the Dumfries Public Library and it may not have survived.

10 James F. S. Gordon, *Journal and Appendix to Scotichronicon and Monasticon* (1869), p. 527.

11 Acts and Decreets, 1581–2, vol. 85–95, p. 95, R. C. Reid Collection, Ewart Library, Dumfries. In Scottish law deforcement refers to resisting officials who are employed in the execution of their legal duties.

12 Ibid., p. 107.

13 R. C. Reid, 'The Culvennan Writs', *Transactions of the Dumfries and Galloway Natural History and Antiquarian Society*, 3rd series, vol. 10 (1925), p. 57.

14 *Register of the Privy Council of Scotland, 1599–1604*, first series, vol. 6, p. 312.

15 Ibid., *1604–07*, first series, vol. 7, p. 318.

16 Ibid.

17 Ibid., *Addendum 1545–1625*, vol. 14, p. 425, no. 208.

18 Ibid., *1604–07*, first series, vol. 7, p. 318.

19 Ibid., *1607–10*, first series, vol. 8, p. 119.

20 Ibid., p. 132.

21 Andrew McCulloch, *Galloway, a Land Apart* (2000), p. 318.

22 *Burke's Peerage* (1847), vol. 2, p. 1244, under heading of Skipton of Beech Hill.

23 Protocol Book of Dumfries, 1609–10, B17/1/3, National Records of Scotland.

24 Old Parochial Registers, Deaths and Burials Index, Dumfries Parish, Part I, 1617–79, p. 35, Dumfries and Galloway Family History Society.

25 Selected Protocols of Herbert Cunningham, 18 Aug. 1596, R. C. Reid Collection, Ewart Library, Dumfries.

26 Protocol Book of Dumfries, 1615–33, B17/1/8 f. 105r, 8 July 1631, National Records of Scotland.

27 Ibid.
28 *Calendar of State Papers of Ireland, Charles I, 1625–1632*, p. 509.
29 Ibid., p. 510.
30 Ibid., p. 511.
31 Ibid., p. 512.
32 *Register of the Privy Council of Scotland, 1607–1610*, vol. 8, p. 132.
33 Abstract of Baird Family Typed Notes, PRONI, T808/898–899.
34 Ibid.
35 William J. Roulston, *Restoration Strabane, 1660–1714: Economy and Society in Provincial Ireland* (2007), p. 46.
36 William A. Shaw (ed.), *Denizations and Naturalizations of Aliens in England and Ireland* (Huguenot Society of London, 1911), p. 333.
37 R. C. Simington (ed.), *The Civil Survey III* (Irish Manuscripts Commission, 1937), p. 385.
38 Ibid., p. 390. Drumnaboy had been mortgaged to David by Lord Strabane.
39 Lodge, Records of the Rolls, vol. vi, Charles I to 1648, p. 231, PRONI, MIC600/4.
40 Indenture, Sir George Hamilton of Nenagh to Patrick Hamilton, 4 April 1676, PRONI, D623/B/13/9.
41 Lease between Sir George Hamilton and Robert Carson, 30 April 1675, PRONI, LPC/771.
42 Chancery Inquisition Juries, PRONI, T1365. Loghmony may be Loch Monann. That lake no longer exists but it evidently used to be at the head of Strabane Glen until it collapsed.
43 Abstract of title of Holy Hill, copied by Warren Loane (photocopy in the author's possession). Holy Hill is presently owned by Hamilton and Margaret Thompson, who have done a splendid job of maintaining the dignity of the house and its beautiful setting.
44 Ibid.
45 *Records of the Scots Colleges of Douai, Rome, Madrid, Valladolid and Ratisbon*, vol. 1 (New Spalding Club, 1906), p. 32.
46 Tom McInally, *The Sixth Scottish University: The Scots Colleges Abroad, 1575–1799* (2012), p. 39.
47 Abstract of title of Holy Hill. Ballyburney is the original Irish name for Holy Hill.
48 *Calendar of State Papers Domestic: Charles II, Addenda 1660–1685*, p. 492. The only two about whom we have any information are David and George.
49 PRONI, D1854/2/19
50 In a remarkable discovery, Fergus McGhee unearthed an article from the April 1953 edition of *Country Life* magazine. In the article is described a cane which must have been one passed down through generations of the family. The cane had the names of John Macghee from Balm Macghee in Scotland and then the names of David Macghee 1628, Jacob (James) Macghee 1670 and George Macghee 1714. On the cane is an engraved coat of arms with three leopard's heads. Not only does this provide confirmation of the line of succession from John to George it also provides a coat of arms just as the one on John's gravestone.

51 *Records of the Scots Colleges of Douai, Rome, Madrid, Valladolid and Ratisbon,* vol. 1, p. 38.

52 McInally, *The Sixth Scottish University*, p. 39.

53 Prerogative Administrations Intestate, G.O. 259, National Library of Ireland.

54 McInally, *The Sixth Scottish University*, p. 191.

55 Gordon, *Journal and Appendix to Scotichronicon and Monasticon*, p. 592.

56 Alexander Browne is possibly the man of that name mentioned in the vestry minutes for Donagheady parish for 16 April 1723. John Rea is possibly the man of that name listed on the Subsidy Rolls for 1664 and 1666, County Tyrone. He owed £2 both years.

57 *Records of the Scots Colleges of Douai, Rome, Madrid, Valladolid and Ratisbon,* vol. 1, p. 53.

58 Knockbeach (probably what is now called Knockbeha, Feakle Parish) and Clouneskeagh (137acres), three cartrons of Tullyglasse, Clonloghan Parish (75 acres), Killines and that part of Lissinrinkea surveyed with it by Capt Webb (135a) and Killulla, Clonloghan Parish (46 acres).

59 John Ainsworth (ed.), *The Inchiquin Manuscripts* (Irish Manuscripts Commission, 1961), p. 352. One of the witnesses to this lease was Nicholas Harrold, who appears in King James' Army List with John's brother, James, and is likely the man of that name, listed as an apothecary, who appears on the same page of Pender's 1659 census with three other Magees, sons of the John (Seamus Pender (ed.), *A Census of Ireland circa 1659* (Irish Manuscripts Commission, 1939), p. 171).

60 Ibid., p. 353.

61 Pender, *Census of Ireland*, p. 171.

62 A John Magee was called upon to furnish his best horses for the army of King James in 1690; a man of that name was a witness to a mortgage deed in Lecarrow, Tulla parish in 1684 and was mentioned in the will of James Roch of Killgobbane as leasing Lassana and Killgobane, Clooney parish – he was still leasing these lands in 1700 (James Frost, *The History and Topography of the County of Clare: From the Earliest Times to the Beginning of the 18th Century* (1893), pp 563, 585; Ainsworth, *Inchiquin Manuscripts*, pp 517, 552).

63 We are grateful to Faye Logue and Len Swindley for their transcription of this will.

Dean Mahomed
Irish-Indian travel writer, curry entrepreneur and shampooer to kings

JAMES BARTLETT

When the British Empire was at its height, India was
known as 'the jewel in the crown' and had a special place in
the hearts of the many who went there to seek their fame
and fortune in cotton, opium and other trades.

Sake Dean Mahomed or Mahomet (the surname spelling varied, but
in Arabic it was Sheikh Din Muhammad, the 'Din' driving from the
Arabic word for 'religion'), was born in Patna in 1759, and grew up a
Muslim in Bengali, northern India. He had watched the area slowly
succumb to the might of the English East India Tea Company, and at
the age of 11 he attached himself as a 'camp follower' or aide-de-camp
to Godfrey Evan Baker, a Protestant-Anglo Irish officer in the British
army. It was a friendship that lasted until Baker's death, and over the
following years Mahomed fought in several battles, moving up in the
ranks. Though there were more Indians than Europeans working for the
Company, Mahomed would have to fight against discrimination for the
rest of his life, and was called an 'Irish Indian' by both the British and
his Indian countrymen.

Baker resigned in disgrace after being charged with embezzlement in
1782, and they both travelled to Cork in Ireland in 1784. Mahomed
worked on the Baker estate for over 20 years and improved his already-
good English language and writing, but he also scandalously wooed and
all-but eloped with a young Protestant gentry woman called Jane Daly,

whom he converted in order to marry. During that time he also secured subscriptions, so that he could write and publish the two-volume book that he had been ruminating over since he arrived on Irish soil. *The Travels of Dean Mahomet: an Eighteenth-Century Journey through India* was written as 'a series of letters to a friend' and recounted the country he had left behind, the peoples and customs he had encountered while marching across north India, and his stories of marriage and family. It was the first book written and published by an Indian in English, and made him a celebrity of sorts, especially among society elite, and also arguably one of the first travel writers.

Even though he was allied with the British regime, his kind representations of Indian people and Islamic beliefs distinguished his work from those of other European writers, though sadly it did not change colonial attitudes, and after over two decades in Cork he left Ireland for London, arriving around 1806. It seems Mahomed came alone, because around that time he entered a (possibly bigamous) second marriage to Jane Jeffreys. Calling himself 'William', at least on the legal documents, they subsequently had a daughter, Amelia, born in 1808, though records show that back in Ireland with his first wife were six more children.

Now Mahomed changed tack and worked briefly as a therapeutic practitioner – then called a 'shampooer' – for a rich nobleman, and then for Basil Cochrane, who had installed a steam bath in his house in Portman Square, and then promoted its medical benefits to the public. In 1809, Mahomed opened the Hindoostane Coffee House, which was one of the first curry restaurants in London and offered 'for the entertainment of Indian gentlemen, where they may enjoy the Hoakha, with real Chilm tobacco, and Indian dishes, in the highest perfection … to be unequalled to any curries ever made in England.'

Although the restaurant had good reviews it did not make enough money, and Mahomed filed for bankruptcy in 1812. In 1814, he and his new family moved to the seaside town of Brighton, where the Royal Pavilion was being 'Indianised' and he opened Mahomed's Baths. His use of the practice of *ch mpo*, a Hindi word referring to a head massage with oils, was possibly the origin of the English word 'shampoo' and here he also practised his 'Oriental medicine', and utilised other luxuries like Indian powder and hair dyes. His techniques of therapeutic oil massage, an early form of aromatherapy, alongside herbal steam baths, were said to be a cure for many diseases including gout, stiff joints and aches and pain, and it was now that he hit the heights of his fame. He was christened 'Dr. Brighton' and became the 'Shampooing Surgeon' to King George IV and King William IV.

Despite never gaining total acceptance in several cultures, his clever advertising skills and two more books – *Cases Cured*, an analysis of all the aches, pains, and maladies that shampooing and steam baths could cure or alleviate (apparently including paralysis, sore throat, and indigestion), and the autobiographical *Shampooing Surgeon, Inventor of the Indian medicated Vapour and Sea Water Baths etc.* – made Mahomed an immigrant pioneer who was years ahead of his time. Today he would in all probability be a successful and wealthy businessman but, back in the 1800s, his celebrity and entrepreneurial skill was not enough, and he was penniless and almost totally forgotten by the time of his death in 1851. One of his sons carried on his traditions, becoming a proprietor of the Turkish Baths at Brighton, while one of his grandsons became an internationally-known physician who was vital in the studies of high blood pressure.

His curry and bath houses are long gone now, and it was over 120 years before Mahomed was fully recognised again, when poet and scholar Alamgir Hashmi drew attention to his achievements in the 1970/80s. In 1997 Michael H. Fisher edited the travel journals, and a year later, Rozina Visram's *Ayahs, Lascars and Princes: The Story of Indians in Britain 1700–1947* shone more light on his life. There have been several academic appreciations since then as well, and the Brighton Pavilion, where he occasionally plied his healthy trade, has his original writings. Despite his Coffee House not being a success, it was honoured on 29 September 2005, when the City of Westminster unveiled a Green Plaque commemorating the site on George Street. Alas you can only see the plaque through the door of the office that is there today.

In 2007, he returned to the public eye once again when he was featured as one of the subjects of *Between Worlds: Voyagers to Britain 1700–1850*, a small exhibition in the Porter Gallery at the National Portrait Gallery in London. It focused on a dozen or so individuals over that period who travelled – mostly willingly – thousands of miles away from their native lands of India, Australia, North America, Africa and others to Britain, where their extraordinary presence, cultures and appearance, even over a short period of time, was to have a lasting effect. Mahomed's small red shoes, waistcoat, advertisements and portraits were on display, and he would doubtless be interested – and maybe surprised – to know that, according to the NPG's exhibition brochure, there are over 300 languages spoken in London today. Most recently, in January 2019 he achieved contemporary immortality when Google recognised him as one of their daily Doodle illustrations on their home page, something Mahomed, who is buried in Brighton, could never have dreamed of, no matter if he was under Indian, Irish or English skies.

FURTHER READING

The Travels of Dean Mahomet: An Eighteenth-Century Journey through India, ed. Michael H. Fisher (University of California Press, 1997).
Michael H. Fisher, *The First Indian Author in English: Dean Mahomed (1759–1851) in India, Ireland, and England* (Oxford University Press, 2000).
Romita Ray, 'Sake Dean Mahomed', in *Between Worlds: Voyagers to Britain, 1700–1850*, ed. Jocelyn Hackforth-Jones et al. (National Portrait Gallery, 2007).
Alok Kumar Das, 'Life and legacy of Sake Dean Mahomet: a forgotten enigma', *Communication Studies and Language Pedagogy*, vol. 2, no. 1–2, Jan–Dec. 2016.
https://www.aramcoworld.com/Articles/March-2018/The-Shampooing-Surgeon-of-Brighton.

Whatever happened to Belfast radicalism after the '98 rebellion?

THOMAS BARTLETT

FERGUS WHELAN
May Tyrants Tremble: The Life of William Drennan, 1754–1820
Irish Academic Press, 2020
pp 352   ISBN 978-1-78855-121-2   hb   €29.95

MARY MᴄNEILL
*The Life and Times of Mary Ann McCracken, 1770–1866:
A Belfast Panorama*
Irish Academic Press, 2019 (first published 1960)
New foreword by Marianne Elliott
and new introduction by Sir Ronald Weatherup
pp 340   ISBN 978-1-78855-082-6   hb   €22.95

It still surprises that until now no full-scale biography of William Drennan has been published (in the English language, at least: Jörg Lahme, *William Drennan und der Kampf um die irische Unabhängigkeit: Eine politische Biographie (1754–1820)* [*William Drennan and the Struggle for Irish Independence: A Political Biography*] Göttingen: Wallstein Verlag, published 2012, remains untranslated. I am grateful to Dr Colin Walker for this information). Drennan's career, from his Belfast birth and upbringing, medical training in Scotland and practice, first in Belfast (1778–82), then Newry till 1789, then Dublin and, finally in 1807, back to Belfast is replete with interest. Moreover, he was prominent in the various reform movements of the 1780s and 1790s, notably the Volunteers and the United Irishmen, and he remained committed to reform – against slavery, and in favour of press freedom and Catholic emancipation – in the increasingly uncongenial atmosphere of post-Union Belfast. In addition, Drennan was a poet (his best-known poem is probably *The Wake of William Orr*), prolific pamphleteer (his 1784 *Letters of Orellana, an Irish Helot* still commands attention), and on his return to Belfast, editor of the *Belfast Monthly Magazine,* and founder of the Belfast Academical Institution ('Inst') – the first university established in these islands since the University of Dublin in the late sixteenth century.

Nor are materials for a full biography lacking: along with his published writings, there is extant some 1,500 letters of a correspondence between Drennan and his sister Martha (Matty), his mother and his brother-in-law Samuel McTier, three volumes of which were edited by Jean Agnew and published by the Irish Manuscripts Commission in 1998, to add to a volume of selections edited by D. A. Chart for the Public Record Office of Northern Ireland in 1931. It is true that a number of individual studies on Drennan have appeared: Mary Helen Thuente has examined his literary output in *The Harp Re-Strung* (1994), John Larkin, *The Trial of William Drennan* (1991) looks at his prosecution for seditious libel, while Ian McBride, *Eighteenth-century Ireland: the isle of Slaves* (2009), Michael Brown, *The Irish Enlightenment* (2016) and the late A. T. Q. Stewart *A Deeper Silence: the hidden origins of the United Irishmen* (1993) all treat of Drennan's thought. And yet, the fact remains that a biography has remained elusive and Fergus Whelan is to be congratulated for being the first to write one.

William Drennan was born in 1770, a 'son of the manse': his father, Thomas, was the 'New light' minister in the First Presbyterian Church, Rosemary Lane, Belfast. 'New light' Presbyterians were intellectually curious, resistant to any attempt to stifle private judgement, committed to justice and lovers of freedom. Hence, they were early opponents of slavery, exponents of brotherhood and enemies of the endemic sectarianism of Irish society at the time. The intellectual/theological milieu into which Drennan was born and reared was to shape his life and work thereafter. As was the norm for Irish Presbyterians – Trinity

College Dublin was closed to them – Drennan travelled to university in Glasgow and then on to Edinburgh where he completed his medical studies. He was a lying-in doctor, or 'man midwife', as he put it, in Belfast, then Newry and Dublin, before his return to Belfast in 1807. However, his career was not all that lucrative, and financial worries would remain a constant with him until relatively late in life.

The late eighteenth century was a period of political and revolutionary ferment in Ireland and in the wider Atlantic world and Drennan was quickly caught up in the excitement. He was avowedly on the side of the American colonists in their struggle against the mother country and he was an enthusiastic member of the Volunteers, seeing in that movement the perfect engine for far-reaching reform in Ireland. His crushing disappointment at the failure of parliamentary reform in Ireland in the 1780s was alleviated by news of exciting events in France in the early 1790s – nothing less than the fall of the French monarchy, the death of Louis XVI and the declaration of a republic. Drennan, like many young men, was caught up in the general excitement and sought to use the stirring events in France to stimulate radical reform in Ireland. From early in 1791 he was advocating the formation of a new type of political society in Ireland – one that would promote brotherhood between Catholics and Protestants, combat sectarianism, and seek parliamentary reform. He has a strong claim to be the 'stable, unseen power' behind the foundation of the Society of United Irishmen in Belfast in October 1791.

Drennan was an enthusiastic member of the Dublin Society of United Irishmen, set up a month later, writing frequently for it and being author of the 'test', or pledge, which all joining had to take. Propagating the cause of the United Irishmen brought him to the attention of the authorities, who from the beginning had regarded the entire reform project of the United Irishmen as simply a cloak for revolutionary change, up to and including separation from Britain and the establishment of an Irish republic. Accused of seditious libel through his writings, Drennan was duly tried but was acquitted. He was lucky: fellow radicals such as Maurice Margarot, were sentenced in Edinburgh to fourteen years transportation to New South Wales for similar alleged offences. Thereafter Drennan appears to have withdrawn from the more militant wing of the United Irishmen: he played no role in the coming rebellion of 1798 and, unlike many of his friends, was not arrested nor sent into exile (nor executed). He opposed Union in 1800 but was soon reconciled to its passing and even saw advantages in a close British link, especially with English reformers.

As Whelan makes clear, his commitment to reform never slackened and he remained a prominent advocate for Catholic emancipation, a supporter of Daniel O'Connell and the anti-slavery cause, all the while using the *Belfast Monthly Magazine* (1808-14) to promote enlightened ideas. Occasionally we catch a glimpse of him: Colonel A. D. Kelly, *aide de camp* to the Duke of Sussex on a tour of the north of Ireland in 1814 met 'Dr Drenning' and others who endeavoured to persuade him of 'the evils which flow from the Orange societies'. His main achievement in these latter years was, in the teeth of opposition, the foundation of the Belfast Academical Institution in 1814. Drennan was a firm believer in the power of education to bring about societal change and the school's motto *Quaerere Verum* (to seek the truth) perfectly sums up his philosophy.

Whelan writes well about these issues and he makes good use of the available documentation. He is, however, over-anxious to scotch all claims that Drennan was simply a 'sunshine patriot' (as Thomas Paine had it) and 'an anti-Catholic bigot' to boot. In this latter regard, Whelan's determination to 'proceed to examine the case against Drennan and assess whether he is guilty as charged' (p. 50) of having 'an obsessive dislike and mistrust of Catholics' (p.x) is surely a mistake. Drennan wanted parliamentary reform and he knew that without Catholic support campaign for it would go nowhere. The Catholics knew this too: but they also knew that the British government was in a position to deliver Catholic relief while the Protestant parliament in College Green was not. Hence there was a good deal of juggling, of allegations of sharp practice, and of politicking between the Catholics and the Presbyterians.

'The Catholics have two strings to their bow' wrote an exasperated Drennan in 1793: one to treat with Irish Presbyterians and the other to treat with the British. Given the history of Ireland since 1600 it could not have been otherwise. Drennan believed that the Catholic capacity for liberty or independent thought was at that time severely limited and he was convinced that only education would bring them to a higher level. Some Catholics also had their doubts about Catholic capacity for liberty, and some had doubts about Presbyterian sincerity in seeking an alliance. Drennan could certainly be cutting in his comments on Catholics – he hated his time in Newry, finding nothing there but 'pigs and papists': but there was no consensus among historians that he was an anti-Catholic bigot.

More seriously, Whelan casts Drennan as a republican separatist from the early 1790s. This is entirely misleading. The crucial document here – Drennan's letter to his brother in law, Sam McTier of 21 May 1791 – is perfunctorily examined by Whelan. In this letter, Drennan calls for a new society to promote reform – 'a benevolent conspiracy - a plot for the people' whose specific end would be the 'rights of man and the greatest happiness of the greatest number', with as its general object 'real independence for Ireland and republicanism its particular purpose'. This does not make Drennan 'a full-blooded revolutionary and Irish separatist' (p.61). Drennan's understanding of 'republicanism' was essentially civic humanism, promoting the betterment of mankind through moral improvement, social reform and above all, education. In this crucial respect, Drennan parted company with Theobald Wolfe Tone whose understanding of republicanism was rooted in the belief that only through separation from Britain could republicanism flourish in Ireland.

In any case, Drennan's formula for achieving his lofty objectives – declaration, publication, communication – would have elicited a scornful 'good luck with that' from Lord Edward FitzGerald, Thomas Russell, Tone and John and Henry Sheares all of whom desired a French invasion force to bring about the desired ends (and all of whom perished in the ensuing struggle). Drennan even sought to reassure his brother in law and, through him, his sister Matty that they were not to imagine 'that I shall neglect my profession or injure my character by keeping bad company'. If Drennan were a 'full-blooded revolutionary', as Whelan claims, then he would surely have given up the day job and actively sought 'bad company'. Drennan was committed to the cause of reform for most of his life, and he never abandoned his former colleagues – he offered, at some risk to himself and to his profession, to appear as a character witness for Arthur O'Connor at his trial in Maidstone, Kent, in 1798, and he was active in promoting the *Press*, successor paper to the ill-fated *Northern Star*; but he was also prudent: better a live reformer than a dead revolutionary.

Mention of Drennan's sister Martha serves to remind us of her important role in Drennan's life; she was eleven years his senior and a valued confidante and advisor throughout his career. She was also in favour of radical reform but, like her brother, drew the line at insurrection. She may have written for the United Irish paper, *The Northern Star*. She was very perceptive: she 'smoked' (=suspected) Leonard MacNally for a government spy from the outset, while brother William carelessly sponsored MacNally's rise in the United Irishmen. Another extraordinary woman in late eighteenth-century Belfast was Mary Ann McCracken (1770–1866), the subject of Mary McNeill's freshly re-issued biography, with a new introduction by Belfast-born Professor Marianne Elliott. As Elliott remarks, the biography of McCracken was 'written by one remarkable Belfast woman about another', for Mary McNeill pursued a notable career as a social reformer in education and the treatment of the poor in twentieth-century Belfast.

McNeill's subject, Mary Ann McCracken, was the brother of the insurgent leader Henry Joy McCracken (executed in 1798) and, as well as rearing her brother's illegitimate offspring, Maria, she devoted her life to improving the lot of the poor in Belfast through her work for the Belfast Charitable Society, Ladies Industrial School, Ladies Clothing Society and much else besides. She also in later life co-operated with the historian R. R. Madden as he sought to assemble material relating to the revolutionary era in Belfast. What we know of her brother Henry Joy McCracken is based largely on Mary Ann's communications to Madden. She also furnished him with material on Thomas Russell (executed 1803) and with whom she may well have been in love. Fifty years after Russell's death, Mary Ann recalled he 'was a model of manly beauty … [whose] mouth was the most beautiful, particularly when he smiled, I ever saw'. McNeill made excellent use of this material, reprinting many letters of Mary Ann *in extenso*. This re-issue of McNeill's biography of Mary Ann McCracken marks the 250th anniversary of her birth.

Ireland's Forgotten WW2 Servicemen and Women

ROBSON DAVISON

DAN HARVEY
A Bloody Dawn: The Irish at D-Day
Merrion Press, 2019
pp 210   ISBN 978-0-178537-241-4   pb   €16.95

A Bloody Week: The Irish at Arnhem
Merrion Press, 2019
pp 152   ISBN 978-0-178537-273-5   pb   €16.95

A Bloody Victory: The Irish at War's End: Europe 1945
Merrion Press, 2020
pp 152   ISBN 978-0-178537-333-6   pb   €16.95

The relationship between the United Kingdom and Ireland during the Second World War was often strained. Historians have in recent times been closely considering this complex relationship, particularly following increased accessibility to relevant archives from the 1970s and 1980s. In the three books under review Dan Harvey, a retired Irish Army officer, tells the stories of Irish participants on D-Day, at Arnhem and in the final stages of the war in Europe. He explains in the final book, 'These Irish men and women deserve our grateful appreciation and to be rightfully honoured – not written out of Irish history … Instead they ought to be put centre stage' (*Bloody Victory*, p. xiii). He is describing those from neutral Ireland. If they wished to fight Nazism they were faced with a difficult choice as a consequence of that neutrality. At the end of the war most service personnel from Northern Ireland returned home to a welcome from their families, friends and neighbours. It was a more difficult experience in the rest of Ireland.

On the outbreak of the Second World War Ireland declared itself neutral, the only Dominion to do so. Neutrality had strong support in Ireland, including all the parties in the Dail. While Ireland's neutrality caused considerable unease in London, Foreign Secretary Eden was assured by Joseph Walshe, the administrative head of the Department of External Affairs, that De Valera, 'wished to be as friendly to the British Government as he could and to go as far as he could to assist Great Britain while maintaining the essentials of neutrality'. This did not, however, include making available to the Royal Navy the Treaty ports of Queenstown, Berehaven and Lough Swilly, given up in the Anglo-Irish Treaty of the previous year.

Historians have focused on various aspects of Ireland's neutrality. There is a broad consensus on why it was adopted. Fisk, for example, suggested, 'it was intimately bound up with freedom from British rule'. For O'Halpin, it 'became the proof and justification of Ireland's title to independent statehood' though it was initially the product of 'sheer pragmatism, national self-interest and the enduring nationalist grievance over partition'. There is a broad consensus on how it was operated. On the formal level, the diplomatic niceties were observed. On a practical level, historians have identified the covert assistance given to the Allies, including the right for RAF aircraft based in County Fermanagh to over-fly County Donegal, the provision of meteorological information and navigational facilities, and the close co-operation in the field of intelligence which continued throughout the war. Many of these concessions were linked to British and, later, American pressure. Neutrality was projected as dogma; in practice, it was complex, and sometimes ambivalent.

An important critique of neutrality is that it represented a moral indifference to the great issues of the war, democracy versus dictatorship, the rights of small nations, the existence of the death camps etc. De Valera's formal visit to Hempel, the German Minister in Dublin, in May 1945 came, for example, after the Allies had made known the horrors of Bergen-Belsen. Most historians agree that neutrality had a negative effect on hopes of ending partition. In June 1940, British proposals on partition foundered mainly because De Valera and his senior colleagues saw a British defeat as almost inevitable. From 1941, air and sea bases in Northern Ireland began to play a vital role in the Battle of the Atlantic, winning support in London for partition, mainly for strategic reasons. This continued after the war.

Despite some practical co-operation between the United Kingdom and Ireland there were still tensions. A police raid in Dublin in May 1940, for example, uncovered evidence of IRA/German links (including plans for a joint attack on Northern Ireland) and of the presence in Ireland of a German spy. A very strong Irish Government response, assisted by intelligence co-operation with London, meant that, after 1942, the IRA no longer posed a significant threat. Churchill was increasingly irritated by Irish neutrality. In early 1941, 'silent' economic sanctions were introduced. British forces in Northern Ireland were increased and, in the spring of 1942, were joined by American troops. In late 1943 and early 1944, the pressure on Dublin came largely from the Americans concerned about leakage of the D-Day invasion plans through the German Legation. However, despite all this, De Valera stuck to neutrality with continued public support. By this stage of the war British demands for access to the former Treaty ports were forgotten with the increasing importance of Northern Ireland's naval and air bases.

Churchill's 13 May 1945 speech made his frustrations clear: 'had it not been for the loyalty and friendship of Northern Ireland we should have been forced to come to close quarters with Mr. De Valera or perish from the earth'. He added, 'we left the De Valera Government to frolic with the Germans and later with the Japanese representatives to their hearts content'. De Valera responded that, if Ireland had accepted Churchill's position on Irish neutrality it would mean, 'Britain's necessity would become a moral code and … other people's rights were not to count'. The exchange illustrated the depth of feeling on both sides.

It helped to sustain the continuing anti-British sentiment in Ireland at the end of the war, including demonstrations in Dublin and Cork in May 1945. The history of the British-Irish relationship, neutrality, the wartime economic hardships and the lack of public knowledge about the wartime relationship with the British contributed to an atmosphere for Irish personnel who returned to Ireland after service in the British forces. A consideration of this issue first emerged in the 1980s and 1990s with Richard Doherty, Myles Dungan, Kevin Myers and others. The Volunteer Project at NUI, Cork in the late 1990s, for example, gathered evidence from over 50 of the surviving veterans. The work of Doherty, McEwen, O'Connor and others suggests that some 70,000 volunteers from Ireland joined the British forces (compared to some 50,000 from Northern Ireland).

Research has adduced a complex mixture of factors among the volunteers such as a family tradition of service in the British forces, the prospect of excitement and adventure, the possibility of better paid employment, peer pressure (particularly in the Protestant community) and, for some, the moral case for fighting against Nazism. While avoiding any acknowledgement of the volunteers in the British forces, the Irish Government did little to stop them leaving. Most made their way across the border to join up in Northern Ireland. In the case of Irish workers leaving to work in the war industries in Britain the Irish authorities co-operated closely with the British Government to regulate the system. It is not known precisely how many service personnel returned to Ireland at the end of the war. However, most received a cool reception on their return. It was similar in some ways to the return of volunteers at the end of the First World War though not in as extreme a form: some 120 ex-servicemen were killed between 1919 and 1923.

In 1945, among those returning were deserters from the Irish forces; they received the full attention of the state. Those service personnel demobbed at the end of the war from the Irish forces received, 'a wide array of financial and employment related concessions', including preferential treatment for jobs, especially in State-owned bodies. Deserters, however, were dealt with through the Emergency Powers Order 362, introduced in August 1945 by De Valera. Immediately, 4,634 men were expelled from the Irish forces with a further 149 in March 1946. They were stripped of their pensions and allowances but, in addition, they were excluded from all Government paid jobs for seven years. They were treated more harshly than personnel dealt with by the military authorities. Fine Gael attempted unsuccessfully to annul the Order in the Dáil 18 October 1945. T. F. O'Higgins described it as an

Order 'stimulated by malice, seething with hatred, oozing with venom'. Brian Girvin has called the action, 'vindictiveness'. Bernard Kelly suggests, however, that, 'Pragmatism, not spite or vindictiveness, informed his (De Valera's) decision'.

In April 1995, the then Taoiseach, John Bruton, paid tribute to the Irish volunteers in the wartime Allied armed forces. Fifty years after the war's end it was the first sign of a changing attitude. In 2001, a campaign began to seek pardons for those who had been affected by the Emergency Order. The campaign was ultimately successful and the Second World War Amnesty and Immunity Bill passed through the Irish parliament on 14 May 2013. The then Minister of Defence, Alan Shatter, assured those involved, and their relatives, that the State fully acknowledged their contribution to the fight against tyranny. This is the key theme of the three books under review.

Dan Harvey has taken on a difficult task in this series of books on the Second World War, attempting to provide an outline of the major events while also integrating the stories of individual Irish men and women. They are drawn from all three services and include occasional Irish-American examples. He has in my view managed this task successfully. There is a consistent emphasis on the lack of recognition for those returning to neutral Ireland. Their stories were never told, their accomplishments were never recognised nor commemorated. They kept their heads down. In Northern Ireland, it was different since it was a belligerent in the war.

The book on D-Day is of reasonable length; the other two books are rather shorter. The author consistently adopts a chronological approach. The books have helpful maps, glossaries, chronologies and bibliographies. Unusually, each book contains a short final chapter on how the events have been captured on film, including by some famous Irish-American directors. Reading the three books together, there is some repetition. The final book, for example, deliberately reprises the events of D-Day and Operation Market Garden, since its readers may not know about prior events. Some characters appear to have a considerable fascination for the author. Otto Skorzeny, a colourful Austrian SS officer who famously rescued Mussolini in 1943, and Kay Summersby, Eisenhower's Irish driver and possible paramour, appear in all three books. A weakness, from a purely historical perspective, is the lack of footnotes; it would be of value if some of the stated facts could be sourced. There are some infelicities in punctuation and the author has something of a predilection for lengthy sentences. However, the author's experience as a former soldier enlivens the stories of the various actions involved and captures, in particular, the excitement and fear of battle. It also brings substance to his descriptions of Allied and German strategy and tactics.

The book on D-Day has a good shape and structure. It is difficult, however, to justify the 18 pages of appendices which provide general information about the war. The author begins with the dilemma faced by the Germans over the appropriate strategy to deal with the Allied landing. While Rommel wished to strike early and seriously contest the landings with tanks, many others, including Hitler, believed that the landing in Normandy might be a feint. This could draw German forces away from the likely main invasion point, considered to be in the Pas-de-Calais. The main Panzer force was held back and only one Panzer division was in action on the day. This was a major strategic mistake. There is a coherent explanation of Allied planning and of how it changed leading up to the invasion. There is a good description of the successful plans for deception and of the importance of Enigma. Interestingly, the timing of the invasion relied heavily on the weather reports from Blacksod Point lighthouse in County Mayo, in neutral Ireland. Reading this part of the book one understands the level of planning that was required and what was at stake on D-Day.

The main part of the book focuses on the landings on the five beaches and the airborne attacks. The author does not flinch from describing the chaos and the failures, as well as the successes. He describes D-Day as, 'a bloody and terrifying battle'. He contrasts the good fortune of the Americans on Utah Beach with the ferocious fighting and bloodbath at Omaha Beach, where the GIs were caught frontally and in enfilade. The descriptions of the landing on Omaha are particularly vivid. The British and Canadian forces had similar mixed fortunes though nothing on the scale of Omaha. At Sword Beach, with the help of the specialised armoured vehicles of the 79th Armoured Division, known as 'funnies', the British made good progress and linked up with the airborne forces at Pegasus Bridge. It was a similar story on Gold Beach where steady progress was made. At Juno Beach, however, the Canadians had to deal with rough seas, a high tide and heavy German resistance and took severe casualties. Overall, the invasion did not achieve all its first day objectives but, after intense fighting, the Allies had a foothold from which to launch the battle for the bridgehead. A defeat on the beaches would have been catastrophic.

The author weaves successfully into the account of the landings the actions of various Irish personnel. One such is Captain Redmond Cunningham, a native of County Waterford, on Sword Beach. The author includes a copy of Cunningham's report on the actions of his Assault Engineer Troop, clearing a way for the disembarking infantry. He was decorated with a Military Cross for his courage. The author picks up on his theme that the Irish men and women involved were fighting for freedom from tyranny and deserve respect. He identifies the number of Irishmen killed in the various theatres of war. This illustrates that the sacrifice of Irishmen, from North and South, was broadly comparable but the detail, across regiments and corps, does not add much to the story of D-Day.

This is a good general account of the planning for D-Day and the epic struggles on the five beaches and in the airborne landing and drop zones. It identifies the many problems and the solutions found and captures the sense of fear and dread that must have affected most of the combatants. It shows how ordinary men and women can rise above that and do extraordinary things. This is all set out in a readable style.

The book on the battle at Arnhem begins with its origins and deals with the fighting on a daily basis. Dan Harvey calls the Operation Market Garden plan 'imaginative, daring and simple'. 'Market' referred to the landings by three airborne divisions to capture a series of bridges and clear the way for the advance of some 65 miles, by Horrocks's 30th Corps ('Garden'). It was to progress up a single road to Arnhem, the furthest bridge. The strategic objective was to win a crossing over the Rhine to open the way for an Allied attack into Germany. It was the brain-child of Montgomery and approved by Eisenhower at a time when the strains between the Western Allies, especially over resources, were beginning to cause difficulties.

The author follows the views of many historians about the reasons for its failure. These include poor planning (the planners had only seven days to prepare for such a complex operation), the single road for 30th

Corps' armoured advance, the serious failures of intelligence (the strength and resilience of the German forces was seriously miscalculated), the need for three airlifts and the lack of air support for the ground troops for much of the battle. Despite these, he suggests that the operation 'almost succeeded'. This is difficult to sustain, given that the strategic objective was not attained, that 1st Airborne Division was almost destroyed, and that the Dutch population was left to suffer severely under German occupation for most of the rest of the war.

The core of the book is the day by day account of the battle at Arnhem and the attempts of the American airborne troops and 30th Corps to link up with the 1st Airborne Division. It uses well the stories of individual Irish soldiers and airmen to personalise the course of the battle. The numerical account of Southern and Northern Irish killed in action is repeated. The author's military knowledge is again helpful for the reader. He describes graphically what he calls 'a disastrous nine day error-stricken engagement' at Arnhem, which resulted in some 1,500 soldiers killed in action and 6,500 prisoners of war, many wounded. He catalogues further errors including the break-down in radio communications and the decision of Major-General Urqhuart, the Divisional commander, to leave his command post and remain out of touch for the crucial early days of the battle. He is critical also of the placing of the drop zones and landing zones so far from the city. In his book 'Arnhem', Antony Beevor quotes 4 Para Brigade's commander Brigadier Shan Hackett's later judgment, 'Everything that could go wrong did go wrong'.

The author tells vividly the story of Lt Col. Frost's seizure of the north end of the bridge at Arnhem and the heroic attempt to hold it against tank and artillery bombardment. He describes very well the chaos and horror of the battle for the perimeter and the significant success of the evacuation across the river of over 2,000 troops, on the night of 25/26 September. It is a powerful story of courage and comradeship. Fighting off successive German attacks with tanks and artillery support for nine days required supreme valour from the men of the 1st Airborne Division, including their Irish soldiers.

This is a good, short account of the Arnhem battle for the general reader. Dan Harvey captures the sense of a glorious failure. The book makes clear the mistakes and failures which led to defeat but the more senior players perhaps deserve more significant censure. Montgomery blamed the weather and insufficient resources; Horrocks blamed Urquhart. Browning blamed the Polish Brigade commander Sosabowski. Urquhart interestingly stayed out of the blame game. As well as the British and Polish airborne troops it was the ordinary Dutch population who paid the price for what Dan Harvey calls, 'a desperately risky undertaking'.

The third book is, of necessity, more diffuse than the others. Instead of dealing with a single day or a single battle, the author covers the period from the autumn of 1944 to the end of the war. Those who have read the first two books will find it irksome to read again brief outlines of D-Day and of Operation Market Garden. These take up around one-fifth of the main text. After Market Garden, the author chooses to cover briefly the Battle of the Bulge, Hitler's last strategic push of the war in the West. It caught the Allies by surprise, made an advance of some 50 miles but was eventually stopped before the River Meuse. The stirring account of the crossings over the Rhine, in March 1945, illustrates the sharp contrast between Montgomery's set piece battle at Wesel and the more fluid American crossings at Remagen, where they found a bridge which could be crossed, and at Oppenheim. The author provides the reader with a concise outline of Allied strategy. He explains Eisenhower's decision after the Rhine crossing to maintain a broad front approach rather than striking for Berlin, as Churchill would have hoped. The Russians eventually took Berlin in fighting described by Dan Harvey as 'brutal and bloody'.

In the broad account, there are not so many opportunities to describe the actions of individual Irishmen but we still learn of Captain Cunningham winning a bar to his Military Cross at the Scheldt. We learn, too, of the O'Donovan brothers from Drumcondra, north Dublin. Fred became an Inquiry Officer with the RAF, attempting to account for individual lost aircrew, including those murdered after escaping from Sagan POW camp in the 'Great Escape'. His brother, Sean, was a serial escapee who, towards the end of the war, fought on horseback with the Cossacks, north-west of Berlin. The author writes about the liberation of the camps in April 1945, including Buchenwald and Bergen-Belsen. He describes also the camp at Friesach where the

Abwehr, helped by the IRA, tried, with little success, to recruit soldiers to operate in Ireland. Almost inevitably, we hear again of Otto Skorzeny and the two Irishmen, Brady and Stringer, who fought with him.

There is a very powerful story at the heart of the three books of Irishmen, from the neutral part of Ireland, who contributed to the defeat of Nazism in Europe but, on their return, received no thanks for their often valiant efforts. In the Acknowledgements, Dan Harvey suggests that he wrote the books 'to make people aware that those Irish men and women who participated in the war were part of a broad, outward-looking, nationalistic narrative, acting for Ireland and standing shoulder to shoulder with the Allies'. This, of course, contrasted with the great majority in the neutral part of Ireland, who continued to support neutrality throughout the war. In Chapter 9, he deals with the treatment of the nearly 5,000 men from the Irish Defence Forces who 'deserted' to join the war. As noted earlier, on their return to Ireland they were summarily dismissed and were disqualified from holding public jobs for seven years. This 'wrong' stood for 68 years until the Dáil passed the law, in 2013, which gave them an amnesty.

Irish nationalism and inclusivity:
a key centenary issue

RICHARD McMINN

CONOR MORRISSEY
Protestant Nationalists in Ireland, 1900–1923
Cambridge University Press, 2019
pp 264   ISBN 978-1-108-47386-6   hb   £75

DONAL McANALLEN
Forgotten Gaelic Volunteers:
Ulster GAA Members Who Fought in World War One
Ó Fiaich Library, Armagh, 2019
pp x, 94   no ISBN   pb   €11

COLUM KENNY
The Enigma of Arthur Griffith:
'Father of Us All'
Merrion Press, 2020
pp 324   ISBN 978-1-785-37314-5   pb   €19.95

PÁDRAIG Ó CAOIMH
Richard Mulcahy:
From the Politics of War to the Politics of Peace, 1913–1924
Irish Academic Press, 2019
pp 352   ISBN 978-1-788-55098-7   hb   €24.95/£22.99

The distinguished literary critic, Edna Longley, in whose tutorials in Queen's University on the Victorian novel I briefly sat in the 1960s, observed in the 1990s that 'Commemorations are as selective as sympathies. They honour our dead, not your dead'. Indeed, as Diarmaid Ferriter has rightly warned us more recently, 'Northern Ireland … will face its commemoration battles soon as the centenary of the foundation of that state looms' (*Irish Times,* 18 January 2020).

After a relatively smooth and uncontroversial series of commemorations to mark the so-called decade of centenaries, the Irish government struck an unanticipated iceberg with the then Minister of Justice Charlie Flanagan's somewhat poorly timed and poorly explained proposal to commemorate, at Dublin Castle on 17 January 2020 the service of members of the Royal Irish Constabulary and the Dublin Metropolitan Police. The timing was curious (the centenaries of their respective disbandments might have been more appropriate, rather than the centenary of the middle of the War of Independence and also of the recruitment of the first Black and Tans) and the fact that their toll of 555 killed during the years of conflict included both members of the Black and Tans and the Auxiliaries, appeared to have not been noticed by the organisers. Indeed, this was also true of the very obvious point that both the 'Tans' and the 'Auxies' were officially elements of the RIC, even if, as Diarmaid Ferriter has pointed out, 'many in the RIC strongly resented the coming of the Black and Tans, whom they regarded as morally and professionally reprehensible' (*Irish Times,* 4 January 2020). David Leeson's authoritative *The Black and Tans* (2011) nonetheless demonstrates that, contrary to popular folklore, 19 per cent of the new recruits, most of whom were ex-servicemen, were in fact Irish.

However, these are the subtleties of history, and the political row at the beginning of 2020 over the proposed Dublin Castle event was such that Minister Flanagan was forced to postpone it. Other historical and political commentators were then drawn into the media firestorm with Fintan O'Toole, for example, arguing that there still would appear to be a 'hierarchy of victims' when it comes to the War of Independence and asking *Irish Times* readers: 'why do we fear the ghosts of dead policemen?' Equally, Fergal Keane, who has family ghosts on both sides of the conflict, warned that the 'RIC row threatens to drag us into a dangerous place' and stressed that while there were legitimate questions about how the postponed ceremony was 'imagined, discussed and organised, these should not blind us to the powerful truth – the majority of RIC men and their IRA opponents were born and grew up to love the same land'. 'They fought for different visions of Ireland but acknowledging the love they shared would be a good place to start'. Dr Éamon Phoenix (a member of Expert Advisory Group) warned that 'the RIC commemoration shows the kind of problems that lie ahead' in 2021–23.

However, what is very clear from this episode is that the issue of Irish nationalism and inclusivity remains very much a live one, for historians as well as the general public. This is brought into sharp focus by Conor Morrissey's *Protestant Nationalists in Ireland, 1900–1923*. Given my own personal interest in, and research on, some of the lesser known Protestant Parnellites and Redmondites, I was particularly looking forward to reading this book, although somewhat dismayed by CUP's decision to put a price tag of £75 on a relatively slim hardback volume of 224 pages of text (including footnotes) and a 24 page bibliography and index. The volume is also bereft of any illustrations, apart from eight statistical tables and a Jack Yeats painting reproduced on the dust jacket. The phrase 'poor value for money' comes to mind.

However, the book itself disappoints in another sense. Rejecting the more inclusive approach of, for example, Patrick Maume and the late D. George Boyce, the author argues that a study of Protestant nationalists must choose between 'moderate and advanced nationalists' (p. 3). The former he dismisses as 'tepid in their convictions, tending to view home rule primarily as another liberal reform, which would ultimately strengthen the Empire'. Thus, Protestant Redmondites are largely ignored and the overwhelming concentration is on 'advanced nationalists' and on Sinn Féin and its antecedents from the Protestant perspective. This presumably explains why Morrissey did not consult a number of key sources, for example the J. B. Armour papers in PRONI. The dividing line between the two groups is not always fully maintained, for example there are occasional, if somewhat dismissive, references, notably in Chapters 2 and 3, to developments such as the rise of the Independent Orange Order in east Ulster and the Ballymoney Protestant anti-Ulster Covenant meeting of 1913. His reliance on a few secondary sources for these two episodes leads him to fail to place them in their proper background context and to overstress the role of the maverick IOO leader Lindsay Crawford, clearly an advanced nationalist who eventually emerged from the Orange closet, and rather simplistically to characterise the Ballymoney meeting of 1913 as a last gasp of the Ulster Liberal Association, given a 'new denominational guise'. Though one would still have to agree with Morrissey that 'those who attended the meeting were certainly home rulers, but they had little sympathy with the more advanced ambitions of its main organisers – 'the eccentric trio of [Roger] Casement, [Alice] Stopford Green and [Jack] White' (p. 115).

Given Morrissey's clearly stated intention at the outset to concentrate largely on 'advanced nationalists', one is led to wonder whether a more accurate title for this book would have been: 'Protestant Advanced Nationalists in Ireland, 1900–1923'? The Protestant Redmondite tradition is largely air-brushed out of the story, a not unfamiliar approach, which persists in some quarters to the present day.

However, having highlighted the limitations of the narrow definition adopted by the author of his topic, I would want to commend the thoroughness of his research and the new light which his combination of a traditional, qualitative biographical approach on and a largely novel, quantitative, prosopographical approach (no doubt influenced by his friend and mentor, the late Professor David Fitzpatrick, the ultimate pioneer in this field), sheds on these alleged 'rotten Protestants'. It is also the case that Morrissey's judgements are fair and balanced: this is particularly true of his exposure of the hostility experienced by Protestant nationalists from some other elements of the advanced nationalist community, who denounced 'synthetic Gaels', as well of course as from their own families and community. The increasing discomfiture they experienced as the advanced nationalist movement became increasingly associated after 1916 with the Roman Catholic church is fully explored, as well as the key role of the Irish Guild of the Church (unpopular with, and excluded by, the Church of Ireland hierarchy) and fascinatingly, the largely previously unnoticed phenomenon of Protestants serving in the new Irish National Army in 1922–23, where again the general ethos was a Roman Catholic one. (251 Protestants in November 1922 out of a total army strength of 33,210). It is intriguing to be reminded that Michael Collins during his early days in London was given, at meetings of the Irish Literary Society, to greet the distinguished writer Robert Lynd with the question: 'And how is the non-conformist conscience today?' Collins was equally flippant with Sam Maguire, the Cork-born Anglican at GAA meetings in London, invariably addressing him as: 'You bloody South of Ireland Protestant'.

Morrissey in his introductory chapter tries to identify the original source of Protestant nationalism and to place it in the wider context of nationalism elsewhere in Europe, where there is a lively debate around the formative role of religion and early or recurrent history (the perennialist approach) versus the view that nationalism is a recent construction deliberately created by social elites to achieve political and economic ends (the modernist approach). Morrissey comes down wholeheartedly on the late eighteenth century as the key moment of 'crystallisation', citing the United Irishmen alongside the Patriots and Volunteers as being responsible for the creation of a Protestant nationalist tradition in Ireland. As to the place of Protestant nationalism in a wider European tradition, having reviewed some possible European parallels, he concludes that 'Protestant nationalism is better understood as a minority response to the history of Irish Protestantism and the growth of Catholic democracy, rather than an expression of a pan-European phenomenon'. Morrissey argues that over-reliance on a biographical approach in the past may have skewed scholarly understanding of the nature of Protestant nationalism in Ireland. More concentration on the networks and associations which it generated is, he argues, the way forward. His new methodology highlights, he believes, that while these individuals may have been politically marginalised in their own religious community, they were able to form 'recognisable networks' and develop 'a distinctive associational culture'. Some 500 Protestant nationalists in total are surveyed in the book (p. 99). Morrissey's dramatic opening description of Protestant female anti-conscription protestors on 9 June 1918 being forced to hold a prayer service kneeling in the rain outside the doors of Christchurch Cathedral, Dublin, which had been closed against them, provides a powerful mental image for his main arguments.

A broadly chronological approach is taken, with a series of terse and punchy chapter headings deployed. In his introductory chapter, the author himself provides readers with quite a comprehensive outline summary of the content which follows in subsequent chapters: What a pity then, given the importance of its subject, the quality of Conor Morrissey's research and the extremely clear presentation of his arguments that his book omits discussion of the Protestant Redmondite nationalist tradition. Nonetheless, this is a significant contribution to the historiography of Protestant nationalism in Ireland. But buy it in paperback!

Another recent publication which highlights the issues of Irish nationalism and inclusivity and the associated historical 'amnesia' concerning the Redmondite/Home Rule strand of the movement is Dónal McAnallen's *Forgotten Gaelic Volunteers* (2019). This 'booklet', as the author modestly describes it at one point in the text, in fact runs to almost one hundred pages and thanks to his painstaking and thorough archival research, especially in a variety of newspaper sources, exposes the hidden, and perhaps for some conveniently forgotten, history of the Ulster GAA members who fought in World War One.

Tantalising hints of this historical reality had emerged previously, notably in Stephen Walker's excellent 2015 account of 'Irish sporting heroes who fell in the Great War', entitled *Ireland's Call*, which I reviewed in *Familia* (No. 31, 2015). With the support of the Cardinal Ó Fiaich Library and Archive and the National Lottery Heritage Fund, McAnallen has now been able to publish the full results of his rigorous research efforts, which in the case of this aspect of GAA history stemmed from his coming upon by chance in 2005 the announcement of Manning's death at the Front in 1918 in an edition of *Ireland's Saturday Night*, the now defunct weekly sporting newspaper, while researching in Belfast's Newspaper Library section of the Central Library. This serendipitous moment was then followed by the discovery of other lost nuggets in that newspaper's microfilm files and with the assistance of a wide variety of other sources, as one would expect from a National Museums of Northern Ireland staff member, he has been able to paint a very comprehensive picture of the scale of Ulster GAA involvement in the First World War.

The core element of the publication is a series of 56 individual biographical profiles of varying length of Ulster GAA players who served in the British forces during the 1914–1918 period – clearly, a vital family history tool. A further 13 individuals are listed where there is insufficient detail to provide full profiles. In some cases photographs have been unearthed and are duly reproduced (pp 32–60). Research on the other three Irish provinces and also of enlistment of British GAA players is still ongoing by McAnallen and others, but a provisional report in the form of a reprinted database is provided as a nine page postscript (pp 86–94).

One of the interesting features of the publication is the introductory Preface (pp v–viii), which outlines the author's trials and tribulations (including a small amount of hostile social media comment directed towards him personally) as he tirelessly completed his research, attempted to overturn the widely accepted notion, especially within the organisation, that the GAA in the early twentieth century was 'a homogeneous phalanx of advanced nationalism'. McAnallen acknowledges that 'this would be difficult territory for many northern nationalists to navigate'. As he somewhat ruefully speculates: 'Perhaps the First World War will ever be a taboo topic for some sections of Irish nationalism'.

The central section of individual personal biographical profiles, noted above, is set within four useful contextual chapters, analysing both the relationship between the war and the GAA in Ulster and the key issues of who the Gaelic volunteers were and why they may have enlisted. The situation confronting those who survived and returned is explored and the key question of 'Why were they forgotten?' is courageously and honestly confronted. The disturbing and sad case history of the fates of the two sons of Downpatrick-born John McKay, the only Ulsterman involved in founding the GAA, and appointed its first secretary in 1884, provides a sombre coda to the book. Paul and Patrick Joseph enlisted in the Crown forces during the First World War and although both survived, their lives ended ultimately in tragedy, a suicide pact with his wife in 1949 in Paul's case and drug addiction and brief imprisonment, followed by an early death (1929) in the case of Patrick Joseph.

In his four contextual chapters, McAnallen does indeed fulfil his claim that his research revealing the 'forgotten Gaelic volunteers' has 'turned much received wisdom on its head'. Some examples include the revelation that 'it became the tacit policy of the GAA in Ulster and indeed nationwide, that the ban on British soldiers from membership would not be strictly enforced for the duration of the conflict in Europe'. The GAA, unlike other sporting organisations that suspended competitions, 'pressed on with its full programme of activities' but was mostly careful 'not to raise any political controversy at this time'. While given the patchy nature of the sources, it is impossible to quantify precisely how many GAA members enlisted, McAnallen points out (p. 11) that 'during Easter 1916 there were more sometime GAA players from Ulster in British regiments on the continent than engaged in insurrection at home'.

McAnallen calculates that 'at least 42 erstwhile GAA members were killed in the war, 20 of them from Ulster', while 28 have been verified as returning home safely. Since he also estimates that a total of at least 150 First World War soldiers were sometime GAA club or county players or officials and of these 70 were Ulstermen, it would follow that possibly another 22 veterans from Ulster would have survived. Sergeant William Manning, the 27-year-old inter-county star, killed with the Royal Dublin Fusiliers during the German Spring Offensive of April 1918, was the most high profile Gaelic sportsman from Ulster to die in the war, although by 1918 coverage of this tragic loss was played down in the nationalist press, dominated by the threat of conscription in Ireland. But even as late as April 1918, while recruitment in Ireland generally had slowed to a trickle, a few GAA recruits were still coming forward. A case in point was the decision of Patrick Holland and John Anthony Mooney of Dungannon to join the newly-created RAF, no doubt attracted by the possibility of learning to fly. Given the limitations of the available evidence, McAnallen concludes (p. 21) that 'the most that can be said with confidence is that the total [GAA recruitment] from Ulster extended well into three figures, and from all sections of the association together, probably stretched close to one thousand, if not higher'. He is also at pains to debunk the popular notion that all or most of the Ulster Catholic recruits joined the Connaught Rangers. He believes no more than 20 per cent did so, the rest joined a wide range of regiments, although only a small proportion appear to have gained any promotion, for a range of reasons which the author fully explores (p. 24).

McAnallen's concluding two chapters of analysis make a further significant contribution to his declared objective of turning 'much received wisdom on its head'. He broadly endorses the accepted notion of a 'strained relationship between Irish nationalism and the legacy of the Great War' and that 'for many of the demobilised soldiers, there could be no return to the GAA' (for practical as well as political reasons). Indeed, 'the retention of the Association's ban on soldiers kept war veterans out too'. For some, their military service led on to cross-community involvement in other sports such as soccer. The foundation by returned military colleagues of former comrades sporting clubs such as Ballyclare Comrades FC (1919) – whose centenary history by Robson Davison makes for an interesting perspective – provided new alternative opportunities (See *The Comrades: The Story of the First Hundred Years of Ballyclare Comrades Football Club 1919–2019)*. However, McAnallen is also able to demonstrate that from April 1920 onwards, a number of former British soldiers were able to re-enter the GAA world and even play in significant matches, aided in some cases by subsequent IRA involvement, but not in all, and by the somewhat chaotic state of disarray of the GAA in Ulster. One striking example of the pragmatic reintegration process was Alexander Donnelly, a former Pioneer with the Royal Engineers, who was appointed to the paid post of caretaker of MacRory Park on Belfast's Whiterock Road, a strong nationalist district. Thomas Bradley, who fought at the Somme, became a star player for Monaghan at inter-county level. As McAnallen eloquently puts it: 'The passage of time forgets'.

As to the allegation of 'national amnesia' on the part of Irish nationalists regarding Irish involvement in the war, McAnallen believes that in many cases it was 'not wilful'. He identifies a range of factors at work, some personal such as the lack of direct descendants, as well as an act of forgetting at communal level in organisations such as the GAA, even if many families still privately held on to photographs, letters and medals. All of this significantly was happening in a political environment within Northern Ireland which was a cold house for nationalists. Some notable erstwhile Gaelic players from Ulster of course were to serve in the Second World War, although in lesser numbers than the First. The author cites a series of examples of the GAA's selective memory at work over the years, with Irish nationalist soldiers in the First World War coming to be viewed by some as 'misguided fools, "soup takers" and traitors' (p. 70). Certainly, it is true that in the immediate aftermath of the Great War, the spirit of amnesia did not immediately manifest itself. The 'On This Day' *Irish News* centenary column, so energetically curated by Dr Éamon Phoenix, the official historian of that newspaper, reminded me of this historical reality, when a description of the Messines Memorial Mass of 7 June, 1920, was recently reproduced. To mark the third anniversary of the battle of Messines and commemorate the involvement of the 16th Irish Division, the *Irish News* reported as follows on 8 June:

> The Irish National Veterans' Association in Belfast commemorated this historic event in fitting fashion. A Memorial Mass was celebrated in St. Malachy's Church ... preceded by an imposing parade of Catholic ex-servicemen. ... Especially impressive was the 'Dead March' rendered by the Hibernian Band in solemn strains, providing the accompaniment to the measured tramp of the men as they passed into the church ... Fr McKinley [the parish priest], who inspected the ranks, was accorded an ovation by the thousands of onlookers.

Dónal McAnallen concludes his analysis as follows: 'If this publication can contribute a little to levelling out the unevenness of historical memory in Ireland, it will not have been in vain'. This modestly produced volume (bereft of an ISBN but benefiting from an excellent selection of historic photographs and other illustrations) deserves the widest circulation. It represents a fitting follow-on from the pioneering 2005 volume, *World War One – Ireland and its Impacts,* through which the Ó Fiaich Memorial Library and Archive, in partnership with the Armagh Diocesan History Society, originally put the issue of the First World War and political inclusivity on to the local history agenda, especially within the nationalist community.

Conor Morrissey, in the volume reviewed earlier in this article, makes the claim that 'Arthur Griffith devoted much of his career to cultivating nationalist sentiments in Protestants, but he was selective: his preference was for middle-class and Ulster Protestants, rather than for more exotic English-born or upper-class variants'. Indeed, he reproduces a comment by the idiosyncratic Captain Jack White, from the recent White biography by Leo Keohane (which I reviewed in *Familia* No. 34, 2018): 'I always thought [Griffith] a very unpleasant little man, to me, he seemed to emanate the suspicion of the professional Gael towards the foreign or Protestant interloper in the "movement".' While there is some truth in the conventional wisdom that Griffith's tragic early death in 1922 and his role as chief negotiator of the controversial Anglo-Irish Treaty, not to mention his lack of the glamour of a Michael Collins or the black-clad austerity of an Éamon de Valera, has resulted in neglect and popular ignorance of his achievements, he has not been entirely ignored by historians. In the 1950s and early 1960s Seán Ó Lúing was the dominant biographical authority and in his Foreword to the 1974 analysis of Griffith's policies and philosophy by Dr Richard Davis, *Arthur Griffith and Non-Violent Sinn Féin*, Ó Lúing stressed that Griffith's Sinn Féin programme was 'the inclusive compound of all the Irish traditions, unionist and nationalist' and that 'official Ireland has been slow to do him honour … whether his actions be in dispute or not, he was great'. For Davis himself, as a Commonwealth historian, born of Irish parentage in India, it was the fact that Gandhi, in pursuing Indian independence, thought so highly of Griffith's pre-1914 commitment to non-violence and passive resistance that was significant. He concluded his 1970s book, written against the violent background of the early Troubles by arguing that 'in spite of all his weaknesses, Arthur Griffith had a positive and sympathetic approach to the problems of his aggressively unionist fellow-countrymen'. The difficulty of course is that Griffith's Dual Monarchy philosophy, as famously outlined in his 1904 Sinn Féin manifesto, *The Resurrection of Hungary: A Parallel for Ireland*, dubbed even by some contemporary fellow nationalists as the policy of 'the green Hungarian band', perished in the flames of the General Post Office in 1916. This was an episode where Griffith was very much on the margins, even geographically, in the safe Dublin suburbs. Thereafter, all Griffith had to offer Ulster unionists was the prospect of being forced into Irish unity through the Boundary Commission rendering a separate Ulster unviable.

Kenny's is by no means the only relatively recent full-scale biography. Brian Maye's *Arthur Griffith* (1997) has been followed by Owen McGee's *Arthur Griffith* (2015) which, like the competing Kenny volume, comes from the Merrion Press stable. McGee chides Maye for underplaying Griffith's economic self-sufficiency philosophy and sees 'Dan' (as Griffith was always known to his wife and family, presumably in homage to Daniel O'Connell) as very much a product of that intellectually fashionable concept of the 'long nineteenth century', i.e., 1789–1914. In reviewing McGee's volume, Brian Maye generously described it as 'a work of superb scholarship' (*Irish Times,* 12 March 2016), while 'not accepting any charge of underplaying the centrality of "economic nationalism" in Griffith's thought' in his own earlier 1997 biography – a charge McGee levelled not only against Maye but all other previous Griffith biographies. Indeed, Maye goes on to suggest that McGee could be accused of 'overplaying (to the exclusion of much else) economic factors'. However, McGee does highlight Griffith's support for non-denominational education and for the right of the working classes to university education, supported by a grant system. For McGee, Griffith, had he lived, would have pioneered the role of the state rather than the churches in areas such as housing, health and social services. Finally, as to the Treaty negotiations in October 1921, 'the inherent inequality in the negotiations led de Valera to give direct personal advice to Griffith that, unfortunately, he would have to assume the role of scapegoat, to a greater or lesser extent, and this was exactly what Griffith accepted', McGee concludes.

So given the existence of two relatively recent biographies of 'Dan', what, if any, justification is there for the publication of yet another similar volume? What new insights has Colum Kenny to offer his readers? Kenny assures us that 'this book is a critical assessment, not the hagiography of a saint. It will contextualise his occasionally problematic attitudes, not seek to excuse them'. … 'He was no perfect Marvel-comic hero. He was a small, limping, lower-middle-class politician with poor eyesight, an unglamourous wife [Mollie Sheehan, whom he married in 1910, following an earlier infatuation with the glamorous Maud Gonne], an aversion to dramatising violence and a tendency to sharp comment'… 'Yet his leadership inspired a generation'. For Kenny, Griffith is both 'an awkward father figure' and also something of a Hamlet – 'a Shakespearian character around whom violence exploded but who was slow to perpetrate it'. One of the strengths of Kenny's book is his exploration of the connections between Griffith and a range of artistic figures. The chapter 'Arthur Griffith and Joyce's *Ulysses*' in particular presents Griffith in a very different light, even if relationships with Yeats and O'Casey, once close, were rather more strained in later years.

Kenny's approach is to a degree thematic, although within a broadly chronological framework and does not hesitate to address controversial subjects such as the allegations of anti-semitism and racism sometimes levelled against Griffith by his critics. Kenny is particularly impressed by Griffith's work ethic as a journalist and his disdain for material success. 'The papers that he edited were for twenty years a wealth of debate and information, and today they merit overdue digitisation and analysis'. He in particular cites the examples of the *United Irishman* and *Sinn Féin* but warns against assuming that Griffith, as the editor, approved or held every opinion expressed in them. Like Yeats, and indeed Owen McGee, Kenny views Griffith as 'anti-clerical', despite his criticisms of *The Playboy of the Western World*. As to the Jewish question, 'he was a Zionist who struggled to overcome within himself contemporary anti-Semitic prejudice'. Clearly, his South African journalistic adventure in 1897–8, his admiration for the Young Irelander and slavery advocate John Mitchel and his support for the Boers during their war with the British, raise some awkward questions for the 'Black Lives Matter' generation. Kenny's chapter 'Griffith, Race and Africa' inevitably cannot entirely acquit Griffith from some blame on this issue and at times reads a little like special pleading on behalf of a man who shared some of the attitudes of his time. Michael Laffan's *DIB* entry for Griffith was probably accurate in its judgement that 'Griffith sympathised instinctively with every anti-British interest and individual, however unworthy they might be'. This ambiguity even extended to the atrocities perpetrated by the Belgians in the Congo!

Kenny, while acknowledging that Griffith was 'sometimes intolerant' and *'petit bourgeois'* in his attitudes, denies that he was either fascist or undemocratic. He was no socialist but 'he cared a great deal about matters that deeply affected the lives of working people' and also was a shy man who sometimes 'rubbed people up the wrong way'. Despite having been privy to a decision in 1914 that foreshadowed the rebellion of 1916 and despite having participated in the Howth gun-running and in 'square-bashing' with his Irish Volunteer unit, the leaders in 1916 in the end excluded Griffith 'apparently for strategic reasons'. Kenny's chapters on the Griffith/de Valera relationship and on the Treaty negotiations are particular strengths, with de Valera seen as the black-suited, austere manipulator who displaced Griffith as Sinn Féin

President in 1917, only to rely on him during his lengthy absence in the USA and who by refusing to lead the Irish negotiating team sent to London in October 1921, avoided 'taking ownership' of the talks process. For Kenny, Griffith achieved his chief political objective in his lifetime – 'the withdrawal of Irish MPs from Westminster in order to re-establish an independent Irish legislature'. But like Patrick Maume and Owen McGee, Kenny believes Griffith was more republican than is generally realised. 'However, he was not prepared to insist on imposing republican status on the whole island regardless of the cost of attempting to do so'. But one would have to add that none of Griffith's biographers have much to say about any engagement with Ulster as opposed to Southern unionists from the Protestant tradition.

Pádraig Ó Caoimh's study of Richard Mulcahy, published in a hardback edition at a very fair price, contains an iconic photograph of the state funeral accorded to Arthur Griffith on 16 August 1922, which shows a group of uniformed senior officers of the new Irish Free State National Army standing and awaiting instructions. Of the two most senior figures in the front rank, the tall, impressive figure of Michael Collins (his own state funeral only 12 days away) is instantly recognisable. But many might struggle to recognise the smaller, lean figure on his left. This is his friend, close colleague, fellow IRB member and organisation man, Richard Mulcahy. Colum Kenny reproduces the same National Library of Ireland photograph in his Griffith biography. Mulcahy, a somewhat shy, less extrovert and perhaps more strongly religious individual than Collins, played an equally key role in both military and political affairs. Yet although he turned out to be both a physical and in the longer term political survivor, after a career blip resulting from his handling of the threatened 1924 National Army 'mutiny', Mulcahy, much more than is claimed for Griffith by Kenny, remains something of a mysterious enigma, as indeed the press release for the new book by Ó Caoimh states.

So is this the 'long overdue new biography', as heralded by that same release? Alas not. While there is some interesting coverage of Mulcahy's early life in Chapter One entitled 'The Socio-Political Milieu, 1886–1913' (born 10 May 1886 in Waterford City), including his education by the Christian Brothers, his early career as a postal official specialising in telegraphy and engineering, his enthusiasm for the Irish language, the influence on his political thinking of Griffith's *United Irishman* newspaper and most notably *The Resurrection of Hungary* (1904) and his deep, if conventional, Catholic religious faith, Mulcahy's second political career from 1927 (after three years in the wilderness) when he served for a period as leader of Fine Gael and held a series of significant Ministerial posts, is accorded only two and a half pages in the summary introduction. However, we do learn in Chapter One how great the influence of Griffith on him was. As he himself later acknowledged: 'Griffith was our great teacher ... our guide', and this was undoubtedly a key factor when it came to finalising his attitude to the Anglo-Irish Treaty of 1921, alongside his pragmatic realism regarding the IRA's military prospects in a renewed war with the British and his faith in Collins' stepping stone theory of government (pp 90–91).

A loyal IRB and Collins man, as Ó Caoimh notes, 'Mulcahy found himself espousing an early interest of his, i.e. Griffith's pragmatic, legalistic, evolutionary nationalism'. Mulcahy was also cautious by nature, at times self-effacing, an individual who liked to reflect on decisions before making them. Even in his more youthful days, he spent Holy Week 1916 on a religious retreat before reporting for duty as an Irish Volunteer and subsequently distinguishing himself when, as second-in-command to Thomas Ashe, he played a key role in the one minor victory secured by the rebels – the attack on Ashbourne RIC barracks in County Meath. It was this achievement which gave Mulcahy subsequent celebrity status amongst the surviving participants of the Easter Rising.

So if this recent book is not a full biography, what then exactly is it? This is indeed an important contribution to the study of the key revolutionary period of 1913–24, incorporating significant new revelations deriving from the author's deep knowledge of his sources and reflecting recent significant contributions to the historiography of the Irish revolution, including those of Owen McGee, the late David Fitzpatrick, Roy Foster, the late Shane Kenna, Fergus O'Farrell, Michael Laffan and John Regan.

Ó Caoimh concisely sums up his core objectives in his Preface: 'This book is a study of two interrelated processes which transpired during the revolutionary period of Irish national liberation, 1913–24, namely the politico-military career of Richard Mulcahy and the struggle for supremacy within the nationalist elite, especially the struggle for supremacy on the vital question of the nature and extent of the emerging government – army relationship'. For me, two particularly impressive themes to emerge from this extremely thorough analysis are the key role which the IRB continued to play in events right up to 1924, a role which Mulcahy, like his mentor and friend Collins, was closely identified with and secondly, the degree of personal rivalry and petty jealousies within the Republican leadership, which would not have been out of place at the Byzantine court. The IRB in a sense operated as an organisation within the wider organisations of the Dáil and Government of the Republic, not to mention the emerging National Army, while behind the veneer of a united band of revolutionary brothers, there were bitter rivalries and constant jockeying for power and control, both *before* as well as after the Treaty split. This reality continued even after the anti-Treaty faction had departed, with the IRB/GHQ element of the new National Army a particular source of internal conflict.

In a judicious final chapter, entitled simply 'Conclusion', Ó Caoimh provides a convincing overview of both the process of government/army tensions and the threatened conflict around the abortive Army mutiny of 1924 and of the somewhat ambiguous and complex role played by Mulcahy, to outward appearances an army enthusiast. While acknowledging Mulcahy's 'scheming IRB ways' and his 'snobbish' regard for the officer corps of the army (Mulcahy choosing to reside in their midst in Lissenfield House in the grounds of Portobello Barracks), Ó Caoimh acquits him of the charge of an interest in the establishment of a military dictatorship. He was no Miguel Primo de Rivera or Benito Mussolini. Ultimately, his desire was 'to build a small, decorous and duteous national army' and he skilfully reduced the bloated 60,000 strong National Army of the Civil War period through a reorganisation scheme from November 1923 to February 1924, and through nipping a mutiny in the bud by authorising the famous raid on Devlin's pub in 1924 (although failing to consult his political colleagues in advance which led to his forced resignation as Minister for Defence (MD)). The late Ronan Fanning and in a qualified way more recently, Diarmaid Ferriter, have praised Mulcahy's role, even if Kevin O'Higgins as Minister of Foreign Affairs, because of his much-quoted declaration that never again would the institutions of the State 'take their stride from a soldier's boot', is often given the credit for saving Irish democracy. O'Higgins of course was no friend and was determined to 'sideline Mulcahy' (Ferriter, *Irish Times*, 15 December 2019). Ferriter has also pointed out that Mulcahy's demobilisation process, while deserving of praise, came with a significant human cost, as the recently released, often moving, appeals preserved in the Army Mutiny files, from the many now 'thrown to the wolves' reveal. 'None of them were reinstated', despite often desperate economic circumstances.

As for Mulcahy, Ó Caoimh finds him to be 'a man of contradictions, yet one who, largely because of the strength of his patriotism, ambition, bravery, self-belief, self-discipline and self-sacrifice, rose to prominence among a most uniquely talented and committed generation of Irish nationalists'. But 'as such, nonetheless, in terms of talent alone, his place in the pecking order placed him in a position below that of Collins, de Valera and Griffith but also below Cosgrave and O'Higgins probably'. Indeed, he concludes that Collins even in death 'continued to upstage Mulcahy'. Mulcahy had none of the Collins charisma. He was 'pedantic and aloof'… 'the even-paced systematic bureaucrat, who invariably took things personally'. A man with a 'penchant for walk outs, retirement threats and acknowledgement requests', a man who delayed over decisions, who even when he finally took action, sometimes forcefully, often favoured oblique 'mind-game tactics, such as segmentation and attrition'. A striking example of this is provided by Mulcahy's role in support of the Collins/O'Duffy proposed IRA military assault on 'Carsonia', as Mulcahy dubbed the six Ulster counties in the early summer of 1922. 'There is a strong possibility that there was a cynical aspect to Mulcahy's thinking throughout' (p. 117) and that he was less concerned about the Ulster situation than he was about giving 'his army the edge over the IRA executive forces in the pending civil war'.

What then of Richard Mulcahy, the devout Catholic and his attitude to Protestant nationalists? Conor Morrissey has pointed out that the new 1922 National Army had a largely Catholic ethos which was in fact formally institutionalised: 'Catholic chaplains were appointed; soldiers paraded outside church on Sundays; days were punctuated with the intonation of the rosary'. However, as noted earlier, there were around 251 Protestants (0.76 per cent) serving in that army. It is therefore interesting that Mulcahy, as Minister for Defence, wrote to the Church of Ireland Archbishop Gregg of Dublin, seeking to create chaplaincy arrangements for Anglican soldiers and made plans to approach other denominations as well in November 1922. Defence Order No. 3 duly created the position of resident chaplains and a Garrison church was established at the Curragh Camp, with Rev. R. C. Madden appointed as its first chaplain. Rev. Ernest Lewis-Crosby had already been appointed officiating clergyman to Portobello Barracks in Dublin.

So we are still left with the intriguing question which Ó Caoimh courageously addresses in this study of Richard Mulcahy. As the press release succinctly puts it: 'Who was the enigmatic man behind the myth? Conspiratorial IRB nationalist; stubborn military tribune; pragmatic, political officeholder; or a fascinating combination of these and other traits?' To all of that, I would add 'the great survivor'. After all, Mulcahy's political career may have seemed to many contemporary observers to have been ended by his lack of consultation in handling the 1924 Army Mutiny. But Mulcahy emerged from the political wilderness in June 1927 as Minister of Local Government and Health and went on to enjoy a long second career as a political representative and party leader, fully committed to democratic principles and narrowly missing the opportunity of serving as Taoiseach in 1948, when he selflessly stepped aside in favour of John A. Costello to enable the formation of the first Inter-Party Irish government. So as Ó Caoimh acknowledges in his introductory chapter, the full Mulcahy story is yet to be told.

CONCLUSION

What do these four books reveal about Irish nationalism and inclusivity? The evidence is mixed. Indeed, while Richard Mulcahy on the one hand may have been quite proactive in securing chaplaincy arrangements for the tiny minority of Protestant soldiers in the new National Army, the Civil War period demonstrates that both he and to a much lesser degree Griffith were prepared to use extreme violence both against their political opponents and former comrades (notably during the Munster campaign and with Mulcahy's key role in the summary execution on 6 December 1922 of McKelvey, O'Connor, Barrett and Mellows in Mountjoy Jail, not to mention his earlier complicity in the planning of the IRA assault on Ulster, possibly as a useful distraction). But as Pádraig Ó Caoimh points out (p. 243), there was much more terror and political violence in other European post-imperial countries in the same period – Finland, Estonia, Latvia, Lithuania and Czechoslovakia all provide good examples.

As McAnallen has shown, not all of the Gaelic volunteers who served in the Crown forces during the First World War, had to maintain a low profile in their communities on their return home and some were to suffer more greatly at the hands of Protestant mobs during the 1920 riots and workplace expulsions in places like Belfast, Banbridge and Lisburn. Conor Morrissey is of the view that while 'Southern Protestants would never achieve the same level of political, social and economic dominance that they had enjoyed before independence … life in independent Ireland was probably better than many had expected'. Whereas, in his view, many of the Protestant nationalists were doomed to have 'melancholy experiences', as the Irish Free State became an increasingly 'Catholic-dominated state' in the 1920s and 1930s.

Harry Clarke's stained glass imagery in the new Ireland

AMANDA CROFT

LUCY COSTIGAN & MICHAEL CULLEN
Dark Beauty:
Hidden Detail in Harry Clarke's Stained Glass
Merrion Press, 2019
pp 270   ISBN 978-1-78537-233-9   hb   €35.00

Lucy Costigan first came across the work of the Irish stained glass designer Harry Clarke on an impromptu visit to Dublin City Art Gallery in 1985. In the preface to *Dark Beauty: Hidden Detail in Harry Clarke's Stained Glass,* illustrated with some 300 photographs by her collaborator, Michael Cullen, she describes her delight on her discovery: 'The delicacy of the robes and finery was simply breathtaking … rare combination of artistic gifts and fantastic imagination'. This encounter was to be the catalyst for a life's work devoted to visiting and cataloguing all of Harry Clarke's stained glass windows and panels found in churches and museums in Ireland, Great Britain, Australia and America.

Harry Clarke (1889–1931) was critically applauded nationally and internationally during his lifetime but after his untimely death at 41 from tuberculosis his reputation and artistic profile faded from public view until it was revived by the art and design historian Nicola Gordon Bowe (1948–2018) whose two seminal texts on Clarke, *Harry Clarke: His Graphic Art* (1983) and *The Life and Work of Harry Clarke* (1989) re-established Clarke's role as a key exponent of early twentieth century Irish stained glass design. In the introduction to the latter, Gordon Bowe observed 'Because Clarke's masterpieces are in the relatively inaccessible medium of glass and have to be tracked down in often remote churches or private collections … the legacy of his short life has been insufficiently recognised'. This reinforced Costigan's resolve to document Clarke's work by undertaking a comprehensive photographic record of all his extant work.

As she explains in the preface, Clarke's 'task as an illustrator of fairy tales and literature, and also as a creator of religious and biblical stories in his stained glass, was to portray moments of heroism and enlightenment but also of weakness and evil … [which] necessitated depictions of illumination and darkness in all its variations'. The title *Dark Beauty* is borrowed from A. Kelly, critic for *The Irish Press* in 1938, who noted that Clarke's 'chief gift is a strange blend of dark beauty and almost spectral luminosity'. Aimed primarily at a non-academic readership, *Dark Beauty* informs but never overwhelms the reader. When Clarke designed a window, whether secular or religious, he embellished the essential narrative with minute details that relate to its symbolism, historical context and geographical setting, treating each window 'as though he was working on a book illustration'. Most of these details are almost invisible to the viewer from ground level but Cullen's photographs illustrate them to perfection throughout Costigan's descriptive text.

Following the introductory chapter, 'Master of Colour and Light', offering insight into the life, influences and techniques of Clarke, each of the following chapters concentrates on themes: fashion and accessories; flora and fauna; settings and décor; borders, tracery and decorative panels; diminutive characters, referencing numerous windows by Clarke from across a wide range of locations that are also listed in the comprehensive catalogue of work at the end of the book.

The chapter on 'Fashion and Accessories' focuses on the myriad artistic influences utilised by Clarke throughout his career. Initially trained in stained glass design in his father's commercial church decorating and stained glass business and at the Dublin Metropolitan School of Art where he was taught by A. E. Child and the painter William Orpen, Clarke also travelled to London and Europe where he saw the richly coloured medieval glass at the Victoria and Albert Museum and Chartres Cathedral that would inform the deep blues and ruby reds of his own work. Costigan and Cullen reference Clarke's use of blues in an early work, *Madonna and Bambino* (1915), a small roundel, and in the portrayal of Mary in *The Nativity* (1924) at the Diseart Institute of Education and Celtic Culture, Dingle, County Kerry. His use of vibrant reds is evident in the light devoted to *Suffer the Little Children* (1924).

Clarke's figures wear medieval dresses, dainty fur edged shoes, elaborate be-jewelled headdresses, silvered and embroidered gowns akin to those found in the paintings of the Pre-Raphaelites and the decadent illustrations of Aubrey Beardsley. The authors note they are also reminiscent of Clarke's own characters in *Fairy Tales by Hans Christian Anderson* (1916) and *The Fairy Tales of Charles Perrault* (1922). An undercurrent of the fairy tale in evident in Clarke's interpretation of Keats's poem *The Eve of St Agnes* (1924) at the Hugh Lane, Dublin, with its shimmering light dancing over the sequinned costumes of Madeline, Porphyro and the revellers.

Clarke also absorbed the stylistic characteristics of the European Symbolists and artists of the decadent *fin-de-siècle*. The organic flow of Art Nouveau can be seen as a source for the floral motifs in the commemorative window, *Our Lady and Child Adored by St Aiden of Ferns and St Adrian* (1919) in Wexford town. The geometric patterning of Art Deco is evident in the black and white borders of the *St Peter and St Paul* (1927) light in the Church of Ireland, Ranelagh and in the 'jagged, angular shapes' of the *Nine Chancel Windows Depicting Angels Bearing Symbols for the Mass* (1929), Bayonne, New Jersey, Clarke's only American commission.

The section devoted to 'Borders, Tracery and Decorative Panels' discusses Clarke's stained glass techniques, and how he manipulated his preferred flashed glass to obtain a full range of tones from each hue. This was achieved by layering thin films or flashes of colour onto still molten hand blown sheets of clear glass. He also employed slab glass, developed in the late nineteenth century to mimic the irregularities of medieval glass. Additional detailing was then hand painted onto the glass resulting in complex layering of colour and imagery. Such techniques are the defining characteristics of Clarke's glass works.

Not all of his glass is figurative. Many borders, tracery and decorative panels employ abstract patterning, often recalling the illuminated manuscripts such as the Irish High Crosses and the *Book of Kells*. Often the lights that display the most abstraction in their decoration are located high up in an architectural setting, so high that any narrative figuration would be barely visible from below. Costigan and Cullen illustrate this with a sub-section devoted to such decorative windows found in Letterkenny, County Donegal; Lusk and Phibsborough, County Dublin and the spectacular rose window at the Dominican Convent Chapel on the Falls Road, Belfast. Commissioned in June 1927, it required 'over a thousand feet of leaded glass' and contains 'twelve decorative panels set within a further twelve panels, representing the twelve apostles'. The central panel depicts a red cross on a white background creating a glorious effect suggestive of Clarke's pre-First World War visit to Chartres.

The majority of Clarke's window lights display a strong sense of place and connection to the natural world as seen in the chapter devoted to 'Flora and Fauna'. A young St Patrick is shown tending his sheep in the predella of *St Patrick* (1928) in Tullamore Church, County Offaly, and a squirrel and rabbits are included in the panel devoted to 'The Wayfarer' by Pádraig Pearse in the *Geneva Window* (1930). Here Clarke makes a direct reference to the poem written by Pearse, one of the leaders of the 1916 Rebellion, on the eve of his execution:

> The beauty of the world hath made me sad,
> This beauty that will pass;
> Sometimes my heart hath shaken with great joy
> To see a leaping squirrel in a tree,
> Or a red lady-bird upon a stalk,
> Or little rabbits in a field at evening,
> Lit by a slanting sun.

Flowers, butterflies and exotic birds abound as do insects and sea creatures as seen throughout the six decorative panels in Bewley's Oriental Café, Grafton Street, Dublin. These windows are arguably

Clarke's best known works, beloved by the public at large and part of the national fabric. Writing in the *Irish Times* in May 2020, Rosita Boland commented 'Seeing Harry Clarke's windows for the first time was an aesthetic shock so profound and joyful I can still recall it. Instead of the Crucifixion ... I was looking at fantastic birds and flowers and butterflies like none I had seen in real life'. Worryingly, the future of the four windows depicting the *Corinthian, Doric, Ionic and Composite Orders of Architecture* and the *Two Decorative Windows* that flank Swan Lane is now under serious threat as the premises have closed permanently.

In the chapter on 'Flora and Fauna' the authors acknowledge that place, in the sense of landscape, is important for a number of key works by Clarke. Most notable are the nine windows (eleven lights) for the Honan Chapel of St Finbarr, Cork (1915–17). This was the project that made Clarke's reputation as noted in the *Irish Times*, 'These windows, in the opinion of the most competent critics, rival in beauty some of the most remarkable products of Continental art'. Today the windows are lauded for their visual references to the landscape, legends, Celtic carvings and culture associated with the West of Ireland and the Aran Islands in particular and have, along with *The Geneva Window*, become part of current academic considerations of the role of artists and designers in the formation of a visual identity for Ireland's cultural renaissance pre- and post-partition.

Clarke made regular trips to the Aran Islands from 1909–15, holidaying (and honeymooning) there. The West of Ireland has long been associated with the search for a 'pure' Ireland. Clarke's association with the West and, in the opinion of some academics, his perceived political engagement with the newly emergent Irish State was discussed by Angela Griffith, Marguerite Helmers and Róisín Kennedy in *Harry Clarke: Artistic Visions of the New Irish State* (2019) reviewed in *Familia* 2019. Clarke's imagery has come under close scrutiny from commentators and art historians seeking to establish 'the complex relationship between visual art and literature' that they believe 'lies at the heart of Clarke's contribution to Irish post-independence culture'.

Throughout *Dark Beauty*, Costigan and Cullen prefer to concentrate on the aesthetics of Clarke's work rather than his engagement with politics. One exception is their brief discussion of the ill-fated *Geneva*

Window (1930) which fell foul of the conservative values of the new Irish State and the Censorship of Publications Act of 1929. Commissioned by the Irish government 'as a gift from the Irish Free State to the International Labour Organisation (ILO) in Geneva', Clarke, given free rein to select a suitable subject, chose literary scenes by fifteen of Ireland's finest writers. Whilst many were considered 'acceptable', associated with the Celtic Revival, the Gaelic League and the Abbey Theatre, James Joyce and Liam O'Flaherty 'were considered licentious and decadent by the Irish church and State'. Clarke's rendition of O'Flaherty's *Mr Gilhooley* smoking a cigar, quaffing champagne and leering at a semi-clad dancing Nelly, the inclusion of lovers and young women 'who oozed eroticism and sexuality', and his depiction of Joxer Daley from Sean O'Casey's *Juno and the Paycock* as a drunkard with a whiskey bottle in his pocket resulted in the whole window being rejected by the State as immoral, inappropriate and offensive.

President Cosgrave asked Clarke to make alterations but the artist died before any work could be carried out and the window was never sent to Geneva. His widow, Margaret Clarke, bought back the window from the Irish State in 1932. In 1988 it was sold by the family to the American collector, Mitchell Wolfson and it is now on permanent display in the Wolfsonian Museum of Art, Miami Beach, Florida in a room that 'deals with national identity'. Clarke's stained glass windows and black and white illustrations may have offended the Irish State in the 1930s but today his legacy is being exploited as cultural tourism. Pre-coronavirus, coach tours took enthusiasts across Ireland, from Dublin to Dingle, Donegal, Cork, Galway, Mayo, Armagh and Belfast to see his windows *in situ*.

Dark Beauty is just one of a growing raft of accessible texts and merchandise based on Clarke's designs. Beautifully illustrated throughout, *Dark Beauty* is a welcome, accessible primer for the general public who will be as entranced and delighted by Clarke's stained glass as Lucy Costigan as a young student in the 1980s.

REVIEWS

DAVID FITZPATRICK

The Americanisation of Ireland:
Migration and Settlement, 1841–1925

Cambridge University Press, 2019

pp 270   ISBN 978-1-108-48649-1   hb   £29.99

It remains problematic to encapsulate neatly the influence of David Fitzpatrick's work as an historian, following his untimely passing in February 2019. It is almost unimaginable that anybody could seek to write anything about modern Irish migration history without reference to his many publications. If Moody, Beckett and Dudley-Edwards dominated the Irish historiographical landscape in the era which culminated in the publication of volume III of the *Oxford New History of Ireland* (1976), Fitzpatrick would undoubtedly be one of a small cadre of historians who helped shape the field from then to the publication, edited by Thomas Bartlett, the *Cambridge History of Ireland* (2018).

This book was his last, poignantly copyrighted to 'the estate of David Fitzpatrick' and published posthumously. As Don Akenson comments in the blurb, 'this is classic Fitzpatrick'. Slaughtering sacred cows was a veritable Fitzpatrick pastime and here he takes double aim at the notions that Irish emigrants always went for good and, more broadly, that the shape of post-Famine modernisation in Ireland was predominantly characterised by the creeping process dubbed 'Anglicisation'.

In what is described in the prologue as a 'design' which is 'deliberately unconventional', the analysis moves from a broad, general survey to the particular interrogation of individual cases drawn from a constructed database of migrants, who sought passports in the US to permit return to Leitrim county 1914–25. Chapter one sets out to frame the research question and offers a more holistic perspective on Irish migration. The author understood fully the universality of the migrant experience and that it was not primarily defined by distance. In truth, the argument specifically concerning return migration here should come as no great surprise to those familiar with the field. The essential case, that permanent return to Ireland from America was somewhat greater than previously acknowledged and that impermanent visits in the same direction had become increasingly common towards the close of the nineteenth century, had been set out by Fitzpatrick in his 1996 survey of Irish emigration, 1871–1921, in volume VI of the *Oxford New History of Ireland*. Indeed, no fewer than four of 31 pages considered the phenomenon of return migration, findings to my knowledge that were never subsequently challenged.

Although ignoring Wyman's 1994 monograph on US immigrants' return to Europe in the half-century after 1880, Fitzpatrick quotes work by Gould suggesting that Irish permanent returnees were outnumbered to a ratio of 16:1 by emigrants heading in the opposite direction, making the Irish return rate the lowest of any major European sending country. Whether return migrants returning temporarily to Ireland had less socio-cultural influence on the sending nation than the permanent returnee obviously remains very difficult to measure with any degree of certainty. The surprising virtual absence of reference to the wider European context is not helpful. Even at its apex in Edwardian Leitrim, whether temporary or permanent, returns from America compared to returns to contemporary southern, central and eastern Europe could only be described as modest. Therefore, if the force of Americanisation was significant in rural, western Ireland it must have been substantially more evident in southern Italy, the Balkans or in Russia.

Calling on impressive research, Fitzpatrick considers, through the census, immigration into Ireland in the seven decades after 1841. Although inward migration was steadily increasing through these decades again there is, disappointingly, no broader European context. It is established that what distinguished the American component was the increasing concentration in the most 'backward' and rural western counties, with a disproportionate number of children within the group. Whether this amounted to an 'American *colonisation* of Connaught' is highly debateable (colonisation is a particularly loaded term in this context) and those born in Britain continued to outnumber the American-born across the island throughout the period.

Using a database of about 1,000 'elite' North Americans in Ireland between 1901 and 1911, Fitzpatrick offers a profile of the group. This reinforces the conclusion that kinship networks were generally crucial to explain their existence in Ireland but the profile reflected the diversity on show. The interrogation of different employment sectors is comprehensive with large numbers of individual cases considered. One professional pathway considered was education and it was surprising that more was not made of the particular potential of teachers to act as 'cultural brokers' on American ways and mores. As Janet Nolan has noted an energetic and consciously developed programme of Americanisation had been underway in contemporary American public schools where Irish teachers, particularly young women, seized the opportunity for upward social mobility. At their height in 1911, however, there were only 87 such personnel across 32 counties. Fitzpatrick points out the 'genuine cosmopolitanism' of his sample, showing connectedness with a range of Irish counties as well as Britain and the Empire. Importantly, he also stresses that individual destinations were not mutually exclusive with significant migrant experience of both Britain and North America. Many of the Americans (including Canadians) in Edwardian Ireland were thus not exclusively reflective of American cultural influence, however that might be defined.

The second part of the book focuses on a case study of County Leitrim. As Fitzpatrick points out, Leitrim by 1911 was the Irish county with the highest concentration of American residents, reflecting its consistently heavy post-Famine emigration rates, particularly directed to the US. However, we should not lose sight of the proportionate significance of all this. Although amounting to 'almost 300', this still represents less than 0.5 per cent of the then county population (or 47 per 10,000 inhabitants). The author stresses that Leitrim's 300 (actually 298) Americans outnumbered both Scottish and English residents but this seems misleading. Combined, the British born contingent (438) in the county was more than 30 per cent greater and setting all other variables aside, one should anticipate the latter's socio-cultural impact to be proportionately greater.

Amongst these Leitrim Americans the author notes the astonishing predominance of children, suggestive of extended family strategies for child rearing. The census schedules, of course, only recorded those born overseas so other 'returned Yanks' went under the census radar. The evidence suggests there was little resemblance to the 'swaggering figure of fiction', with most returners more likely to be classified as needy losers than brash winners in any crude dichotomy. Predominantly represented in small farm households, some returned to inherit or purchase smallholdings whilst in many cases the 'surplus' children of extended family in America were accommodated 'at home'. The gradual establishment of primogeniture in a county like Leitrim must have had significant bearing on migration strategies and it is curious that Fitzpatrick has so little to comment on the subject. Was the returning sibling, now not assured of a share of the family farm not potentially problematic in light of these changing inheritance customs?

In drawing on US passport applications made between 1914 and 1925, Fitzpatrick utilises what he describes as the 'most extensive and representative source for any study of Irish return migration'. In doing so he acknowledges the pioneering work, using this source, undertaken on return migration to Connacht by Diane Dunnigan for her 2012 NUI Maynooth PhD thesis. Fitzpatrick, with the aid of some painstaking searching on variant spellings (wonderfully including 'latrine'), generated a sizeable database of some 600 Leitrim native applicants and offers a comprehensive profile. The use of the data is masterly and includes an interesting consideration of physical characteristics, taking advantage of the enclosed portrait photographs. The consideration of Edwardian moustache styles is very Fitzpatrickian. The 600 were deemed to be broadly representative of the population of 'backward' western Ireland in general.

Exploring the declared motives of the sample, almost four-fifths reported a desire to visit family members. No less than 31 applicants mentioned pursuit of health and there might have been greater scope to consider the particular role of tuberculosis or consumption here. One very interesting sidelight revealed in the course of the applications was the apparently fairly widespread trend by which emigrants confessed to routinely burning or destroying letters previously sent across the Atlantic from home (little hint of sentimentality there). Readers of this journal might be interested to note that the author, who enjoyed a complex relationship with family historians, uses sources such as Ancestry.com to augment his research. That one of these radical Leitrimonians, James

Gralton, returned as a member of the Communist Party serves only to illustrate the fallacy of any simple depiction of 'Americanisation' being imported to Ireland. The author reproduces over seventy portrait photographs of the subjects with a pithy commentary on what these might tell us.

A final short but poignant epilogue concludes the volume. The author, very importantly, reminds us that what he describes as 'this demographic study' was not originally intended to stand alone and that a second accompanying volume was conceived as a way of broadening out the exploration of what is framed as 'Ireland's forgotten Americanisation'. Frustratingly there are almost half a dozen references in just over two pages to Europe here and it is a shame that this continental comparative context was not developed in the preceding 200 pages. Even today, if you walk through the landscape of rural Italy, Portugal or Norway you will fairly regularly encounter material, physical markers to the influence of earlier returned Americans, the 'American House' being just the most sizeable and tangible of these. The parallel does not apply in rural Leitrim which in itself raises some interesting questions concerning the manifestation of 'Americanisation'.

So whilst this book makes for an interesting read and complements the research of Dunnigan, the proposition that a thorough-going process of Americanisation acted as a counter-weight to Anglicisation in turn-of-the-century Ireland remains, in the eyes of this reviewer, largely unproven. If Americanisation did take hold in twentieth-century Ireland it perhaps did so during the 1960s, when television sets delivered into Irish living rooms American-made programming which impacted significantly on millions of peering sets of young eyes. David Fitzpatrick was always a very dedicated and supportive teacher: one feels confident that many of his former students will continue to play an active and important role in pursuing the equally important themes and questions raised by his work.

PATRICK FITZGERALD

ALICE JOHNSON
Middle-Class Life in Victorian Belfast
Liverpool University Press, 2020
pp 376   ISBN 978-1-78962-031-3   hb   £80.00

Belfast's growth as the pre-eminent manufacturing town on the island of Ireland was marked by gaining city status in 1888. Over the preceding 50 years the town's prosperity had been consolidated by the mechanised production of linen and its export world-wide. This study reconstructs the social world of its upper middle class and provides an intriguing counterbalance to the more commonly explored themes of working-class employment patterns, housing and social conditions.

By 1881 Belfast was four times bigger than it had been in 1831. The upstart nature of its civic growth was evident in its absence of resident aristocracy, a cathedral, or (until 1845) a university – all features of established urban life elsewhere in Ireland, Britain and Europe. It developed as a middle-class run town whose leaders displayed a conscious pride in being hardworking and entrepreneurial. Business interests dominated town affairs and public discussions of political, religious and social issues, particularly following the municipal reforms of the 1840s. Belfast professions – lawyers, doctors and educationalists - were considered as social equals to the industrialists and merchants, but their numbers were fewer and their wealth so much less that their influence in civic matters was correspondingly weakened.

Johnson's analysis of the 'civic elite' gains its very real warmth and solidity from her plundering of two main sources of material. One is a compilation of names and collection of biographical information of over 800 individuals identified as members of the town's key organisations – the Harbour Commissioners and magistracy or on the committees of charities and voluntary philanthropic societies. A 'group portrait' of the elite emerges which takes in education, wealth and standards of living as well as geographical, religious and class origins. Victorian Belfast was a town of outsiders with people moving in from the countryside in every decade; over 20 per cent of the most heavily involved members of the 'civic elite' were from Great Britain.

In addition, three families in this elite, the Workmans, the Corrys and the McCances, are portrayed in detail over the generations through the availability at PRONI of family memoirs and correspondence. All three families were Presbyterians (the McCances were Unitarians or Non-Subscribing Presbyterians). Johnson notes that though her search was in vain for a comparable substantial middle-class Church of Ireland/Anglican family archive this does not imply that Presbyterians dominated public life. Just over one third of the 'civic elite' were Anglicans though they comprised one quarter of the town's population. Although Catholics formed one third of Belfast's population at mid-century their middle class was generally under-represented in public life, instead serving its own community by constructing new church buildings and providing schools.

The Workman brothers, from Ayrshire, John and Robert, commenced as muslin manufacturers in Belfast during the 1830s, no doubt with connections already established in the Ayrshire sewed muslin trade. The next generation wisely moved into mercantile shipping and, in 1880, Robert's grandson, Frank, formed the shipbuilding firm of Workman Clark & Co. with his cousin, George Clark. The second family group, the Corrys, from Newtownards, established a small timber business in 1814. In the 1820s a son, Robert, leased a quarry site at Scrabo, and Scrabo stone rapidly became the most widely used building material throughout Ulster. Robert and his brother, John, became building contractors, later J. P Corry & Co., undertaking private housing and municipal contracts such as the Ormeau gasworks. They also became shipowners importing tea and sugar as well as timber. Corrys ordered their ships from Harland and Wolff but when Workman Clark opened they switched allegiance. The McCance family was part of the older elite of linen bleachers and merchants. Their country location at Dunmurry indicated the continued reliance throughout the nineteenth century on the water power in the Lagan valley for bleaching, beetling, dyeing, printing and finishing linen. The McCances intermarried with other wealthy Lagan Valley linen families such as the Charleys. They were also connected to the old elite of Belfast bankers and merchants.

Many of the 'civic élite' were initially educated privately or at local schools, RBAI or Belfast (Royal) Academy or both. The ties with Scottish universities, as in the eighteenth century, remained strong. When Queen's College opened, its main initial intake was not from

Belfast schoolboys but from rural Ulster, sons of small farmers, shopkeepers, country doctors and Presbyterian ministers. In late eighteenth-century Belfast, the middle and professional classes had lived cheek by jowl with ordinary working people in the centre of town. With the deteriorating environment caused by the construction of mills and factories in overcrowded districts, new housing in healthier neighbourhoods was built on the outskirts of Belfast for those who could afford to move. This suburbanisation was a common feature of nineteenth-century cities.

The wives, mothers, daughters and sisters in this 'civic elite' have left a lighter record but their initiatives in the philanthropic and educational spheres were influential. Many were members of voluntary societies and charitable associations where civic duties quietly supported the plight of poor women and children and the Belfast Naturalists' Field Club admitted women as full members from its inception in 1863. Correspondence in the Workman archive and a diary kept by young Mary Watts, who lived in Upper Crescent during the 1860s and 1870s, next door to Robert Corry, paint a lively picture, not only of family life, but also of women who took on public responsibilities in a range of spheres and were far from being passive adjuncts to their husbands. Family and kinship networks through intermarriage were a vital part of the business community; there was huge emphasis on safeguarding and passing on the family business to the next generations.

This is a rich book. Its breadth and depth of referenced material place it as a source book in its own right and this review has been selective in the themes explored. The story of Belfast's middle classes has many similarities to other British towns. 'Linenopolis' was comparable to 'Cottonopolis' (Manchester) though it differed principally by its displays of sectarianism. However, even while presenting a face to the world of fashionable cultural expressions of Celtic imagery such as harps, round towers and shamrocks in the patterns of Ulster's damask linen tablecloths, Belfast's 'dual Irishness' remained, in Johnson's phrase, an anomaly in a rural island.

BRENDA COLLINS

SEÁN ENRIGHT
The Irish Civil War
Law, Execution and Atrocity
Merrion Press, 2019
pp xvi, 286   ISBN 9781785372537   pb   €18.95

Whatever principles guided the leaders of the fledging Irish state, the right to a fair trial and respect for the sanctity of human life were evidently not uppermost. From June 1922–June 1923 83 prisoners were executed and over 125 more fell victim to extra-judicial killings carried out by the state. The book opens in November 1923 with the trial of Jock McPeake, a Scot, who had been a machine-gunner on the 'Slievenamon' – the armoured car used in the fatal ambush of Michael Collins, one of the most contentious events of the Civil War, where myth and legend are almost inseparable from fact. Despite a lack of evidence against him, McPeake (wisely) pleaded guilty on the basis that prison was the safest option – it was abundantly clear that, if freed, he would have been immediately killed by a group of Collins' former army officer colleagues attending the trial. That a case was conducted in such an atmosphere demonstrates the extent to which, as Enright says, 'the rule of law had just fallen by the wayside'.

In order to understand what had led the country to this point, the author examines the preceding events and the principal actors involved. Michael Collins, for all his reputed ruthlessness, was instinctively opposed to the proposed execution policy. Richard Mulcahy, who succeeded him as Commander in Chief of the Army and Minister of Defence, argued in the Dáil in favour of an execution policy, fearing that the already shaky discipline of the new national army would break down entirely and soldiers would take the law into their own hands. However, by far the most enthusiastic proponent of the execution policy was not a soldier, but a lawyer, Kevin O'Higgins, who argued for 'on the spot' shooting of men captured carrying arms and for regular executions in every county. Between 1922 and 1923, he personally confirmed the death sentences of 77 republican prisoners, including Rory O'Connor who had been the best man at his wedding the previous year. In reprisal for O'Higgins's role in the executions the Anti-Treaty

IRA murdered his father and burned his family home in Stradbally, County Laois. O'Higgins himself was shot dead in July 1927. His last words were reported as, 'I was always a diehard'. (His granddaughter Iseult O'Malley, the current Irish Supreme Court judge, has been a strong proponent of due process and fair procedural rights throughout her legal career.)

Enright analyses the court martial and failed *habeas corpus* application which preceded the execution of another famous 'diehard', Erskine Childers, found guilty of possession of a small revolver, reputedly a present from Michael Collins. He argues that it is unfair to lay full responsibility for the dubious legality of the execution on O'Higgins personally, but accepts that Childers had become a hate figure of the Executive Council and 'being English and not a hero of 1916, was rather easier to vilify'. Enright accepts that O'Higgins' description of Childers as 'bent on the complete breakdown…of the country' is accurate, but points out that this was nothing more than orthodox anti-Treaty policy, namely to make the country ungovernable and 'to seize a republic from the ruins'.

The author insightfully analyses the motivation behind the execution policy, concluding that the principal reason was mundane – the economy. One quarter of government revenue was spent on the army bill alone. A fall in tax revenue was further exposing government weakness – in effect the anti-Treaty faction was seeking to drive the government into bankruptcy. It was against this background and driven by the fear that the state would become ungovernable, bankrupt and chaotic, and that the British might again send in troops, that the Executive Council finally agreed to allow the army to set up military courts to try prisoners and to carry out executions.

The vast majority of those executed were in their teens or early twenties – boys and men of 'of low rank or no rank'. With the exception of Childers, there were very few TDs or men of rank executed – several were sentenced to death but were either not executed or given the opportunity to save their lives by signing a typed 'surrender note', encouraging others to give up the fight. The background is of course complicated by the fact that less than a year earlier, many of these men had been comrades in arms fighting against the British presence in Ireland. Enright concludes that the evidence suggests it was 'not considered politic to execute TDs or heroes of the War of Independence and that occasionally a prisoner with friends on the other side might avoid trial entirely'. Although not drawn out as a specific theme in the book, the relative youth of all of the main protagonists is striking. Liam Lynch, Chief-of-Staff of the anti-Treaty forces was killed aged 29 and Michael Collins was 32 when he died. Kevin O'Higgins became Minister of Justice and Vice-President of the Executive Council aged 30, and General Richard Mulcahy was 36 when he became Minister of Defence in Commander in Chief of the Army, both in 1922. Like many of their fellow officers and colleagues, these men had in quick succession served in the War of Independence and then on one or other side of the Irish Civil War. Many had also fought through World War One. The fact that such men had extensive combat experience but very little experience of peacetime leadership and governance may be seen in the brutal pragmatism of the execution policy.

Clearly a line must be drawn between the dubious legality of the executions ordered by military tribunals and instances where prisoners were simply killed out of hand, without any veneer of legal process. The worst atrocities appear to have occurred in Dublin and the south-west, where the fighting was fiercest, but the Kerry landmine massacres stand out in the national consciousness as particularly barbaric. Enright assesses these events with forensic scrutiny and effectively demolishes the army's version of events, that three separate groups totalling 17 prisoners (plus one survivor) had been accidentally blown up by their own booby-trap landmines, while clearing barricades. The appalling truth, and its subsequent cover-up, reflects no glory on the national army.

This remarkable book is important for another reason. Just before Eamon de Valera came to power in 1932 Desmond Fitzgerald, Minister of Defence (and father of Garret Fitzgerald, Taoiseach 1981–2 and 1982–7) signed an order for the 'destruction by fire' of 'the proceedings of Military Courts and Tribunals and reports on and details of executions 1922/23'. The stated reason was to destroy material which might lead to a loss of life. The destruction of the formal records of state legal proceedings surely betrays serious misgivings about scrutiny of their contents. This slim but rewarding volume is well served by the chronology of key events and the pen portraits of the main protagonists.

I would have welcomed a map or two. I would recommend it not only to those intrigued by this period of Irish history but also to anyone with an interest in what happens when the rule of law and due process break down and necessity arguments and egg and omelette metaphors start to drown out less bellicose voices.

PATRICK BUTLER

GLADYS GANIEL & JAMIE YOHANIS
Considering Grace:
Presbyterians and the Troubles
Merrion Press, 2019
pp xiv, 264   ISBN 978-1-78537-289-6   pb   €16.95

The origins of this book lie in a research project of the Presbyterian Church in Ireland which itself was derived from a statement issued by the General Assembly after its meeting in 2016. That might sound like an unpromising starting point for a book but *Considering Grace* is well worth engaging with, particularly for those who want to understand and participate in peacemaking in Ireland and for those, both inside and outside the denomination, who want to understand more about the theological make-up of Presbyterians particularly in relation to the legacy of the Troubles. One of the 'big three' denominations in Ireland, Presbyterianism has declined from 29% of the population of Northern Ireland in 1961 to just 19% in 2011, according to the census. That is still a significant section of the populace but throughout this period Presbyterianism has suffered in terms of the articulation and public expression of its message through the annual change of moderator. Churches with bishops have spokespeople who stay in position for long periods, are able to acquire more effective media skills and can express – and are expected to express – with authority, what their church thinks. Strangely this lack of what one person calls 'a settled voice' (p. 199) is mostly identified by non-Presbyterians in this book but undoubtedly this examination of Presbyterian thought, theology and response to the Troubles is all the more valuable for giving voice to such a significant yet frequently overlooked or misunderstood faith tradition.

The book is based on interviews with 120 people, most of them Presbyterians. These interviews are divided into nine separate chapters covering ministers; victims; security forces; those affected by loyalist paramilitarism (including ex-combatants); emergency responders and health care workers; quiet peacemakers; politicians; those who left Presbyterianism; and critical friends. The authors are experienced researchers and writers in this field and they present the often harrowing and moving accounts of personal experiences of the Troubles in a sensitive way, creating a narrative that allows the interviewees to speak for themselves. What is new about their approach is the asking of questions about people's theological understanding of what has happened as well as their feelings about peacemaking, reconciliation and the building of relationships across the divides. The participants reflect on how this has been done – or not done – both by congregations and by the whole denomination. But the experiences recounted in the different sections often remember a time when there was no counselling or support for anyone caught up in the brutality of the early years of the Troubles. Many struggle in different ways with notions of forgiveness, some speak of a belief in ultimate judgment, many worked to break down barriers in the search for peace.

The PCI itself established a Peacemaking Programme from 2006–09 and had a system of 'peace agents' in local congregations whose job it was to lead peacemaking initiatives. But most 'quiet' peacemakers felt the denomination itself did not do enough (p. 156) although they, and some others, often mention the leadership given by some prominent Presbyterians, usually ministers and often ex-moderators, whose names recur throughout the book. It is interesting how names such as John Dunlop, Ken Newell and Norman Hamilton and others crop up as inspiring leaders. Some names evoke starkly different responses from the interviewees but no individual gets name-checked more frequently than Ian Paisley. Indeed his personality and his Free Presbyterian Church are always in the background, often threatening to draw people away or restraining those who might have wanted to be more vocal in the direction of a conciliatory approach. So 'it was difficult for PCI to do much publicly, especially with Rev. Ian Paisley criticising its every move' (p. 134) or 'the church has had a tough time trying to compete with the

Free Presbyterians. Paisley took no prisoners' (p. 202). Views like these are repeated throughout the book.

It was perhaps the influence of Ian Paisley that led to many PCI ministers preaching what one ex-Presbyterian describes as 'a strange Troubles-related theology' (p. 217) which laid great stress on Christ's second coming. A number are critical of a preaching of the gospel that is 'too small'. As one Presbyterian peace activist asks: 'Who are the keepers of the story of the common good within Presbyterianism? All our stories are about private salvation' (p. 186). The authors attempt to share the diversity of Presbyterian experiences of the Troubles, 'to extend an invitation to everyone on this island to *consider grace*' (p. 242). They recognise that this is a challenging endeavour for everyone but the stories told reveal people who have done just that and whose expression of grace is something that can help to build a better future.

DAVID STEERS

RICHARD J. BUTLER
Building the Irish Courthouse and Prison:
A Political History, 1750–1850
Cork University Press, 2020
pp 652   ISBN 978-1-78205-369-9   hb   €39.00

This is a most original, well researched, well written and beautifully illustrated book. The small quarto format provides the flexibility to reproduce the illustrations exactly where they should be in the text, and ample captions summarise their relevance. The quality of reproduction, partly in colour and partly in black-and-white, is high, and the selection of the illustration has been made from as wide a range of (sometimes obscure) sources as the evidence on which the text itself is based.

On the face of it, the building of courthouses and, especially, prisons is not a subject to make the heart beat faster. But Dr Butler, in a judicious blend of architectural, political and administrative history, spiced by examples of eccentric or perverse human behaviour, establishes the centrality of the subject. He also documents the uneven and by no means parallel steps by which central government eventually took over responsibilities which had once been exercised by the grand juries and other local government agencies. It is not too much to say that no future study of Irish local government in the period covered by this book will be attempted without reference to it.

The plan of the book is straightforward and effective. A well judged introduction stimulates interest without giving too much away, and defines the courthouses concerned as county or assize courthouses, not those of lesser jurisdiction, and the prisons as county or civic prisons, not bridewells, houses of correction and lesser lock-ups. Part one relates to courthouse-building, its three chapters dealing with definable phases 1786–1817, 1817–31 and 1831–55. The first phase is one of unrestrained expenditure by the grand juries of counties and county boroughs, financed out of local rates buoyed up by the wartime boom then in full swing. The second is one of post-war recession and austerity, in which greater central-government control was brought to bear upon the grand juries, but which was also characterised by generous government loans at low rates of interest; thus, paradoxically, the years of austerity were 'the peak years of courthouse building'. The last phase is one of grand jury reform and, because so many courthouses had been built already, a much-reduced rate of courthouse-building, but also a phase which witnessed some new, major and necessary examples of the *genre* – in Tullamore, Waterford, Nenagh and Belfast.

Part two relates to prison-building, and is also divided into another three chapters, covering the periods 1770–1810, 1810–21 and 1821–38 (though actually more like 1821–*c.* 1860). Here the story is different from that of courthouse-building because of the earlier intervention of central government in prison-building, the persistent presence of outside theoreticians and pressure groups calling for penal reform, and the championing by these groups, and by government officials, of new (and ever-changing) designs for 'model' prisons. In the period 1770–1810, grand juries were in effect at liberty to ignore the behests of the newly constituted (1786) prisons inspectorate and of the penal reformers, and also to ignore the restrictions arising from a considerable body of pre-Union legislation. Thereafter, following Prisons Acts of 1810 and, particularly, of 1821, the grand juries found their area of discretion severely limited by the reconstituted prisons inspectorate, by a Board of Works with extended powers and, as before, by penal reformers (who included members of parliament, members of the Dublin Castle administration, and a hitherto underestimated Irish pressure group founded in 1818 and laboriously entitled the Association for the Improvement of Prisons and of Prison Discipline in Ireland).

It is impossible within the scope of a review to summarise the content of a book of this wide-ranging complexity and sheer quality. Selected highlights, however, must include some of the quirks and paradoxes which emerge. It is, for example, surprising that there was little correlation between the building of courthouses and, especially, of prisons, and an escalation of crime rates in the jurisdiction concerned; sometimes such a correlation appears to exist, but it then transpires, under Dr Butler's microscope, that the reasons for the building initiative lie elsewhere. These less than rational explanations include: the architectural enthusiasms of individual grand jurymen (e.g. the projectors of Dundalk courthouse, 1813–*c.* 1821); a determination among some grand juries not to be outdone by the building achievements of neighbouring counties; and the tempting availability of government loans. In other cases, the need for expenditure on a courthouse or prison was palpable, but the timing of the work was entirely due to the attitude of the assize judge; in County Carlow, for example, the grand jury inertia was encouraged by the relationship of mutual, anti-Emancipationist admiration which it enjoyed with its circuit judge, Lord Norbury, but as soon as Norbury retired in 1827 it was forcibly reminded by his successor, Charles Kendal Bushe, that the government possessed powers to require it to expand the county gaol and build a new county courthouse (which it duly did).

Another surprising revelation is that, although some well known architects combined prison-design with a diverse and general architectural practice – Richard and William Vitruvius Morrison, George Richard and James Pain, John Hargrave, John Benjamin Keane, William Murray and Charles Lanyon, for example – other big-name architects were abject failures at prison-building. Thomas Cooley's Newgate prison, Dublin, completed in 1781, was a disaster from the start, although it was not abandoned until the 1840s. James Gandon's Waterford gaol of 1784–7 (the evidence for which has been dramatically reinterpreted by Dr Butler) was another failure. Most expensively and embarrassingly of all, Francis Johnston's Richmond penitentiary and, on the other side of Dublin, Richmond bridewell, were long out of date and almost unserviceable by the time they were completed, *c.* 1820. They cost the enormous sums of £32,415 and at least £41,300 respectively, and undermined Johnston's credibility as the architect to the Board of Works with responsibility under the 1810 Prisons Act for approving or rejecting designs for new prisons countrywide. After the 1810 and 1821 Acts, prison-design was reduced to a succession of penal-reform models, and little was left to the architect (even if he were freelance and not employed by the Board of Works) except the design of the façade. By contrast, courthouse-design remained very much the architects' sphere of influence and opportunity to shine. Gandon's Waterford courthouse, built at the same time as his unsuccessful Waterford gaol, was such a success that it influenced courthouse-design far into the nineteenth century.

The fact that architects retained the freedom to design the facades of prisons is significant. This meant that prisons, like courthouses (generally and for obvious reasons in close proximity), might contribute architecturally to the visual enhancement of a townscape. Some facades, it is true, were designed to look grim and forbidding. But the compensation for that was the boost to the local economy which a prison provided. Both courthouses and prisons were a major source of employment and profit during the period of their construction. Thereafter both, but especially prisons, continued to enrich their locality. Dr Butler has estimated that in the early 1830s the running costs of the county gaol and bridewells of County Clare together amounted to £2,000 p.a., or five per cent of the county's annual budget, much of it presumably being spent locally. It is not surprising, then, that a gaol was regarded as an asset to a town and not as an affront to the genteel sensibilities of the inhabitants. No wonder towns like Philipstown and Tullamore and Dungarvan and Waterford vied furiously with each other for designation as the county towns of Offaly and Waterford respectively. The effect of courthouse- and prison-building on local economies might, as Dr Butler suggests, profitably become a subject of research.

A final and indeed paradoxical reflection is that, although prison-building was brought much earlier under central government control than the building of courthouses, this did not necessarily make the former more economical than the latter. Corrupt and/or extravagant grand juries built unnecessarily lavish courthouses, but the high-minded penal reformers and their allies in parliament and government were also blame-worthy because they kept changing their minds as to what constituted the perfect model of a prison. They were unanimous in thinking that the rectilinear-plan gaols of the 1780s and beyond were out of date and unacceptable, but much less so about what should replace them. Thus, in the early nineteenth century, the respective merits of radial and polygonal designs were debated and, from *c*. 1838 onwards, the 'separate-system' (i.e. a separate cell for every inmate) was preferred.

The closing feature of the book is a series of appendices, running to *c*. 200 pages. The fullest and most important is a building history of each county's courthouses and prisons, with details of all the associated printed and manuscript sources. This is of vital interest to the local historian (among others), and bears out Dr Butler's claim that the book is not intended as the last word on his subject, but rather as a means of opening it up to further research on this and related topics.

A. P. W. MALCOMSON

LINDE LUNNEY, JAMES QUINN & WILLIAM ROULSTON (EDS)
Transatlantic Lives:
The Irish Experience in Colonial America
Ulster Historical Foundation, 2019
pp 184 ISBN 978-1-909556-64-5 pb £11.99

The Dictionary of Irish Biography (2009) has been a consistently trustworthy and widely consulted resource for historical research in Ireland, even beyond. Selecting biographical portraits from the volumes and drawing them together, as here, on a particular theme and/or period serves to create a prosopography – an investigation of the common characteristics of a group of people – which can shed new light on the theme. The editors describe those selected as 'a representative sample of some of the more notable figures among these emigrants' (i.e. those of the colonial period). However, their very 'notability' inevitably means that they are less representative of the migration stream in its totality.

For example, of the 59 subjects presented here only two (Matthew Lyon and George Taylor) are noted as travelling across the Atlantic as either indentured servants or as redemptioners (whose fares were paid on arrival in colonial America), when we know that the majority of Irish migrants to colonial America actually deployed these mechanisms. As always in the early modern period, those without literacy and drawn from a lower social strata remain particularly elusive to the biographer: it is important to recognise that point.

On the issue of gender, of the 59 individuals considered here, only three are female but, again, we have to recognise the inadequacies of the sources. Although women were somewhat less prominent in Irish trans-Atlantic migration in the colonial era than they would later become, they constituted significantly more than the mere five per cent presented here. To the editors' credit, however, consistent consideration is offered to the marriage patterns within the group, usefully shedding light on the kin networks operating powerfully across the sample and the ocean. The general impression is that, while the majority adhere to the near-truism that most Irish migrants to North America were young adults quite a number of migrants were aged over thirty. Of these more mature migrants, a significant proportion were churchmen, including Matthew Clerk, who left Kilrea, County Londonderry for America in his seventieth year.

In terms of the migrants' geographical origins and denominational background, there is, overall, a refreshing diversity. A significant core of this sample are Ulster Presbyterians. No fewer than 17 (29 per cent) were Presbyterian clergymen. Nonetheless there is a particularly strong representation of Episcopalians, representing their involvement in the colonial administrative, church and military strands of the first British Empire, both in the American colonies and the territory that would ultimately become Canada. In addition Loyalists during the Revolutionary War are well represented. Methodists, Quakers, those of smaller Protestant sects and Catholics are included whilst some migrants' religious identity remains obscure or ambivalent. Migrants drawn from Leinster and Dublin are well represented with only Connacht unrepresented amongst the provinces. It is instructive how widely spread across the Atlantic coast of North America the Irish were. We should note that migrants continued to migrate within North America and, more than might be imagined, even prior to the Revolution, a nascent urban America.

A number of other points about this sample caught this reader's eye. Although very few left Ireland from a genuinely impoverished background, there were many who made substantial material progression in the New World (not always honestly!). Many who rose to prominence in the patriot cause did very well financially and we can detect much financial acumen in these pages. The older argument, that Ulster or Irish migrants had little connection to the slave trade, is challenged here with both participants and opponents represented. Also, a more nuanced representation of relations with and understanding of Native American society emerges from the portraits offered in comparison with the developed stereotype. The concept of social networks and their influence permeates the book and we can see how many of the early eighteenth-century Ulster migrants looked back to the seminal event of the 1689 siege of Derry as an experience that both stood out in their memory and served to bind them into a Protestant imperial world. History is often rich in ironies and one could not help a wry smile on learning of the firebrand Reformed Presbyterian minister from Ballykelly, County Londonderry, who preached first in America to a congregation known as the Catholic congregation at Rocky Creek in South Carolina. Perhaps, it was this which drove him to an over-indulgence in whiskey, or even whisky!

Although clearly this publication is a welcome addition to the literature this reviewer has two concluding caveats. The first relates to the explanatory interpretation of emigration, particularly from Ulster prior to 1750. Graeme Kirkham has elsewhere stressed the marked extent to which the peaks in these trans-Atlantic departures correlated closely with periods of subsistence crisis or famine. Whilst the better known famine of 1740–41 is noted in the timeline, the evidence suggests that in Ulster the years 1727–31 and 1744–5 may have been equally severe. Similarly, it is worth highlighting the marked extent to which leases drawn up in the mid 1690s fell in around 1717–18. We no longer neatly isolate 'economic' factors from 'religious' in explaining migrant motivation and the question of tithes, paid to the Anglican church, represents just one issue where the spheres clearly overlap.

The second caveat relates to the need to recognise the extent to which the period covered here, 1660–1791, even in Ulster represents a mere prelude to an era of mass migration after 1820. The fact remains that more Ulster Presbyterians crossed the Atlantic 1840–60 than during the entire eighteenth century. A future companion volume charting some of these Famine-era migrants and sharing their experiences would extend our understanding of the true sequencing of outward migration from the northern province. The pattern of emigration from Ulster, historically, was indeed different from the other three provinces but the difference was not as pronounced as has traditionally been portrayed. Nonetheless, and taking these caveats into account, this volume, by illustrating personal examples of the emigrants' dream, warts and all, adds considerably to our understanding of the migration stream from Ireland to Colonial America.

PATRICK FITZGERALD

BRIAN M. WALKER

Irish History Matters:
Politics, Identities and Commemoration

The History Press, 2019

pp 256   ISBN 978-0-75099-129-2   hb   £20.00

Competent Irish historians are not uncommon and talented political scientists specialising in Irish matters are not unknown. However, Brian Walker has the rare distinction of having achieved excellence in both fields of scholarship. This is amply demonstrated in the series of essays and articles presented in this publication which reflects over 30 years of scholarship dealing with Irish matters. The information and enlightened insights presented are timely and relevant to anyone who has Ireland's true interests at heart. The four parts of the book – Part 1 'Past and Present'; Part 2 'Commemoration'; Part 3 'Identities' and Part 4 'Politics, 1885–1923' – are scholarly distillations of Walker's work and influence in modern Ireland – North and South.

In Part 1 'Past and Present', he weaves a clever amalgam of the thoughts of many of the leading figures involved in Irish affairs in recent decades. For example, he focuses (p. 40) on the public statements of

President Mary McAleese, particularly during the royal visit to Ireland in May 2011: Queen Elizabeth spoke of 'the complexity of our history'. McAleese's stirring response was, 'We cannot change the past, we have chosen to change the future'. This could be taken positively or negatively. Perhaps Brexiteers should take note? Part 2 dealing with 'Commemoration' is informed and erudite and its objective presentation of clear historical evidence may not appeal to anniversary zealots on both sides of the main Irish political fault line.

Chapter 6 'The Lost Tribes of Ireland: Diversity, Identity and Loss Among the Irish Diaspora' in Part 3 'Identities' brings a timely reminder based on recent revisionist (to some) research of scholars such as Donald Akenson, of the significant Protestant element in the Irish Diaspora in the USA. Walker (p. 137) subverts the popular image of 'Irish Americans' as the descendants of mainly Catholic refugees from poverty-stricken Ireland by pointing out that 'Protestants of Irish descent experienced significantly lower levels of educational standards, family incomes and high prestige jobs than Catholics of Irish ancestry in the 1980s and 1990s. His assertion that Protestants with an Irish background were more likely to be working class than were Catholics is a useful myth breaker. The role of Irish Protestants in the Diaspora to Australia is a timely contribution which Walker has synthesised and distilled, again from the research of people like Donald Akenson and by so doing brings it to a wider audience in this publication.

Walker's assessment of changed perceptions of Irish Identity in Part 3 is balanced and insightful. It is vital for anyone who seeks to understand the nature of the new multicultural society of Ireland – particularly the Republic. He quotes *Irish Times* columnist Fintan O'Toole's assertion in 2017 that 'Twenty years ago Irish society was relatively homogeneous but at present some 17% of those living in the state were born abroad'. This issue of a more pluralistic and international Irish identity was also addressed at Queen's in August 2017 by Leo Varadkar: 'I passionately believe that being European is an essential part of the modern Irish identity'. This was, of course, before Brexit.

Part 4 'Politics, 1885 – 1923' is an important reminder of the pivotal role of the elections in Ireland in 1885 and 1886 in determining the basic dynamics of politics North and South up to the present day. This material is based on Walker's original research as a political science doctoral student at Trinity. Chapter 9 'Southern Protestant Voices During the Irish War of Independence and the Civil War' redresses a long standing imbalance in the story of the evolution of the modern Irish state: the acknowledgement of the persecution of the Protestant minority in its early years. The earlier parts of the book contain much insight and synthesis. However, Chapter 9 slides occasionally and disappointingly into 'reportage' as we are treated to a blow by blow account of the proceedings of various synods of the Church of Ireland in the 1919–1923 period.

Many of the chapters have 'Final Observations' sections. A final synopsis of observations for the whole book would have been a daunting but perhaps necessary task for such a seminal publication. *Irish History Matters* is a *tour de force* publication which gives Irish Protestants their rightful place in the history of Ireland. It redresses decades of one-sided histories of the island.

GERRY CLEARY

CONNIE KELLEHER
The Alliance of Pirates:
Ireland and Atlantic piracy in the early seventeenth century
Cork University Press, 2020
pp 552   ISBN 9078-1-78205-365-1   hb   €30.00

On 30 June 1631 a number of ships commanded by Jan Janszoom, also known as Murad Reis, put into Baltimore harbour in west Cork. Their mission was essentially plunder, and in the ensuing attack two people were killed and over 107 men, women and children were carried off into slavery. A pub in Baltimore, the Algiers Inn, not mentioned here, commemorates the onslaught. As Connie Kelleher makes clear in this gripping and engrossing book such an attack was by no means unique. On the contrary, from their bases in North Africa – principally Algiers, Tunis and Salé (on the Atlantic coast) – these 'pirates' sallied forth on extensive sea voyages as far north as Iceland and the Faroes, west to southern Ireland and across the Atlantic to Newfoundland.

They were generally described, and denounced, as 'Turks' but in fact the pirate crews comprised many nationalities. For example, Janszoom, the leader of the Baltimore attack was likely Dutch-born but had converted to Islam and taken the name Murad Reis. Almost certainly, he was guided in the waters of Roaringwater Bay by Irish sailors who willingly or not acted as pilots. Kelleher situates her account of piracy in Irish waters in the context of the increasing globalisation of the world economy in the seventeenth century, as the riches of the East and the treasures of the New World drew the pirates out of the Mediterranean in search of fresh booty.

Building on work by Clive Senior and especially John Appleby, Kelleher adds a new dimension by making good use of her researches as an underwater archaeologist with the National Monuments Service of Ireland. As well, she examines the complex legal world inhabited by pirates, privateers, corsairs and seadogs: governments might condemn them in public but in private acknowledged that they had their uses especially if war was to break out. There is a useful glossary of terms for those who might not know their carrack from their kedge: but it was surely unnecessary to gloss 'alehouse' as 'a place where drink (i.e. ale) was sold'. A minor quibble: the names of those carried off by the Janszoon/Murad Reis raiders are listed in the relevant collection of State Papers: perhaps it might usefully have been added as an appendix here? Splendidly illustrated and handsomely produced, this volume is a significant contribution to the growing literature on Ireland in the Atlantic world in the early modern period.

THOMAS BARTLETT

DERIC HENDERSON & IVAN LITTLE (Compilers)
Reporting the Troubles:
Journalists tell their stories of the Northern Ireland conflict
Blackstaff Press, Belfast, 2018
pp 256 ISBN 987-1-78073-179-7 pb £14.99

This is not just a surprisingly good book; it is outstandingly good and an important and moving contribution to the history of the Troubles. I say surprisingly good because the prospect of almost 70 journalists – hacks, as some might call them – given a free hand to reminisce about how they scooped the field, how, as it were, they liberated Bagdad ahead of Stormin' Norman, or how they were first into Port Stanley ahead of the troops who had routed the Argies, was far from enticing. But clearly they were not given a free hand, and some credit must go to the 'compilers' for restricting the length of each contribution to, as I reckon, one thousand words. While Deric Henderson and Ivan Little eschew the title of 'editors', they must, I assume, take credit for exercising deft editorial control where needed. Credit, of course, to the 68 contributors, recalling their personal involvement in witnessing, reporting on and reacting to, mainly, acts of appalling violence. There are also more intimate – and unreported – accounts of the impact of such acts on families and on the writers themselves.

Though an entirely different exercise, the book is in many ways a worthy companion to the monumental *Lost Lives,*(1999) that detailed catalogue of all those who died in the Troubles, one of whose authors, David McKittrick, contributes here his own story of how *Lost Lives* was written. Reading *Reporting the Troubles* is, for those of us old enough, re-living the Troubles. We are reminded not just of Bloody Sunday (1972), Narrow Water (1979), Enniskillen (1987), Omagh (1998) and other major atrocities, but of isolated killings, even in one instance of the journalist's own near assassination in his own home, in front of his family. Reading the contributions over a period of two weeks, in no particular order, I must confess that I was repeatedly close to tears.

With 68 contributors it would be invidious to comment on individual pieces. Most are extremely well written, with restraint and deep understanding, almost never judgemental. They are eyewitness accounts of evil deeds done to individuals, families, communities and which inflicted untold harm and damage on all of us. Someone in the book is quoted as describing the events of the 30 years as 'dirty little war'. It was none of those. In terms of length of years it was generational. The totals of dead and wounded and of physical and economic damage in relation to the size and population of Northern Ireland were calamitous. If you try to think of it as a war, it was a very odd one. The armed groups doing the killing and bombing – even if you insist on including state forces – killed far more civilians than they did each other.

The strength of the book is to serve as a stark reminder of how awful the Troubles were, particularly as a text book for new generations who are encouraged to regard them as a closed chapter, time to move on and get on with life. So what, if youths of one sort shout 'Up the Ra' at Gaelic football games, or youths of another sort build enormous bonfires in defiance of the law and hurl sectarian insults. But what about senior politicians, even government ministers, who are still ready to honour the IRA and commemorate their deeds, and what about a lingering reluctance by some on the unionist side to break all ties with loyalist terror groups, and still honour the UVF or the UDA? Do we again say 'so what'?

One hopes the impact of *Reporting the Troubles*, particularly on younger generations, is not lessened by some well-intentioned but, to me, rather inappropriate contributions. One is the very short foreword by Senator George Mitchell in which he links the publication of the book to the twentieth anniversary of the signing of the (1998) Belfast Agreement and lauds the work of the many people, including journalists, who helped bring the killing frenzy to an end. The intention of this, and one or two other pieces, could have been to add some sense of closure; having told in stark and frightening terms the evil of the Troubles it was appropriate to tell how they ended in agreement to stop the killing.

I think the essence, and value, of the book is better conveyed by the closing words of two other contributions. Richard Kay concludes his account of the murder of Mary Travers, killed during an IRA assassination attempt on her father as they came home from Sunday morning mass: 'She loved music, played the harp, helped with the school choir … A life of opportunity stretched ahead. Her death was one more senseless murder'. Chris Moore ends his account of the murder of

Terence McKeever by the IRA in 1986, reportedly because his electrical company had done work at some security bases. The reporter saw Mr McKeever's body still lying on a border road. Moore's final paragraph is an apt summary of the book: 'Death is ugly in whatever form and for more than three decades the people who endured life during the Troubles encountered it more than three thousand times. And now we ask – to achieve what exactly?'

DENNIS KENNEDY

MARY PETERS

Passing the Torch: Sportswomen who Inspire
Foreword by HRH The Princess Royal
Gateway Publishing Limited, Belfast, 2019
pp 180   ISBN 978-1-902471-16-7   pb   £12.99

Lady Mary Peters remains one of the most iconic figures anywhere in the sporting world, not least as a role model for the participation of girls and women in the field of athletics. Olympic gold medallist at the 1972 Munich Olympics she has since then worked tirelessly to provide opportunities for young people, principally by means of the Trust she has established and for which she has raised £1 million to provide bursaries for young sportsmen and women, both able-bodied and disabled.

The esteem in which she is held throughout the world of athletics and beyond is very evident in her new book. It seeks, as its title indicates, to inspire a new generation of athletes, in many fields, by letting established sporting figures, all female, tell their individual stories. Nearly 100 women of all age levels have responded positively to Mary's idea and have, in many cases very simply, outlined their own stories and, in particular, what or, more often, who has helped them attain their personal best. They represent not only the field of athletics and paralympic athletics but also an impressive range of outdoor and indoor sports: rowing, hockey, tennis (Christine Truman, Wimbledon finalist 1961, and Rosie Casals!) powerboat racing, bowls, camogie, golf, football, eventing, horse racing, cycling, motorcycle racing; rugby union, judo; gymnastics, swimming, table tennis, curling, ice dancing ... this list is by no means complete.

The personal testimonies are almost uniformly admirable, even ... inspiring. It would be invidious in a short review to select any one but Fatima Whitbread's (p. 167) opening sentence, 'I spent the first 14 years my life in children's homes having been abandoned as a baby although some might say left to die' betokens a remarkable story. None is more remarkable that Lady Mary's own testimony (pp 131–9) especially the grim sequel to her Olympic triumph. Having been welcomed back to Belfast, for whom she proudly professed she had won the medal, she was not allowed back into her flat for some considerable time: this was 1972, the worst year of the Troubles in terms of deaths (over 400) and there were grounds for suspecting a terrorist attack.

However, there is much else here to embody the Olympic ideal of intense but respectful competitiveness. This is best summed up in Mary's own story: she was so neck and neck with her great rival Heide Rosendahl of West Germany that even at the end of the final pentathlon event, 'I didn't know if I had done enough. Then I saw Heide coming towards me and she gave me a hug and I knew that I had won.' It's enough to restore your faith in human nature.

TREVOR PARKHILL

LIAM BECKETT

Old School: Beckett, Bikes, Balls and All

Colourpoint Books, 2019

pp 176   ISBN 978-1-78073-235-0   pb   £9.99

In this engaging memoir of a book Liam Beckett entertainingly outlines the principal components of his sporting career, particularly in the field of soccer in which he, for a self-described 'journeyman' player, had reasonable success in the 1970s, as a player with Crusaders F. C and then with Coleraine FC and Dundalk FC and rather less as a manager. However, it is the other aspects of his life story that deserve most attention. His family background – father dead at 26, leaving Maud, his mother, to rear Liam and brother Lawrence; and his stirring association with the iconic motor-cycling Dunlop family, also in his native Ballymoney, which forms the first section of the book, is made all the more poignant by the deaths, both during road races, of first Joey and then more especially Robert, to whom Beckett, as mechanic and mentor, was especially close over many years.

Becket is best known as a commentator on football, on radio and in the Sunday press, both of which feature in this memory-laden account. However, it is his charitable work, for which her was been deservedly honoured with a MBE, as Black Santa in Ballymoney town centre at Christmas, through which he has raised thousands of pounds for a range of charitable causes, and the inspirational account of his visits, past and forthcoming, to Burkina Faso, probably the poorest country on earth and about which I'd have liked to learn more, that leaves the reader with a strong sense of admiration for his energy, compassion and humanity. The only disappointing feature of the book is that, unaccountably, he misses out the time when we both played, in the late 1960s, in the Coleraine and district summer league, for Mosside ... perhaps a sequel?

TREVOR PARKHILL

DARAGH SMYTH
Earthing the Myths:
The Myths, Legends and Early History of Ireland
Irish Academic Press, 2020
pp 386   ISBN 978-178855-135-9   hb   €29.95

This handsomely-produced and nicely-illustrated (hardback) book looks at first sight as it if might fall into the dreaded 'coffee-table' category. Not a bit of it. It is a thoroughgoing county-by-county (within each of the four provinces) guide to archaeological sites throughout the island of Ireland – and a section on related sites located in western Scotland to boot. There is the added value of the narration of stories associated with the legends for which Ireland has been famed – monsters (*ollphéists*, in the Irish language) wailing banshees (of course), even a king with horse's ears – are all to be found therein.

It could well become an oft-referred-to work of reference, listing as it does more than 1,000 locations on the island, many of which are accompanied by suitable photographs and drawings, enhanced by a thorough and clearly laid-out 14-page index. This reviewer's eye was naturally enough attracted to the Ulster counties. For Antrim, one of the legends associated with Lough Neagh, the largest freshwater lake in Ireland and Britain and which features here, is the one that every schoolboy/girl knows, that 'Finn mac Cumhail threw a large chunk of earth from here to form the Isle of Man and the resulting depression eventually formed the great Lough Neagh'. Interestingly, however, Smyth claims (pp 263–4) that 'Geology tells a similar story but from a scientific viewpoint – that a large mass of basalt dropped down and created a basin in which a lake was formed. The deposits under the waters of Lough Neagh extend back over millions of years'. In illustrating that 'giants play a big part in Irish mythology' (pp 265–7) Smyth needs to look no further than the Giant's Causeway on the north coast, 'now recognised as one of the wonders of the world', though it does not, as he observes, feature in many of the annals. Perhaps the annalists thought, like Dr Johnson, that it was worth seeing but not worth … etc?

'Armagh', says Smyth 'is the only county in Ireland to be named after a goddess' (macha). The excavation of Emain Macha (commonly known as Navan Fort) was excavated for eight years from 1965 by (Dudley) Waterman is 'generally regarded as a masterwork in excavation and has led perhaps for the first time to providing a physical context for life and legend in the Late Bronze Age and Early Iron Age'. It is also 'the location for the opening of the great romantic tale of Deirdre and Naoise … the original saga is recorded in the *Book of Leinster* as one of the three sorrowful tales of Ireland, the others being 'The Fate of the Children of Lir' and 'The Fate of the Children of Tuireann'.

Cavan is represented here (p. 284) as 'The crucible in which many of our pre-Christian deities found their origin'. Smyth also focuses on the role of sweathouses of which 'there are far more in north-western Cavan' and their value for local communities until the introduction of dispensaries from the early and middle years of the nineteenth century. 'At Moneen, sweathouses were used in autumn for their healing powers. As many as six people entered the houses at the same time, and after about an hour they went and plunged in a nearby stream; after their "sweat bath" they went to bed'.

The county listed here as Derry (formerly the county of Coleraine) is well represented by significant archaeological finds, not least the Broighter Hoard, uncovered near Limavady in 1896 by ploughman Thomas Nicholl who explained that the find, some 15 inches below the surface, 'one part just catched on the nose of the plough and it turned out of line'. It is now in the National Museum of Ireland. The Bann Disc, in the Ulster Museum, represents the Iron Age from the first and second century AD. It was dredged from the River Bann at Loughan Island near Coleraine in 1929 (p. 303). The naming of the Grianán of Ailach, that iconic location in County Donegal where Nuadu, an ancient king of Ireland, is said to have been buried, is thoroughly examined, as is its poetic traditions from the tenth and eleventh centuries. The largest fort ring in Ireland is the Giant's Ring, listed under 'Down' but only four miles from the centre of Belfast in the townland of Ballynahatty is, according to Lalor in *Ulster: its Archaeology and Antiquities*, 'the best example of a great circular or oval wall' (p. 320).

The rich folklore tradition of County Fermanagh is contained in a mere six pages (pp 330–35) focusing principally on White Island and Boa Island, in addition to the intriguing story Slieve Beagh on the border with County Monaghan, reputed to contain the burial site of of the first man to arrive in Ireland, Bith or Bioth, in Irish *Beatha*, the fourth son of Noah expelled by his father and instructed, in the modern idiom, to 'go west young man ...'.

In Monaghan itself looms the Black Pig's Dyke. 'Linear earthworks', says Smyth, 'are a feature of the southern areas of Ulster, the most common and best known of which is the Black Pig's Dyke'. In 1835 John O'Donovan wrote 'It must have been a tremendous Ollphéist ('huge worm') that ran across the country when she formed so deep a track but her coils, voluminous and vast, cannot have been more terrible than the tusks of the huge boar that rooted the Valley of the Black Dyke'.

In Tyrone, two miles south-east of Cookstown is the Tullaghoge a ring fort and, most importantly, an inauguration site. Smyth (pp

340–01) says that 'Traditionally this was the inauguration site of the O'Neills and the capital of medieval Tyrone … The great Hugh O'Neill was said to have been the last king installed there'.

This review also carries a health warning. The attraction, if that is the right word, of banshees in the long-established folklore tradition is perhaps best evinced by a description of Bronach of the Burren, a banshee from Lough Rask, who had '… a bossy, wrinkled, ulcerated brow, the hairs of her eyebrows like fish hooks, bleared watery eyes peered with malignant fire between red inflamed lids' … try reading that to the weans at bedtime.

TREVOR PARKHILL

Researching
Presbyterian
Ancestors in Ireland

William J. Roulston

Major-General Oliver Nugent

*The Irishman
who led the
Ulster Division
in the Great War*

NICHOLAS PERRY

ROGER BLANEY

Presbyterians
Preispitéirigh
and the
agus an
Irish Language
Ghaeilge

An absorbing account of an
integral but little-known strand
in the fabric of Presbyterianism

Aodán Mac Póilin

Our
tangled
speech

essays on language and culture

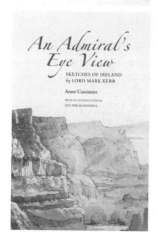

*An Admiral's
Eye View*

SKETCHES OF IRELAND
by LORD MARK KERR

Anne Casement

WITH AN INTRODUCTION BY
HECTOR McDONNELL

Ulster Transformed
Plantation in early modern Ireland
*c.*1590–1641

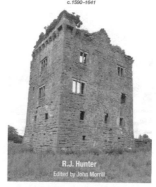

R.J. Hunter
Edited by John Morrill

www.booksireland.org.uk

Family names
in the
Glens *of*
Antrim

BRIAN S. TURNER

ARTHUR McALISTER
ESTD 1890
GLENS OF ANTRIM HOUSE

Irish Names
and Surnames

sloinnte
gaedeal is gall

WOULFE

Place names
in Ulster

JONATHAN
BARDON

Researching
Scots-Irish Ancestors
The essential genealogical guide
to early modern Ulster, 1600–1800

SECOND EDITION

William J. Roulston

Researching
Farming
Ancestors in Ireland

William J. Roulston

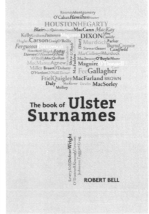

The book of Ulster
Surnames

ROBERT BELL